M

Clinton's World

CLINTON'S WORLD

Remaking American Foreign Policy

WILLIAM G. HYLAND

PRAEGER

Westport, Connecticut
London

Library of Congress Cataloging-in-Publication Data

Hyland, William, 1929–
    Clinton's world : remaking American foreign policy / William G.
Hyland.
      p. cm.
    Includes bibliographical references and index.
    ISBN 0–275–96396–9 (alk. paper)
    1. United States—Foreign relations—1993– . 2. Clinton, Bill,
1946– . I. Title.
E885.H95   1999
327.73′009′049—dc21   98–37155

British Library Cataloguing in Publication Data is available.

Library of Congress Catalog Card Number: 98–37155
ISBN: 0–275–96396–9

First published in 1999

Praeger Publishers, 88 Post Road West, Westport, CT 06881
An imprint of Greenwood Publishing Group, Inc.

Printed in the United States of America

The paper used in this book complies with the
Permanent Paper Standard issued by the National
Information Standards Organization (Z39.48–1984).

10 9 8 7 6 5 4 3 2 1

Contents

Clinton's World

1

The Legacy

No other modern American president inherited a stronger, safer international position than Bill Clinton. The Cold War was over. The nation was at peace. Its principal enemy had collapsed. The United States was the world's only genuine superpower. The major threats that had haunted American policy for nearly fifty years had either disappeared or were rapidly receding. To be sure, there were problems abroad and threats to national security, but they were manageable. The most intractable problems were at home. The presidential election campaign of 1992 demonstrated that domestic issues were at the center of the nation's attention. George Bush's skills in handling foreign affairs had been less important than the growing concerns over domestic crises. Bill Clinton understood this and capitalized on it.

Nevertheless, Bush's legacy in foreign policy was impressive. Within a year of his inauguration in January 1989 he had confronted a daunting array of problems swirling around the end of the Cold War. Between 1989 and 1991 the core structure of the Soviet empire in Eastern Europe had imploded and disappeared in less than six months. Forty-five years after its defeat in World War II, Germany was again united. Then the Soviet Union itself had splintered apart. In its place was a conglomeration of independent states, some of ancient origin, some completely new. For the first time in several hundred years, Russia stood alone, separate from Ukraine, from Byelorussia, the Baltic States, and the nations of Central Asia and the Caucasus. It was not even the empire of Peter or Catherine. Indeed, only a tiny sliver of territory, the former German city of Königsberg, tied Russia to

Central and Western Europe. There had been few periods of comparable change in modern European history. It had been much like the end of World War I, when the three great European empires collapsed almost overnight. The changes had been of "biblical proportions," George Bush said later.

On a pleasant Parisian day in November 1990, George Bush declared that the Cold War was over. It was over, he explained, because he and the Soviet president Mikhail Gorbachev, as well as all of the European leaders, had just signed the Charter of Paris, proclaiming democracy and human rights to be the way of the future. The Cold War had begun as a battle of ideas between two different views of how to organize and govern society, and the new charter, Bush asserted, signified an end to that struggle.[1]

Others could argue that the Cold War did not end until August 1991, when an imprisoned Mikhail Gorbachev, freed from his would-be captors of the Soviet old guard, returned from the Crimea to Moscow and dissolved the Communist Party of the Soviet Union, which had betrayed him. But there could be no doubt at all that by December 8, 1991, the Cold War had definitely ended: on that day the Union of Soviet Socialist Republics was finally and officially dissolved.

The conventional wisdom had been that the Cold War was a conflict destined to continue for a protracted period, ending either in a nuclear bang or an evolutionary whimper. Reality defied both views, and the sudden end of the Cold War created considerable confusion. Inside and outside Washington there had been little or no intellectual preparation for this sweeping reversal of history. A few observers had sensed that a revolutionary upheaval was in the making, but by and large political and strategic planning for the end of the Cold War had been minimal. It was reminiscent of 1953, when Stalin died; President Eisenhower complained that for years there had been talk of the post-Stalin era, but when it was actually at hand no one really knew what to do. The Washington bureaucracy was still debating whether and how much to help Mikhail Gorbachev when he fell from power.

Bush believed that the post–Cold War era was comparable to the periods beginning in 1918 and 1945, following the termination of the two great world conflicts, and that it would take years to work out a post–Cold War settlement. Several "think tanks" drew similar conclusions: for the third time in this century history was at a crossroads, from where the political leaders could set new directions.

The fluidity that had marked the two earlier postwar periods had congealed in an American consensus: isolationism in 1919–1921 and internationalism in 1945–1947. Many observers saw this third chance as a choice between 1919 and 1945. Ideas that had been rank heresy could be entertained, and various theories began to emerge. There were renewed forecasts of a decline of the West, as well as predictions of a new anarchy. It was speculated that creating a "new world order" would be to the Bush presidency what the New Deal had been to Franklin D. Roosevelt. The problem was stated best in a happy phrase by Jeane Kirkpatrick, former ambassador to the United Nations: the objective of foreign policy was to permit the United States to become a "normal country in normal times."[2]

But what was normal? Would the United States return to the 1920s and once again turn its back on the world's troubles? Or more plausibly, would it return to the 1940s, when World War II ended and the country edged toward new international commitments? If the United States was the only remaining superpower, how should it use its power? Should it reorder the world in its own image? Was America bound to lead, as many argued? Or should the country veer more toward the old isolationist slogan of America First?[3] Some foreign observers, perhaps too mindful of American history, leaped to the erroneous conclusion that isolationism would sweep the country. The London *Economist* (September 28, 1991) speculated that by the mid-1990s one of the two political parties, probably the Democrats, would be as "committed to isolationism as American parties can be."

Isolationism was never a viable alternative. The vintage isolationism of the 1920s and 1930s was long gone. The United States had become deeply entangled in the world's economy, in global technology, in international politics and institutions, and in at least a half-dozen security alliances. It would probably have taken at least a decade of dedicated effort by both the Congress and the president to extricate the United States enough even to approximate the isolation of the 1930s. The result would be a global crisis of unimaginable proportions in a world of a dozen or more nuclear powers. No one wanted that.

Still, isolationism was a convenient whipping boy for political candidates. President Bush could hardly pass up a chance to attack the new isolationists for their "stubborn fantasy that we can live as an isolated island surrounded by a changing and developing world." Nevertheless, even the so-called Realists began to redefine the concept of the national interest in terms more circumspect than heretofore: as Henry Kissinger put it, "more discriminating in its purpose, less cataclysmic in its strategy and, above all, more regional in its design."[4] A wariness of new commitments also became evident.

The real debate was between two categories of international Realists: between those who conceived the national interest in broadly traditional terms—to protect the nation's territory, wealth, and access to necessary goods—and those who would pursue policies of disinterested globalism, asking in effect what needed to be done. The United States would have to "thread its way between an overly brutal realpolitik and an unworkable idealism," as one observer described the choice.[5]

The Bush administration was never much inclined to engage in intellectual debates over theories of foreign policy. Nevertheless, in many respects George Bush was ideally suited by background and training to deal with the post–Cold War world. He knew the issues, was well acquainted with the major personalities, and presided over a talented and aggressive staff. Bush dealt with the real world, tolerant of various concepts but not dominated by them. He was far more intrigued by interaction with the world's leaders he came to know. He saw international politics in terms of his relations with Mikhail Gorbachev and Boris Yeltsin, with Deng Xiaoping, or with Margaret Thatcher and Helmut Kohl. He doubted that there could now be a single overriding doctrine, equivalent to containment in the Cold War. At first his pragmatism was an asset; later it would be more of a liability, when he had to confront more philosophical questions concerning tensions between interests and values.

The greatest impact of the end of the Cold War was in Europe. The United States and its allies immediately faced the enormous challenge of reconstructing Europe after the fall of the Berlin Wall. The central issue in Europe, however, was not how to deal with the former communist states, such as Poland or Czechoslovakia, but the unification of Germany. Bush seized on the German question, and despite reservations in Paris and London, he persisted in negotiating German unity with Mikhail Gorbachev. He insisted that a neutral Germany, maneuvering between East and West, would be a major threat to European stability; a united Germany ensconced within the NATO alliance would be safer. Rather amazingly, he succeeded in winning Gorbachev's agreement not only to German unification but to continued German membership in NATO. Despite various theories advising the contrary, a critical piece of the post–Cold War structure was created by a skillful exercise in practical diplomacy.

The second critical piece of post–Cold War architecture was the Gulf War. It crystallized a central foreign policy issue: for what purposes and to what end would America use its unrivaled power?

For almost fifty years those questions had been answered in the name of containing communism and the Soviet Union. The United States had intervened both openly and clandestinely around the world. There had always been some degree of risk that intervention would escalate into highly dangerous confrontations or even a major war. Suddenly, such fears were no longer determinants; the United States was essentially free to intervene abroad without fear of confrontation with Moscow. This was a new and important dimension to foreign policy.

Nevertheless, the question remained: intervention for what? The debate over the Gulf War demonstrated that protecting American interests was not necessarily a persuasive answer. The United States obviously had important interests in the Gulf, but when Secretary of State James Baker said that the war was about "jobs," he was roundly criticized. The national interest demanded a more rigorous definition. In this case the security and stability of the region and the protection of Israel were more persuasive answers, because they appealed to the American public's desire to justify its actions on more than crass, commercial grounds.

Bush, however, chose to go much further. He justified the Gulf War not only as a challenge to the regional balance of power (which it was) but as a challenge to the entire post–Cold War order (which was debatable). The United States was determined to support "collective security" against aggression. Thus, victory in the Gulf War meant that the world had passed the first test of a post–Cold War order. New strategic opportunities, comparable to the opportunities after World War I and World War II, would follow the success of Desert Storm. After the war Bush said:

> We can see a new world coming into view, a world in which there is the very real prospect of a new world order . . . a world where the United Nations—freed from Cold War stalemate—is poised to fulfill the historic vision of its founders; a world in which freedom and respect for human rights find a home among all nations.[6]

This, then, was the vague and slightly idealistic outline of what Bush called a "new world order." It was hoped that the primary instrument for creating and enforcing it would be the United Nations. In disrepute during the Cold War, the UN had been resuscitated by the vigorous role of the Security Council in the Gulf crisis. For the first time since 1945 there was a chance that collective security would replace unilateralism. Even Ronald Reagan, in a speech to the Oxford Union (December 2, 1992), had called for a new UN army, an "army of conscience."

Nevertheless, the Gulf War had provoked a long debate over the use of force and the president's power to go to war. A small army of commentators ominously predicted that a military campaign would produce heavy casualties for American forces. A strong political faction favored continuing economic sanctions rather than resorting to war. Congressional votes were much closer than anticipated: reliance on sanctions alone was turned down 46–53 in the Senate, though more decisively, 183 to 250, in the

House. The ranking Senate Democrat on national security affairs, Senator Sam Nunn, took the position that the use of force was justified but was not necessarily in the national interest; he voted against the immediate resort to force. (He later said that he regretted that vote.) Former President Jimmy Carter opposed the use of force, because he thought it would destroy America's position with the Arabs. Patrick Buchanan, preparing for his presidential bid, said that Kuwait was not worth sacrificing the 82nd Airborne Division.

The quick military victory and the low level of casualties effectively ended the debate. The Gulf War, however, did not usher in the new era of international cooperation, as had been hoped. By definition, collective security rests on a close identification and common interests among the countries involved. Even during the Gulf crisis it was obvious that congruence of the interests of the great powers was shaped more by specific conditions than by exalted, universal principles.

Russia (still the Soviet Union), for example, had reluctantly abandoned its one-time client, Iraq, in order to maintain links to Washington. But in the Balkans, Russia was not prepared to abdicate its historical interests. Similarly, the Europeans were ready to follow America's lead in the Gulf, but not in the Balkans. The ideal of collective security was threatened by a rising nationalism, evident in the breakup of the Soviet Union, in the attack of one Arab state against another, in Iranian fundamentalism, and in the ethnic conflict in Yugoslavia. Nationalism was at least as potent a force as internationalism.

Bush became a prisoner of his own success. The United States was free to act without much fear of confrontation, and it did so in the Gulf War. On balance, however, it turned out that the United States now had less genuine freedom of action than it had enjoyed in the Cold War. In the Cold War the lines had usually been sharply drawn, especially in a crisis, and much of the world had deferred to Washington's judgment; after the Cold War, the political lines became far less distinct, both at home and abroad. In 1990 Bush was attacked for acting too precipitately, for refusing to let economic sanctions take their course. On the other hand, at war's end he was attacked for stopping the fighting before overthrowing Saddam Hussein.

The controversy over intervention led to a debate over what the criteria should be. There was almost unanimous agreement among both theorists and practitioners that each situation had to be addressed on its merits, but there were several efforts to lay down guidelines. In January 1993, after his electoral defeat, Bush elaborated a set of criteria: that the stakes warranted the use of force; that force could be effective; that no other policies were likely to prove effective; that the application of force could be limited in scope and time; and that the potential benefits justified the potential cost and sacrifice. This formulation was so broad as to be a recipe for inaction. General Colin Powell, Chairman of the Joint Chiefs of Staff, offered a similar approach, but he was probably closer to reality when he observed there were no fixed set of rules. Indeed, both Bush and Powell had violated their own guidelines when in the Gulf War they opted not for the limited use of force but for its massive application.

The Gulf War even led to demands that other countries bear their share of the financial burden of international security. For the first time since the Revolutionary War, America sought foreign aid to fight a war (a humiliation, but nevertheless consistent with American public opinion).

America's allies, if still dependent on Washington, could and would seek greater autonomy. Like the United States, they were under domestic pressures to assert more nationalistic positions. While the United States was clearly the dominant power, the new concert of nations was still tenuous: Japan and Germany, for example, remained on the sidelines in the Gulf War, and the new Soviet-American partnership was fragile.

The concept of a new world order was thus quite vague. In Europe, the United States was still the linchpin in a security system resting on U.S. treaty commitments to defend its Atlantic allies. On neither side of the Atlantic was there any sentiment favoring American disengagement. The advance of Germany's borders to the east settled the so-called German question but raised a new (or old) issue: the security of the lands between a new and potentially more powerful Germany and a weakened Russia—a problem Bush carefully finessed and left to his successor.

In Asia, America could still not define its proper role almost twenty years after the end of the war in Vietnam. The fundamental problems were the same as they had been for almost a century—maintaining uneasy relations with Japan and with China. Whereas the American alliance with Europe had deep cultural and historical roots, that with Japan was more superficial and dictated by expediency on both sides. Festering disputes over trade were now souring the alliance.

China was even more of an uncertainty. By the 1980s China had clearly returned to the ranks of the great powers. By the early 1990s China's economic policies were transforming it into an economic giant. In an era of global democratization and liberalization, however, the Chinese communist oligarchy remained an anomaly, especially after the clashes in Tiananmen Square. With the demise of communism in the Soviet Union, the geopolitical arguments that had favored close relations between Washington and Beijing were losing their force. It was ironic that George Bush, who had been ambassador to the UN when the People's Republic of China was admitted and who had served as ambassador in Beijing, would be attacked more for his mishandling of China than over any other foreign policy issue.

The other area significantly affected by the end of the Cold War was the Middle East. The United States had become the only outside power of any consequence in this area. Here, too, pragmatism rather than principle was beginning to govern conduct. Bush believed that victory in the Gulf War had created a new chance for Arab-Israeli peace. The war neutralized Iraq, a principal enemy of Israel; it revealed the impotence of the Soviet Union as a patron of the radical Arabs; it exposed the dependence of the moderate Arabs on Washington; finally, it demonstrated that the United States could and would defend its interests in the area by force if necessary. A strategic window of opportunity seemed to be opening.

In sum, the end of the Cold War was indeed a significant opportunity to build a new international order, reflecting both American interests and its principles. How to grasp such a strategic nettle was a question ideally suited to a presidential debate. After all, Cold War issues had figured in every election campaign since the end of World War II. The Great Debate over post–Cold War foreign policy, however, never took place in 1992.

As the presidential campaign unfolded, George Bush was placed more and more on the defensive. The boldness of his actions in the Gulf crisis did not translate into new political gains at home. Indeed, the early Republican primaries suggested that he was getting little credit for his handling of the Gulf War. The public wanted a change in priorities: opinion polls showed that foreign issues were of much less importance than the economy and other domestic concerns.

How to strike a balance between assigning higher priorities for domestic concerns while continuing an effective foreign policy was a serious issue. It was trivialized, however, by defensive claims from the foreign policy establishment that the foreign threat had not really changed, that the world was even more dangerous than during the Cold War. Ronald Reagan claimed that "evil still stalks the planet"—the world had traded a "single monolithic threat" for a "host of smaller, yet no less deadly, flashpoints."[7] In a flight of rhetoric, even President Bush claimed that the challenges were as daunting as Stalin's army had been forty years earlier. The conflict over domestic and foreign priorities was further trivialized by the charge that President Bush was spending too much time on foreign affairs. It did not help much when a new White House chief of staff, Samuel Skinner, announced that "the baton" had been passed from foreign to domestic policy.

Bush's foreign policies were also attacked within his own party. Conservatives who had never really been reconciled to Bush as Reagan's successor began to take shots at his foreign policy. Patrick Buchanan, in particular, mounted a neo-isolationist assault from the right. Ambassador Jeane Kirkpatrick joined in, questioning what exactly was Bush's vision of world order. She argued in March 1992 that there was no center of gravity to Bush's policy, that neither Bush nor Secretary Baker seemed to attach much importance to the character of foreign regimes, separating American policy from the country's "deeply held political values."[8] Kirkpatrick's complaints were not very different from the Democratic Party's platform, which accused Bush of "corrosive policies" rooted in the past, "divorced from American values, fearful of change and unable to meet America's challenges." In response, the Bush camp emphasized more and more the value of "prudence" in the conduct of foreign policy:

> We need not respond by ourselves to each and every outrage of violence. The fact that America can act does not mean that it must. A nation's sense of idealism need not be at odds with its interests. Nor does principle displace prudence.[9]

Prudence was scarcely designed to electrify the electorate, but it was in fact Bush's election-year policy. Washington adamantly refused to intervene in Yugoslavia, leaving that problem to the Europeans. In Haiti, there seemed to be an opening for vigorous American intervention to restore democracy, but Bush insisted that no vital interest was threatened and that military action was therefore not justified. The same sense of caution also governed the question of aid to the former Soviet Union. There was a strong case that it was in the American interest to aid Russia; Richard Nixon had made that case while Bush was still in office. But Bush was reluctant to go very far.

It became fashionable to mock Bush's new world order, which critics called the new world "disorder." Some saw Bush's vision as much too timid, laying too much emphasis on maintaining stability rather than promoting values. Others concluded that the UN could not be the center of a new world order of collective security and democratic ideals: most of its member governments were oligarchies or dictatorships with abominable records, scarcely suitable agencies for establishing world democracy.[10] Leading geopoliticians felt it was too soon to dismiss the perennial struggle for power, even though they acknowledged that the American public would not rally to some "desiccated" notion of international stability or balance of power. Henry Kissinger admitted that the public could not be won over to policies based an "apparent moral neutrality." Nevertheless, the new world order, Kissinger argued, was anti-historical; centuries of the balance of power could not be brushed aside in favor of a new system that defied definition.[11]

The new conventional wisdom was that economic power would become the decisive factor in international politics. Both American and European leaders foresaw a new era dominated by economics. For example, observers confidently predicted that the post–Cold War world would be shaped by the relative decline of American power and the rise of European and Japanese power based on their economic prowess. The Big Two of nuclear competition would be replaced by the Big Three of economic dominance. Similarly, Margaret Thatcher forecast a trifurcation of the world power into three blocs based on the dollar, the yen, and the Deutsche mark. (This turned out to be wildly wrong.)[12]

Bush, however, echoed these themes. In an address to the UN General Assembly on September 23, 1991, he declared that "economic progress will play a vital role in the new world." He warned that a "new wave of protectionism could destroy our hopes for a better future. I cannot stress this enough."[13] Almost a year later, in his acceptance speech at the Republican convention (August 1992), he said, "The defining challenge of the 90s is to win the economic competition—to win the peace." His warnings against protectionism were well taken, for protecting trade now had much greater support than at any other time since the 1930s. This became evident in the surprising presidential candidacy of Ross Perot and the inflammatory rhetoric of Patrick Buchanan. With the end of the Cold War, Buchanan argued, there were only two claimants to its legacy: either Bush's new world order or America First.

Bush's policy of prudence was therefore dictated in part by economic realities. The country had emerged from the Cold War burdened by a massive debt and seemingly endless budget deficits. There was a consensus that the United States urgently needed to put its economic house in order, to reduce the deficit, and eventually balance the budget. Balancing the budget, however, created a painful dilemma for Republican candidates in that it meant reducing national defense. Republicans had always cited national defense as one of their party's strong points; weakness on defense matters had been a favorite charge against the Democrats. The intricacies of the nuclear competition had given every president since Harry Truman extraordinary power. Now that relative freedom for the chief executive had ended; the United States could no longer afford to support countries or ventures without regard to the economic consequences. The halcyon days of large defense buildups or grandiose Marshall Plans were past.

What would be the new defense strategy? In early 1992 the Bush administration toyed with a bold new concept: that the United States would plan its defense in such a way that no other country could approximate American power. If some other nation did challenge American predominance, the United States would act to block it. The nation would build a new world order based on "convincing potential competitors that they need not aspire to a greater role or pursue a more aggressive posture to protect their legitimate interests."[14] These words were from a draft policy directive which went so far as to specify Germany and Japan as the most likely competitors. This aimed, of course, at outright hegemony. When these ideas were leaked to the public (through the *New York Times*), there was an outcry against what seemed an open-ended commitment to competition and coercion. It had to be dropped.

In its place came a strange new strategy that assumed the United States might have to fight two regional wars at the same time (Korea and the Gulf were the favorite scenarios). If so, the United States would fight them seriatim: having defeated the first enemy, the United States would turn and deal with the second. This of course provoked terror in South Korea, which feared that it might come second. In typical Washington fashion, the entire matter was blurred enough to satisfy both hawks and doves. The armed forces were reduced and streamlined into something called the Base Force, which reflected budgetary constraints rather than grand strategy. The net effect was to add to the confusion over national security.

By election day in November 1992 there was no clear consensus over the direction of foreign policy. The elites still favored a policy of international engagement, albeit a more "selective" engagement that would recognize the limits posed by public opinion and the constraints imposed by resources. To be sure there was a new enthusiasm for the UN and collective security, but there was a lingering nostalgia for unilateral action as well. No multilateralism without unilateralism, was how one observer put it. Moreover, there were numerous predictions that democracy would prove to be the wave of the future. There were dissenters, however, who still believed that foreign policy would and should be governed by the relations between states regardless of their internal orders. Even the Realists, however, recognized the growing impact of idealism on foreign policy.

In short, as Bill Clinton took the oath of office there was intellectual confusion over the nature of the post–Cold War world, and therefore over what the aims of American foreign policy should be. The Bush administration had failed to develop a clear view of the future. Having proclaimed a new world order, Bush came to ridicule the "vision thing." He had concentrated instead on solving problems—Germany, Russia, China, the Gulf War. As the only superpower, the United States could make strategic decisions for the world at large. A "new world order that breaks the old rules and makes new ones," is how one proponent put it.[15]

But the power of the presidency to dictate this new world order was waning. The Cold War had helped to create the "imperial presidency." The end of that historical period meant the end of an era of virtually constant national emergencies, confrontations, and wars. The Gulf War debates represented a challenge to the institution of the presidency in its traditional dominance of foreign affairs. It was becoming clearer that the president could not sound the trumpets and call the nation to action if the enemy was a petty Middle Eastern dictator, not the evil empire of communism. If the nation was no longer to be fixed on the presidency, congressional supremacy would return.[16]

The decline of the presidency was one of the messages of the 1992 election. In Cold War elections the candidate who adopted the strongest foreign policy position usually won. Clinton's victory and Bush's defeat therefore marked a turning point. Clinton was not reconciled to the diminution of the office he would inherit; indeed, in the election campaign he had occasionally adopted a crusading spirit and tone worthy of the Cold War. For example, he declared (April 1992): "I believe it is time for America to lead a global alliance for democracy as united and steadfast as the global alliance that defeated communism."[17]

Beginning on January 20, 1993, he would have a chance to lead this new global alliance.

NOTES

1. Statement by President Bush, Paris, November 21, 1990, Office of the White House Press Secretary.

2. Jeane J. Kirkpatrick, "A Normal Country in a Normal Time," in Owen Harries, ed., *America's Purpose* (San Francisco: ICS Press, 1991), p. 155.

3. Charles Krauthammer, "The Unipolar Moment," *Foreign Affairs*, Winter 1991.

4. Henry A. Kissinger, "What Kind of New World Order?" *Washington Post*, December 3, 1991; Zbigniew Brzezinski, "Selective Global Commitment," *Foreign Affairs*, Fall 1991; Robert W. Tucker, "Realism and the New Consensus," *The National Interest*, Winter 1992/93.

5. Francis Fukuyama, "The Beginning of Foreign Policy," *The New Republic*, August 17 and 24, 1992.

6. George Bush, "The World after the Persian Gulf War," address before a Joint Session of Congress, Washington, D.C., March 6, 1991, in Stanley R. Sloan, "The US Role in a New World Order: Prospects for George Bush's Global Vision," *CRS Report for Congress*, March 28, 1991, p. 19.

7. "Reagan: "Evil Still Stalks the Planet," Associated Press, Oxford, England, *Washington Post*, December 5, 1992.

8. Jeane Kirkpatrick, "What Are the President's Foreign Policy Goals?" *Washington Post*, March 16, 1992.

9. George Bush, "Remarks by the President to West Point Cadets," U.S. Military Academy, West Point, N.Y., January 5, 1993, Office of the White House Press Secretary.

10. William Pfaff, quoted in Sloan, "The US Role in a New World Order," p. 29.

11. Henry Kissinger, "False Dreams of New World Order," *Washington Post*, February 26, 1991.

12. C. Fred Bergsten, "The World Economy after the Cold War," *Foreign Affairs*, Summer 1990.

13. Excerpts in *New York Times*, September 24, 1991.

14. Patrick E. Tyler, "Pentagon Drops Goal of Blocking New Superpowers," *New York Times*, May 24, 1992.

15. Krauthammer, "The Unipolar Moment."

16. George Will, "The Miniaturized Presidency: A Casualty of Peace," *Washington Post*, May 30, 1993.

17. Remarks by Governor Bill Clinton to the Foreign Policy Association, New York, April 1, 1992.

2

Mandate for Change

William Jefferson Clinton was better educated in foreign affairs than many of his predecessors. He had graduated from the prestigious School of Foreign Service of Georgetown University. There he had imbibed the political atmosphere of the nation's capital for four years, serving part-time on the staff of the influential Senator William Fulbright, from his home state of Arkansas, then the powerful chairman of the Senate Foreign Relations Committee. Clinton also studied abroad for two years at Oxford, where he was occasionally tutored in Russian and Eastern European affairs. Also, as everyone would find out, he had visited Moscow as a student and in London had been an activist in opposing the Vietnam War. Back in the United States, he graduated from Yale Law School and returned to Arkansas.

Over the decades that followed, however, as the attorney general and twice the governor of Arkansas, he had no reason to be at the center of the nation's foreign policy debates. His political timing, however, turned out to be fortuitous. Whereas in 1988 Michael Dukakis's lack of foreign or defense policy experience counted against him, the end of the Cold War made Clinton's inexperience in foreign policy much less important. In the 1992 campaign Clinton wisely chose not to mount a wholesale challenge to Bush's foreign policy; there was little to be gained by playing into his opponent's strength. His campaign, therefore, gave only occasional glimpses of the foreign policy that Clinton would in fact employ. His rhetoric suggested a minimalist approach, spiced with some of the liberalism of the 1960s. In the campaign he did not stray far from the mainstream.

When taxed with his inexperience in foreign affairs, he offered glib rebuttals: times had changed with the end of the Cold War; the most urgent task was to rebuild American strength at home; if the country was not strong at home, it could not be strong abroad. In this view his service as state governor was relevant. In that capacity he had been concerned with international economics, which now would be the core of the new post–Cold War foreign policy.[1]

Even before he became the challenger to Bush, Clinton carefully sought to neutralize potential criticism of his lack of foreign policy credentials and ingratiate himself with the foreign policy community, by adopting a strong position on security issues. It was suggested later that serving in the George McGovern campaign he had learned a valuable lesson: never be caught too far to the left on national defense. Early in his campaign (December 12, 1991), in a speech at his alma mater, Georgetown University, Clinton discussed national security at length. His principal theme was the necessity to maintain nuclear deterrence. This was a safe enough subject, but somewhat an odd choice at that particular moment, when both the United States and the Soviet Union were reducing their nuclear arsenals. His traditional, even slightly hawkish, treatment of the issues provoked both interest and enthusiasm from the so-called Eastern Establishment. That, of course, had been his intention. The speech was overloaded with cliches, such as the need to "keep our guard up" while developing a "smaller, more flexible mix of capabilities." He advocated not only maintaining nuclear deterrence but creating rapid deployment capabilities, while maintaining a technological edge and securing better intelligence. All of this was to be achieved while reducing the defense budget by about one-third over five years (by 1997). Clinton was offering something for almost every faction, except the extreme right and left.[2]

In other early speeches as well he emerged as a thoughtful moderate, a far cry from the anti-Vietnam "peacenik" he was accused of being later in the campaign. His position was close enough to the conventional wisdom that he earned the praise and, more important, the endorsements of some neo-conservatives. Indeed, his occasional potshots at Bush had a neo-conservative tinge:

- He criticized Bush for failing to provide a broad vision of America's world role and thereby "fueling" isolationism from both the left and the right.

- He attacked Bush for coddling the dictators in China; it made little sense, Clinton argued, to play the "China card" when "our opponents have thrown in their hand."

- He attacked Bush for siding with the "crumbling" Soviet center and failing to call for aid for that nation until goaded by Richard Nixon.
- He took Bush to task for failing to challenge the blockade of Sarajevo, for giving "short shrift" to the yearnings of those seeking freedom in Croatia and Bosnia.

Nevertheless, Clinton and Bush were not as far apart as the heat of the campaign often suggested. Both agreed, mistakenly as it turned out, that economics would replace politics as the dominant factor in international relations. Both agreed on the importance of maintaining NATO, helping Russian democracy, and resolving trade disputes with Japan. Both supported a new General Agreement on Tariffs and Trade (GATT), and agreed on the importance of a free trade treaty with Mexico and Canada (the North American Free Trade Agreement, NAFTA). Both agreed that America had to lead, and to resist the temptations of isolationism.

To be sure, there were differences, not only over tactics, as of handling China, but on a strategic level. Bush tilted toward what was called the Realist school of international relations, which defined the national interest in terms of geopolitics rather than universal principles. Clinton, however, insisted that U.S. foreign policy could not be divorced from "the moral principles most American share." He argued that for the first time in his lifetime it was possible consistently to advocate freedom, democracy, and human rights. His inaugural address described a concept of the new world:

> Today, a generation raised in the shadows of the cold war assumes new responsibilities in a world warmed by the sunshine of freedom. . . . Our hopes, our hearts and our hands are with those on every continent who are building democracy and freedom. Their cause is America's cause.[3]

This reflected a stronger internationalism than had been evident in his campaign pronouncements. It had a Kennedyesque ring: John Kennedy had said that the country had to be ready to "bear any burden, pay any price" in the defense of liberty. But like Kennedy's more eloquent phrase, Clinton's "cause" was not easy to translate into operational policies. At what price and at what risk would Clinton champion democracy? He carefully avoided spelling out the answers.

Bush had witnessed the turmoil of the post–Cold War world with sharp misgivings. In an address on April 13, 1991, at Maxwell Air Force Base, he advocated a policy designed to "keep disorder at bay." He had, after all, lived through the delicate and dangerous period when the Cold War was ending in Eastern Europe and a Soviet military intervention could not be ruled out. He had navigated the shoals leading to German unification when his principal allies had been willing to settle for a new status quo. He had witnessed the tense days of the coup that almost restored the old guard to power in Moscow. He had seen Yugoslavia fall completely apart. And, of course, he had gone to war in the Gulf. Thus, keeping disorder at bay made a good deal of sense to Bush.

In Clinton's view, Bush had sided with the status quo against "democratic change"; with "familiar tyrants" rather than those who would overthrow them; with the old geography of repression rather than a "new map of freedom." The test of leadership, Clinton proclaimed in August 1992, was to grasp how the world had changed. Clinton saw a window of opportunity to abandon "business as usual." There was an inconsistency, he claimed, between Bush's preference for stability through personal relationships with foreign leaders and the American impulse to support freedom and democracy. As a candidate, Clinton could get by with such campaign bromides as, "We will to stand up for our interests, but we will share burdens, where possible, through multilateral efforts to secure the peace, such as NATO and a new voluntary U.N. rapid deployment force."[4] Some of this was the usual political posturing, but there was a genuine clash between Bush's emphasis on maintaining stability and candidate Clinton's "new vision" of America's role in a "dynamic world."

Soon after the election, President Clinton made a nearly fatal decision: he chose to turn over his foreign policies to subordinates. Commenting on foreign policy to his close colleagues, he said that he "didn't see a winner in the whole lot." The job of his foreign policy aides was to keep the issues away from the president so he could concentrate on domestic matters. Keep the president informed, his aides were warned, but "don't take too much of his time."[5]

Clinton's new team was drawn largely from the Carter administration. The Democrats had been out of power for twelve years, but the members of Carter's first team—former secretary of state Cyrus Vance, former secretary of defense Harold Brown, and Carter's national security advisor, Zbigniew Brzezinski—all were still quite active. Clinton, however, passed over this group, and he was probably wise to do so, since they would have badly overshadowed him. He dipped down to the second echelon of the Carter administration, choosing as secretary of state Warren Christopher, who had served as Vance's deputy. Christopher had the advantage of having worked with Clinton during the campaign and having advised the selection of Albert Gore as vice president. He had kept his hand in foreign policy as vice chairman of the Council on Foreign Relations in New York, while serving as a highly respected lawyer in California. There was criticism from Democrats who regarded him as too laconic and passive; since foreign policy was not thought to be an urgent concern, however, Christopher's low-key approach seemed ideal.

Strobe Talbott, a close friend and classmate of Clinton's at Oxford, but better known in Washington as a leading journalist for *Time* and an expert on Russia, was named a special ambassador. The post of ambassador to the United Nations was upgraded to cabinet rank (Bush, who had served in the UN, had downgraded the post). It was awarded to Madeleine Albright, who had served in the Carter administration but more recently had been a professor at Georgetown University and was regarded as a protegé of Brzezinski. Christopher chose as one of his under secretaries Peter Tarnoff, the president of the Council on Foreign Relations and formerly a key aide to Cyrus Vance in the State Department. The Far Eastern account was assigned to Winston Lord, also a former president of the Council on Foreign Relations, who had been Bush's ambassador to China and many years earlier a key member of Henry Kissinger's staff.

The real surprise was Clinton's choice for secretary of defense—Congressman Les Aspin, the highly intelligent but volatile chairman of the House Armed Services Committee. He was well liked in Washington, almost a legend for his having successfully challenged the old guard and taken over the leadership of the critical Armed Services Committee. He was a genuine policy "wonk," interested in everything, examining all issues from every standpoint, and highly sensitive to political currents. Nevertheless, his friends considered him ill suited for a bureaucratic job. Characteristically, Washington insiders predicted that Aspin would quickly dominate the administration because of his intimate knowledge of the Congress. In fact, within the year he was nudged out and replaced by his deputy, William Perry, who had also served in the Carter administration. Perry was no strategist either, but he operated in a lower key and became a steadying influence.

The one holdover of importance was the Chairman of the Joint Chiefs of Staff, General Colin Powell. In terms of recent hands-on experience, Powell was clearly well ahead of the rest of the administration. He had served in both the Reagan and Bush administrations. He was in a unique position to compare the new advisors; perhaps it was an ominous portent of things to come that he found the new group frustratingly undisciplined. Meetings of the previously solemn National Security Council were like college bull sessions, he wrote later in his memoirs.[6]

The new director of CIA was James Woolsey, a Washington lawyer with long experience in policy positions, especially in arms control and security affairs, gained in several previous administrations. He too would eventually resign, and he would endorse Robert Dole for president.

For national security advisor in the White House Clinton chose Anthony Lake, who had been the chief of policy planning in the State Department under Vance. He had been brought into the campaign as a speech writer by his former colleague in the State Department, Sandy Berger. Lake, a former Foreign Service Officer, had served in Vietnam—but for the State Department, not the military. Later he had become an important aide to Henry Kissinger in the White House. He and his colleague Roger Morris had resigned from Kissinger's staff in 1970 to protest the Cambodian incursion. (Morris would write in 1996 a searing book attacking Mr. and Mrs. Clinton.) After service in the State Department under Vance and Warren Christopher in the Carter administration, Lake had returned to private life and taught at Mount Holyoke.

Lake assumed the position occupied earlier by such luminaries as MacGeorge Bundy, Kissinger, Brzezinski, and Brent Scowcroft (twice). He was well aware of the built-in tensions between his prestigious office and that of the secretary of state. His position gave him almost daily access to the president. Given Clinton's lack of interest in foreign policy, however, Lake cut down his daily briefings; he was told not to expect Clinton to invest much political capital on foreign matters. For his part, Lake vowed to avoid any Kissinger-like feuds. Nonetheless, this truce with Warren Christopher would last for only a few months before Lake began to make major policy pronouncements. He explained that he did so because the Clinton team was so friendly they had lost their "edge."

This, then, was the professional group, led by a young, inexperienced president, that inherited George Bush's foreign policy legacy. Clinton's supporters were not necessarily happy with his team. The *New Republic* (January 18, 1993) asked to be forgiven for feeling a "little duped" because in foreign policy the new Democrats were looking like old Democrats. The foreign policy team was "utterly undiversified and brings no refreshment," the editorial concluded. On the right, there was also some disappointment that no "neo-cons" had been appointed; a group of them had supported Clinton. Their objections to Christopher, according to Fred Barnes, also writing in the *New Republic*, were Christopher's obsession with negotiations, his fear of the use of force, and lack of intellectual firepower.[7]

On the whole, however, the new team seemed qualified and experienced, if a few years out of date. The real problem was not their previous service together but their common views, which were woefully unrealistic. Several threads bound them together:

- Their aversion to the "cynical calculus" of pure power politics: a balance of power and traditional geopolitics were ill suited to a new era, no longer sufficient reasons to spend national treasure or send American troops to foreign lands.
- Their belief that American policy had to pursue more noble humanitarian goals: enlarging the realm of democracies became a major priority, as did the protection and advancement of human rights. America would support "every prisoner of conscience, every victim of torture, every individual denied basic human rights," as Warren Christopher announced to the World Conference on Human Rights in Vienna (June 14, 1993).
- Their belief that the use of force should not be limited to the defense of vital interests but extended to disinterested intervention in the name of moral principles, when the will and conscience of the international community were defied: force should be discrete and carefully applied.
- Their belief that the test of a policy's validity would be whether it could garner both domestic and international support: going it alone was wrong; the era of multilateral foreign policy and collective security, centered on the United Nations, had finally dawned.

The intellectual wellsprings of the Clinton administration's policy flowed mainly from three individuals: Lake, Talbott, and Albright. They agreed on most fundamentals, but there were differences. Lake and Talbott represented the Vietnam syndrome. They saw the Vietnam War as a catastrophe; they not only feared another "quagmire" but, more positively, wanted policy to represent high-minded ideals. Lake believed Vietnam had reduced the United States to "just another nation," tremendously powerful but "almost as vulnerable to others as they have been to us."[8] To correct this deplorable state of affairs it was necessary to adopt a righteous foreign policy.

Madeleine Albright saw events through the prism of the pre–world war disaster of appeasing dictators, i.e., the Munich syndrome. That was her personal experience, as a Czech-born refugee forced to flee her homeland twice, when the Nazis came to Prague and after the war when the communists seized power. Her preoccupation with Munich inclined her toward collective security as the bedrock of American policy. This in turn meant an inordinate reliance on the United Nations. As for the use of force, she once challenged General Powell as to why the nation had large armed forces if it were unwilling to use them—a remark that caused a near "aneurysm" on the general's part.[9]

Whereas Lake and Talbott were determined to define the limits on the use of American power, Albright believed that the problem was how to legitimize the exercise of power. She argued that legitimacy would be conferred if actions were taken with international support. Talbott and Lake did not dissent, but on the whole they were less hawkish.

A natural defining point for any student of foreign policy was the Cold War. Lake was loathe to give either Reagan or Bush credit for ending the Cold War, let alone winning it. Lake fell into the revisionist camp; he blamed both sides, Washington as well as Moscow, for sustaining the Cold War. For Lake the ideological and strategic rivalries imposed by *both* powers had done much to expand and intensify the bloodshed. Consistent with this view was his conclusion that the Cold War had ended more because of domestic political pressures and economic necessity than by "enlightened choice."

Talbott's views on the Cold War were even more radical than Lake's. Writing in 1990, before the demise of the USSR, Talbott concluded that the Soviet threat was not what it had once been. Had he been content with that statement, in the Gorbachev era, he would have been in been in good company. But he went much further: "The real point, however, is that it never was. The doves in the Great Debate of the past 40 years were right all along." Had the advice of the dovish side been heeded the Cold War would have ended "considerably sooner." This, of course, outraged his critics. His conclusion that it was not too soon to think about downgrading NATO and "rolling back" U.S. security commitments elsewhere would prove embarrassing to the new administration.[10]

This was not Albright's position; this was not the lesson of Munich. Nonetheless she was circumspect in dissenting from her colleagues. Not surprisingly, they all agreed on the importance of the UN. Albright said the UN would be elevated to the center of Clinton's new internationalism: history would record that the end of the Cold War marked a new beginning for the United Nations. Lake agreed that one of the startling international changes was the growing involvement of the United Nations in peacemaking and as well as peacekeeping.

During the campaign Clinton had urged the creation of a UN Rapid Deployment Force that could be used for purposes beyond traditional peacekeeping, such as standing guard at the borders of countries threatened by aggression. Albright went further. Following Clinton's vague lead, she supported creating a UN military capability for "combat operations." This would be one of the "greatest challenges" for the United States in building a collective security system. A viable system of collective security, she said later, would be a more potent weapon for maintaining international peace than the traditional right of self-defense. Finally, she made the rather startling point that "state-building operations" would be another dimension of collective security.[11]

The Clinton's administration's overall strategy was characterized by Lake as "pragmatic neo-Wilsonianism." For America the choice was either isolation, with all its predictable disasters as evidenced by history, or a new doctrine of internationalism—not the crusading idealism of Wilson but a practical application of his principles of democracy.[12] Wilson's core beliefs—spreading democracy to other nations, adhering to the importance of principles, and stressing the need for engagement—were more vital than ever, according to Lake. Americans could not fully embrace doctrines of power politics, as represented by Theodore Roosevelt, but they could rally to Wilson's "deeper resonance," allowing the United States to lead the world in the name of principle. Wilson had understood that what happened within nations was fundamental to what happened between them, Lake argued. Therefore, American security would be shaped by the "character of foreign regimes."[13]

Talbott, who probably had more influence than Lake on Clinton's foreign policy views, reinforced Lake's Wilsonian vision. Talbott asserted that while the internal affairs of a nation had once been off limits, that was no longer the case. Moreover, the principle of "humanitarian intervention" was gaining greater acceptance. The American people, Talbott wrote later, wanted their country's foreign policy rooted in "idealpolitik as well as realpolitik." Lake concurred: among the instances that might require force were "overwhelming violations of human rights." Rectifying human-rights abuses was a completely new rationale for American military intervention.[14]

In the Clinton administration the Realist school of foreign policy would take a severe beating. Joseph Nye of Harvard University, who later served in the CIA and the Defense Department under Clinton, wrote eloquently about the new liberal dispensation in foreign policy. The evolution of transnational communications, economic integration, and interdependence were making more relevant the "liberal conception of a world society of peoples, as well as states and of order resting on values and institutions as well as military power." Liberal views, once regarded as Utopian, now seemed less far-fetched: international order would be preserved by the creation of a UN force, Nye wrote, "an idea worth detailed practical examination" in the aftermath of the Cold War and Gulf War.[15]

Some outside policy groups reinforced the administration's basic philosophical bent. A group of former officials and scholars under the chairmanship of Winston Lord created a report for the Carnegie Endowment for International Peace that supported Clinton's emphases: the United States was free to move away from the "armed truce" of the Cold War toward a more "livable planet," a safer and freer world. America had to build democracies through "multilateral pressures and incentives." This Carnegie group included many future Clinton appointees: Richard Holbrooke, John Deutch, Alice Rivlin, David Gergen, Admiral William J. Crowe Jr., and Richard Gardner.[16]

The Progressive Policy Institute, a creation of the Democratic Party, strongly advocated putting "commercial diplomacy" at the center of America's new security strategy. Trade policies and other leverage could be used to encourage political and economic change in China, for example. Among the other recommendations were to give aid and encouragement to democratic forces abroad, struggling to hold free elections; to revamp foreign aid, shifting from country-by-country assistance to broader goals; to replace the Cold War military establishment with more mobile and flexible forces capable of rapid deployment to regional trouble spots; and finally, to reinvigorate the institutions of collective security.[17]

All of these musings were converted into a policy statement publicly delivered by Lake at Johns Hopkins University on September 21, 1993. He declared that the purpose of American power was to preserve, promote, and protect democracies. The strategy of "enlargement" of democracies would replace the doctrine of the containment of communism. (Ironically, the Carnegie Report argued that no single doctrine such as containment would serve as an organizing principle for American foreign policy.) Therefore, Lake argued, America's security mission was to promote the enlargement of democracy as well as of market economies. The strongest argument for this thesis was that democracies did not fight each other. This view had been adopted by Bush and James Baker, and for a time it had had a substantial intellectual following after the end of the Cold War. Inevitably, scholars began to pick it apart; they pointed out that democracies did not necessarily mean reliable partners and that there were many important instances when democracies had come close to fighting each other, such as England and France in the late nineteenth century. Democratic wars had been averted by an appeal to national interests rather than common political ideologies. A "democratic peace" was a triumph of hope over reality.[18]

Nevertheless, Lake insisted that the United States should not only help democracies but support the liberalization of states hostile to democracy. "Backlash" states, such as Iran and Iraq, would have to be isolated. He weakened his case, however, by adding a caveat: the United States would "at times" be required to befriend and even defend nondemocratic states for "mutually beneficial reasons."

In effect, Lake elevated abstract moral and ethical concepts to the same level as national security interests. Morality was the broad rationale for peacemaking (as opposed to peacekeeping), for "humanitarian" intervention, and for conducting an ethical foreign policy, one that rested not on American power but on the international legitimacy of multilateral institutions, such as the United Nations.

All of this was a witches' brew, too vague to be a guide to practical policy. A note of cold reality was injected into this Wilsonian litany. It came from Peter Tarnoff, the new under secretary of state for political affairs, usually considered the number-three position in the department. Tarnoff had been president of the Council on Foreign Relations when it had completed a long study of the post–Cold War period, entitled *Sea Changes*. Tarnoff had been one of the mentors of the project, which emphasized the limits on American resources and competing domestic concerns.

Shortly after taking office Tarnoff talked off the record about American policy to a group of correspondents. He suggested that the United States could not pursue the expansive liberal agenda being hawked in Washington: American resources were quite limited, and the United States would have to consider retrenchment in its foreign policy. "We simply don't have the leverage, we don't have the influence, we don't have the inclination to use military force," Tarnoff is reported to have said. Not only was this a jarring note in the utopian rhetoric of the early Clinton administration, but it reflected the realism of Clinton's predecessors. Adjusting aims to capabilities was, after all, a basic maxim.

When these remarks became public, Tarnoff was quickly disavowed by Christopher. The secretary of state insisted that despite limits on resources, the United States needed to lead. Reporters counted the use of "lead" and "leadership" twenty-three times in a hastily redrafted speech Christopher gave in Minneapolis. The United States, Christopher declared, had to be "more engaged, not less; more ardent in the promotion of democracy, not less; and more inspired in our leadership, not less." Tarnoff was presumably chastised and chastened. State Department aides were ordered to clear their remarks in advance. Unfortunately, the issues Tarnoff raised would not be debated.[19]

Thus, the new administration brought with it some heavy intellectual baggage. It was not the radical chic of the 1960s, as some critics quickly asserted. Its core was the more traditional liberal critique of American policy: that the nation had been too preoccupied with power; that its foreign policy had failed to reflect the ideals of Americans; that it had failed to support human rights abroad; and that it too often had acted unilaterally in furtherance of a national interest too narrowly defined and commanding only thin public support.

The new team vowed that it would not simply refine or remake Bush's new world order. Rather, it would create its own design. By personality and experience, however, Bill Clinton was not well suited for such a task. His supporters pointed out that he was quick study, but it turned out that he was also impatient with dissent and quick to blame others for his failures. The long transition from the Cold War would prove a difficult period for him.

Even as this team assumed office, the seeds were sown for major trouble. The president and his advisors were comfortable with flashes of Wilsonian rhetoric; indeed they were determined to pursue its lofty goals. But Clinton himself was more of a centrist. True, his interest in foreign affairs was vastly overshadowed by his preoccupation with domestic concerns. His advisors, however, mistook this as a green light to pursue their own policy predilections. When their views clashed with the real world, they needed the firm support of their president. Clinton, however, was not inclined to run political risks for policies he never fully embraced.

Neo-Wilsonianism was appealing to a nation exhausted by the battles of the Cold War and yearning for a respite. But Wilsonianism was a utopian island in a world dominated by a new, virulent nationalism, religious fanaticism, the disintegration of empires, the demise of ideology, regional wars, and great-power disarray. Clinton's interest in foreign affairs was sporadic for too long, and it would cost him heavily.

NOTES

1. Interview, June 25, 1992, *New York Times*, June 28, 1992.

2. Governor Bill Clinton, "A New Covenant for American Security," Georgetown University, Washington, D.C., December 12, 1991.

3. President Clinton, "Inaugural Address," January 20, 1993, in U.S. Department of State *Dispatch*, January 25, 1993.

4. Bill Clinton, "Address to the Los Angeles World Affairs Council," August 13, 1992, in *New York Times*, August 14, 1992.

5. Tom Matthews, "Clinton's Growing Pains," *Newsweek*, May 3, 1993; Douglas Jehl, "Clinton, Unlike Recent Predecessors," *New York Times*, February 8, 1994.

6. Colin Powell, *My American Journey* (New York: Random House, 1995), p. 57.

7. Editorial, "The Quiet Man," *New Republic*, January 18, 1993; Fred Barnes, "Neoconned," *New Republic*, January 25, 1993.

8. Quoted in Peter Grose, *Continuing the Inquiry* (New York: Council on Foreign Relations, 1996), p. 53.

9. Powell, *My American Journey*, p. 57.

10. *Congressional Record, Senate*, February 22, 1994, p. 154.

11. Madeleine K. Albright, testimony, May 3, 1993, House Subcommittee on Europe, in *Dispatch*, May 10, 1993; and "Myths of Peacekeeping," statement before the House Subcommittee on International Security, June 24, 1993, in *Dispatch*, June 28, 1993.

12. Anthony Lake, "From Containment to Enlargement," remarks at Johns Hopkins University, School of Advanced International Studies, Washington, D.C., September 21, 1993.

13. Ibid.; Thomas L. Friedman, "Clinton's Foreign Policy," *New York Times*, October 31, 1993; Jason DeParle, "The Man inside Bill Clinton's Foreign Policy," *New York Times Magazine*, August 20, 1995.

14. Strobe Talbott, "Spreading Democracy," *Foreign Affairs*, November/December 1996.

15. Joseph S. Nye, "What New World Order?" *Foreign Affairs*, Spring 1992.

16. Carnegie Endowment National Commission, *Changing Our Ways: America and the World* (Washington, D.C.: Carnegie Endowment for International Peace, 1992).

17. Will Marshall and Martin Schram, eds., *Mandate for Change* (New York: Beverly Books, 1993), pp. 317–318.

18. Christopher Layne, "Kant or Cant: The Myth of the Democratic Peace," *International Security*, Fall 1994.

19. Steven A. Holmes, "Christopher Reaffirms Leading U.S. Role," *New York Times*, May 28, 1993; Daniel Williams and John N. Goshko, "Administration Rushes to 'Clarify' Policy Remarks," *Washington Post*, May 27, 1993.

3

Intervention

Since the attack on Pearl Harbor, no new administration has enjoyed the luxury of a honeymoon, however brief, before being plunged into the real world of policy and politics. Truman had immediately to confront the decision to drop the atomic bomb. Stalin died less than two months after Eisenhower's inauguration; Kennedy ordered the ill-fated Bay of Pigs invasion in his fourth month in office. Mindful of such examples, new administrations have launched official new studies of issues as soon as possible, in part to assert that the White House would be in charge, but also to get a handle on the policy process. Kissinger, Brzezinski, and Alexander Haig (for Reagan) had been skillful in using this device. Thus, it was no surprise that the Clinton administration announced new studies, called Presidential Study Directives (PSDs). One of the first concerned the situation in Bosnia.

For over forty years Washington had worried about Yugoslavia. The fear had been a relatively simple one: that once the communist dictatorship of Josip Broz Tito was weakened or removed, Yugoslavia would start to break apart into its ethnic components. The Soviet Union would then intervene to restore "order." What would the United States do? No one really knew.

Ironically, when the breakup did come, the Soviet Union was already mortally weakened by its own final crisis. This changed the whole American approach. The greatly diminished likelihood of Soviet intervention allowed the Bush administration to abdicate its responsibilities in favor of the overly eager Europeans, who were determined to prove their independence from American tutelage. The era of Europe had dawned, the foreign minister of Luxembourg exclaimed with relish, at the thought of the end of

American domination. The president of the European Community (EC), Jacques Delors, went further, hoping aloud that since the EC did not interfere in American affairs, the Americans would have enough respect not to interfere in European affairs.

The United States and the Europeans failed to prevent the breakup of Yugoslavia. Neither the United States nor its allies favored a breakup, but they were not prepared to take forceful action to stop it. Moreover, the situation was confused by a clash between two principles: self-determination and territorial sovereignty. The Europeans insisted that force could not be used by outside powers, even to promote self-determination. Without a threat of force, however, diplomacy was impotent. In 1990 the CIA predicted that Yugoslavia would break up within eighteen months.[1]

The summer of 1991 may have been the last and best chance to preserve Yugoslavia; a strong outside political intervention might have worked. Secretary James Baker, while in Belgrade that June, warned against a breakup, announcing that the United States would not recognize any resulting new independent states. This threat of nonrecognition may have been read in unintended ways. It was not meant as a green light to the Serbs to act against the secessionists, but it may well have been taken that way in Belgrade. In any case, the Yugoslav strongman, Slobodan Milosevic, may well have concluded that he had nothing much to fear from Washington; he turned first on Slovenia, which declared its independence the day after Baker left Yugoslavia. Both Baker and Warren Zimmermann, the last American ambassador to Yugoslavia, now insist that no green light was given; but Zimmermann also notes that there was no red light either.[2]

The war between Yugoslavia and Slovenia was mercifully short and ended without much damage. The Yugoslav army withdrew from Slovenia in order to concentrate on a much more important enemy—the Croats. Fighting erupted in Croatia in July 1991, and the European Union (EU) tried to mediate, selecting former British foreign secretary Peter Lord Carrington as their emissary. The United States acceded to Europe's determination to take the lead in Yugoslavia. The principal EU countries, especially Britain, France, and Germany, wanted to keep the diplomatic controls in their own hands. This meant NATO had to be sidetracked; a leading position for NATO would have meant a major American role. By relying on the EU, the Europeans leaders could effectively exclude Washington. A Bush administration official later admitted that American willingness to relinquish responsibility was a tragic mistake. The war between Croatia and Yugoslavia inevitably worsened.[3]

In a typically Pavlovian response, the UN decided to impose an arms embargo against *all* parties—an action that grew out of an original intention to block Russian support for Serbia. Obviously, such an embargo would favor the strongest-armed party, the Serbian-Yugoslav forces. Having voted a general arms embargo, as well as economic sanctions against Yugoslavia, the presumed aggressor, the UN Security Council enlisted a former American secretary of state, Cyrus Vance, as its intermediary. Vance joined forces with Peter Carrington, and together they negotiated a cease-fire between Yugoslavia and Croatia in November 1991; it left Serbian forces in control of about 25 percent of Croatian territory. The cease-fire, in turn, led to the dispatch of a large contingent of UN peacekeepers to Croatia, mainly British and French soldiers.

Some Europeans, however, still wanted to recognize the new states. In particular, there was German pressure to recognize Croatia. Vance pleaded with the Europeans and with Washington to hold off; he was particularly upset by German foreign minister Hans Dietrich Genscher's insistence on immediate recognition. Vance's pleas were brushed aside. Germany granted recognition of Croatia and Slovenia in December 1991, despite American misgivings. The rest of the European Union members then followed the German lead. Washington had no real choice but to fall into line. This left the two other successor republics, Macedonia and Bosnia, in limbo. Eventually the Bush administration recognized their independence as well, arguing that the threat of further violence in Bosnia might be averted by recognition, which might be seen as a stabilizing gesture.

Yugoslavia had ceased to exist. The overriding question for Western policy, however, became how to stop the fighting, or at least limit it. There was a growing fear that the fighting would spread to the Yugoslav province of Kosovo, inhabited by a large majority of Albanians. If the fighting did in fact spread, it could draw in Albania. Refugees might flee to neighboring Macedonia, with the Serbs in hot pursuit; fighting between Serbs and Macedonians would begin. In that case, rather than acquiesce in a Serb predominance, the Greeks and Bulgarians, both claimants to Macedonia, might decide to intervene. Inevitably, the Turks would become involved. The nightmare of a huge Balkan war loomed. This fear was a more compelling argument in Washington for intervention than the war between Serbia and Croatia. Before it left office, the Bush administration sent a stiff warning to Milosevic against taking any actions in Kosovo.

Nevertheless, the Bush administration was adamantly opposed to military intervention by American ground forces. It saw not another Desert Storm but another Vietnam, a bloody conflict with no clear exit. And even if an exit strategy could be devised, the administration saw no threat to vi-

tal American interests. After the Bush administration left office its last secretary of state, Lawrence Eagleburger, declared that "from beginning to
end, to right now, I am telling you I don't know any way to stop it except
with the massive use of military force."[4] This was also the view expressed by
Bush's national security advisor, Brent Scowcroft, after he left office. Others were more critical, suggesting that perhaps the United States could
have halted the fighting if it had put in peacekeeping troops along with the
Europeans after the Croatian cease-fire.

The European/UN forces on the ground inside the country became virtual hostages. In both London and Paris it was argued that any threat of
more vigorous action, such as air strikes, would put these forces at risk.
Since these troops were lightly armed, they were highly vulnerable. As
one State Department official explained to Ambassador Warren Zimmermann, Yugoslavia had become a "tar baby": no one wanted to touch it.
Thus the Serbs gained a free hand. Zimmermann concluded later that
"the refusal of the Bush administration to commit American power
early . . . was our greatest mistake of the entire Yugoslav crisis. It made an
unjust outcome inevitable and wasted the opportunity to prevent over a
hundred thousand deaths."[5]

A new mediation, this time focused on Bosnia, began under Cyrus
Vance and a former British foreign secretary, David Lord Owen, who had
replaced Peter Carrington. It was becoming clear that there was no chance
for American or European military intervention in the fighting. Any settlement therefore would not roll back Serbian gains and restore Bosnian
integrity but would partition Bosnia into its ethnic components. Moreover,
the Bosnian Serb military forces had taken about 60 to 70 percent of the
territory under their military control. Without the threat of outside military intervention, they had no incentive to withdraw.

Nevertheless, Vance and Owen devised a peace plan. It was based on a
division of Bosnia into ten separate cantons, to be presided over by a nominal central government in Sarajevo. Owen argued that this solution made
the best of a bad situation. Negotiations among the parties began in Geneva, but there was no enthusiasm for the plan. Indeed, in the United
States it was denounced as another Munich, rewarding the aggressors.
Vance and Owen were highly indignant at such charges, Owen in particular. He pointed out that if the United States wished a different outcome it
would have to put in troops, which he knew was virtually impossible. Talks
in Geneva between the various parties bogged down; Vance and Owen
shifted their efforts to New York and the UN.

This was the Balkan political situation confronting the incoming Clinton administration. The Bush administration had narrowed American op-

tions by denying that there was a threat to American interests and declaring that outright military intervention was unacceptable without a clear exit strategy. The U.S. stake was not in restoring Bosnia but in ending the war and keeping the combat from spreading. Under Bush—and then under Clinton—the American military establishment in particular was adamantly against an armed intervention, citing the Powell doctrine that any use of force should be massive enough to be decisive. In Bosnia, it argued, there were no clear political objectives justifying massive force.

There was no real pressure on Clinton to intervene with combat forces. Even hawks who favored vigorous action argued for only limited measures, because they knew there was no public support for ground force intervention. On the other hand, the Clinton administration could not easily accept the Vance-Owen plan. Given the new president's history of anti-Vietnam dissent as well as the dovish reputation of some of his key advisors, the new administration was quite sensitive to charges of being soft. The administration accordingly did not reject Vance-Owen but refused to endorse it. Clinton officials privately argued that important principles would be violated: the plan not only rewarded aggression (which it did) but was a thinly disguised partition (which it was); most tellingly, it violated the old Wilsonian principle of self-determination. The United States could not and would not impose a peace settlement on the parties. The practical effect of this principled position was virtually to invite any and every party to the conflict to veto any proposed settlement.

Clinton confronted a confusing alignment of political forces. A humanitarian disaster loomed, and there were increasing reports of atrocities by Serbs. Washington could try to persuade the parties involved to stop fighting, but diplomacy would have to be backed by some threat of force. Given the skeptical state of congressional and public opinion, such a threat was unlikely. Public opinion polls indicated strong opposition to American involvement (60–70 percent against).

Confusion reigned: heated rhetoric, threats, and warnings. Some observers, such as the *Economist* (December 19, 1992), thought that once in office Clinton would nevertheless be inclined to intervention by force, as the most "humane response" to the Serbian regime's "systematic nastiness." The need, the *Economist* continued, was for a "world cop." Clinton had no intention of assuming the role of world cop, even though his natural liberal constituents were increasingly militant: Stop Serbia Now! was their war cry. A powerful argument was the analogy of the atrocities in Bosnia to the Nazi Holocaust; most liberals, however, still balked at the use of ground forces. On the right there was also strong opposition to the use of American ground forces. Some conservative commentators, however, were alarmed by the vehemence and nature of opposition in their ranks to any intervention—it smacked of neo-isolationism. The columnist William Safire proposed perhaps the most outlandish new principle: that collective security should be no longer limited to defending national borders; a "nascent understanding grows that ethnic minorities are entitled to international protection."[6]

If there was a consensus it centered around a combination that came to be known as "lift and strike"—that is, lift the arms embargo against Bosnia to create a level playing field and threaten NATO air strikes against Serbian forces. This option seemed appealing when compared to doing nothing or joining the fighting.

Clinton's team was divided. Richard Holbrooke, who would later play a major role in the Bosnian crisis, argued that the inadequate American reaction was planting seeds for another era of tragedy in Europe. In a memorandum to Clinton he endorsed campaign speeches that were being interpreted as signaling that Clinton would "follow a more vigorous policy against Serb aggression."[7] In the Pentagon, however, both civilian and military leaders were against intervention, and they doubted the effectiveness of air power as well. This had been General Powell's opinion in the Bush administration, when he had been supported by the secretary of defense, Dick Cheney. Powell took the same position with Clinton officials and was supported by the new secretary of defense, Aspin. The chief difference, Powell would note later, was the meandering style of the Clinton team. Anthony Lake was the most hawkish, probably more as a devil's advocate than a genuine convert; in one exchange, for example, he compared Bosnia to Vietnam. Christopher was also opposed to intervention, but rather than rejecting it outright he posed a series of prior conditions that made it inconceivable.

Christopher met with Vance and Owen, but afterward he publicly questioned their plan's "practicality and feasibility." Owen was indignant. He found Christopher ignorant of many of the details and poorly prepared. Unfortunately, Owen aired his indignation to an American reporter, R. W. Apple Jr., who promptly printed it in the New York Times: the Clinton administration's opposition to his plan was going to "scuttle the chances of ending the war."[8] European foreign ministers urged Washington to give an unqualified endorsement to the Vance-Owen plan, but President Clinton, through his press secretary, took the position that he would agree only if all the parties agreed—an obvious signal to the plan's opponents. The Bosnian Serbs did in fact reject the Vance-Owen plan.

Deliberate leaks suggested that Clinton would soon adopt a new diplomatic approach. Clinton himself publicly speculated that the United

States might be prepared to send in troops as peacekeepers if there was a genuine settlement. Administration spokesmen quickly corrected him, emphasizing that American "peacekeepers" would be contemplated only after a final settlement.

On February 9, 1993, Clinton announced a new plan, upon which Christopher elaborated. [9] First, a new American special envoy would be appointed to join the peace negotiations. The United States would press for stronger sanctions and tougher enforcement of the "no-fly zone." A new international war crimes tribunal would be established. There was still no endorsement of Vance-Owen; instead, Christopher's pronouncement indicated, any peace plan would have to be agreed to by all parties. For the moment, Washington ruled out bombing or military intervention.

This statement of policy was generally welcomed. Some believed that it gave some version of the Vance-Owen plan its only chance of success. Others, such as Zbigniew Brzezinski, were critical of what appeared to be "toothless and essentially procedural steps." Republicans in Congress were also skeptical. Former UN ambassador Jeane Kirkpatrick also found the Clinton response inadequate and argued for bombing, even if the United States had to act unilaterally. [10] On the other hand, a *New York Times* editorial (February 11, 1993) sharply warned against the "slippery slope" of military engagement: "Is anyone around the Oval Office reading history books?"

Clinton was simply buying time. The American initiative in itself did not rule out the Vance-Owen plan, but as American officials explained, the plan would have to be renegotiated. Despite earlier hints by the president, the administration had made no clear commitment to insert American troops even as peacekeeping forces; the United States would only "do its share," Christopher said. On a more pressing issue, the arms embargo would not be lifted. The new plan covered all bases, but without any real undertakings.

Buying time did not work; the situation on the ground was deteriorating too rapidly. Several towns in Bosnia were cut off, food was running out in some areas, the fighting was continuing, and there were reports of grisly atrocities. Over the next month the situation became more confused. Margaret Thatcher delivered a particularly strong speech denouncing the West's hesitation: "I never thought I would see another holocaust," she declared, implying that her successor, John Major, was playing the role of Neville Chamberlain. About this time, twelve U.S. State Department officers revolted, sending Secretary Christopher an "impassioned" letter claiming that diplomacy had failed and calling for firm military action. [11] A "private" memorandum from Ambassador Albright to the president was conveniently leaked; in it she urged the use of air power to slow Serb advances. The press again rehearsed differences inside the administration: General Powell was still against using air power, but Secretary Aspin was leaning more in that direction. Both were against a commitment to use American forces for peacekeeping.

A basic decision had to be made. Opinion polls were still running against forceful action, and congressional sentiment was opposed as well. Throughout April the Clinton administration agonized over how far it could go. Some of Clinton's supporters saw Bosnia as a personal test of the president. One observer described the endless policy sessions as "group therapy" rather than a decision-making process. In late April the press reported that the president had turned down any further thought of intervening to impose peace by force. It had never really been an option, but after April 19—the day of the tragic inferno in Waco, Texas—it was off the scope.

As Clinton's options narrowed, the "lift and strike" plan was more and more appealing. The two measures would be complementary, and minimize the risk to American forces, but they would exert new pressure that might conceivably create a cease-fire. On May Day, Christopher reported that there was a new presidential decision; he would leave for Europe that very evening to consult with the allies on the new plan. Details of Clinton's decision were withheld, but the essence was a version of lift and strike.[12]

It should have been obvious that even as the decision was announced in Washington, Britain and France would resist the new Clinton plan. The Clinton tactic to overcome allied resistance was to announce the new decision with a great flourish and hope that Christopher could sell lift and strike as the only way to preserve a united NATO front. The Clinton administration, however, had neglected to prepare a consensus in private before Christopher left for Europe—a lapse that would prove a major blunder. Perhaps it was also a mistake to announce that the final American decision would be made after the consultations and after Christopher had returned to the United States. This left a large loophole, and in his public statements Christopher adopted the ambiguous position that the United States would play its part as long as the others played their roles. In short, Christopher scarcely exuded determination.

A number of commentaries suggested that Clinton had put his presidency on the line. Bosnia was a threat to his domestic initiatives: the economy, the budget, health care, all would be swallowed in a Balkan black hole.[13] Such analyses apparently provoked second thoughts. The more Clinton mulled over Bosnia, the more dangerous his own decision appeared. Even limited air strikes might lead to escalation, and the United States would have assumed the responsibility for the final outcome. Since a superpower could not risk defeat, the United States would have to go in deeper. Christopher encountered European resistance, and Clinton began to have serious doubts, according to Elizabeth Drew's account in her *On the Edge*. The president was "going south" on lift and strike, was how she described Les Aspin's conclusion after he met with Clinton privately during Christopher's trip.[14]

While in Europe, Christopher was informed that the president was wavering. Whether this had any effect on his consultations is unclear, but it could not have helped. A reporter traveling with Christopher to London and Paris had the impression that he was not selling very hard. The French announced their unconditional rejection of lifting the arms embargo and again criticized America's absence from the peacekeeping forces. The French were also hurriedly developing a counterplan: Paris proposed to designate certain areas as "safe havens," which would be protected by UN troops. While Christopher was still traveling, the British and French agreed to designate Sarajevo and six other areas as "safe havens." What this meant was not well defined, but it undercut Christopher's mission. Britain, France, and Russia were united in opposing lift and strike, and Clinton was not willing to override their veto.

The administration had gambled and lost. Having put forward its own plan, for Clinton to back away was to risk humiliation—but that is what happened. Christopher returned home with no endorsement of his plan. The secretary put on a brave face, but within a day of his return it was obvious that the administration had caved in. The president immediately convened a National Security Council meeting to discuss alternatives, thereby discarding the Christopher initiative. Even before the meeting White House officials were spreading the word that the most important factor was to preserve allied unity. In other words, the French-British-Russian veto would not be challenged.

After the NSC had discussed Christopher's report, the word from the White House was that Clinton would not order any military measures but would wait. The White House shifted the blame to the Europeans. The Europeans replied that they could have been persuaded and indeed had expected new pressure from Washington, not a retreat. The Europeans claimed they had only been "nudged" by Christopher, not pushed. They were probably right. Christopher could not go very far, because the heart of his principal, the president of the United States, was not his own policy. Clinton might have taken to the airwaves to promote his plan and stimulate public and congressional support; during the Christopher mission he was strangely silent. This convinced the Europeans that they were being set up: that Clinton would in the end refuse to act decisively and would then blame the Europeans.

Britain and France pressed the new plan for UN contingents to protect six designated "safe havens," which included the towns of Goradze and Srebrenica. American officials reluctantly went along, in the name of preserving allied unity. The foreign ministers met with Christopher in Washington, and the French plan was endorsed on May 22, 1993. It sounded the death knell for Bosnia.

Clinton's first serious foray into great-power politics had failed. It had been handled amateurishly by the White House and the president's lieutenants. It had been put forward with an air of hesitation and reluctance; it was less a concrete plan than a proposed "direction." It had been offered, as one reporter described it, not only for discussion but for amendment. When, inevitably, it was rejected, the president ordered a retreat. Indeed, there seemed to be a sigh of relief in the White House.[15]

Obviously, Washington was determined not to act alone. Consistent with the administration's basic philosophy, it would act only within the safety and comfort of allied or international support. The Clinton administration, however, could not determine its own vital interests. Lacking a firm objective, it relied on tactical maneuvering, influenced by domestic politics. Clinton's hesitation seemed vindicated by the lack of political recrimination at home; even the conservative *National Review* conceded that the United States had no vital interests at stake and that therefore only "modest risks" were justified.[16]

After this doleful episode, the United States had no real strategy: Vance-Owen was dead; lift and strike was dead; military intervention had been ruled out; there was no prospect of a settlement. Bosnia was closer than ever to disappearing as a state. It was reported that Christopher had advised the president to "stay the course"[17]; but no one seemed to know what that course was, or even what it should be. (Later, after the 1996 elections, American officials became historical revisionists. Christopher admitted that his original mission of May 1993 had been badly handled and that backing down had been a mistake. Secretary Perry said that the administration should have been prepared to use NATO at the "beginning" and that prospect had implied the commitment of U.S. forces.)

Bosnia nevertheless dogged the Clinton administration. During 1994 there were sporadic crises—attacks by Serbs, some NATO bombings—but no basic change occurred. An important American policy reassessment, however, took place in the late November. A number of officials feared that continued squabbling over Bosnian tactics was eating away at the foundation of the Atlantic alliance. Under the guidance of National

Security Advisor Anthony Lake, a significant reversal of policy was instituted. In effect, the Clinton administration decided that NATO unity was more important than Bosnia. Washington would not "break" NATO over such Bosnian issues as bombing Serb forces, or lifting the arms embargo. A new policy directive was issued confirming the new order of priorities.[18] It was reported, however, that President Clinton did not bother to attend the NSC meeting that reached the decision; Bosnia had been relegated to the twilight zone. Richard Holbrooke, now assistant secretary of state for European affairs, later recalled that during his first ten months in that office most high-level meetings on Bosnia had a "dispirited, inconclusive quality; there was little enthusiasm for any proposal for action."[19] In early December, during the annual meeting of NATO, Secretary Christopher said that the crisis was limited to Bosnia and the former Yugoslavia: it was "not about NATO."[20] This was a complete reversal of policy.

DAYTON

By early 1995, however, Bosnia had become a symbol of Clinton's failed foreign policy. There was increasingly serious talk of a complete UN withdrawal, in which case American combat troops might have to intervene to protect the UN forces as they withdrew. Several new factors, however, began to change the situation in a way that made a peace settlement feasible.

First, Clinton officials secretly gave a green light to a Croatian plan to import Iranian weapons. Second, the Congress passed a law forbidding the U.S. Navy from enforcing the UN arms embargo. Third, the Croatian forces, now obviously much stronger and better equipped and trained, began to defeat Serb forces; by early August their offensive had recovered almost all Croatian territory lost in the war. The fourth new factor was a ferocious bloodletting resulting from a Serb counteroffensive against UN outposts around the "safe havens" of Srebrenica and the nearby town of Zepa. In both areas there was a horrendous slaughter.[21]

If there was one single turning point in Bosnia, the mass killings in Srebrenica may well have been it. Public opinion was outraged. When Srebrenica fell, a "jolt of electricity" passed through the Clinton administration.[22] Srebrenica was the catalyst of a 180-degree turn in President Clinton's attitude and policies. He was reported to be frustrated and angry and to have berated his NSC staff. Clinton, spewing profanity, shouted at NSC officials Sandy Berger and Nancy Soderberg, "I'm getting creamed," according to an account of journalist Bob Woodward.[23]

What one official had called the "free fall" of American policy came to an end. Clinton finally recognized that deferring to the Europeans, the strategic rationale for much of American policy, was a failure. For Clinton it had meant putting his presidency at the mercy of allies, who would follow their own interests. Particularly irritating to Clinton was a widely quoted, devastating comment by the new French president, Jacques Chirac, after a visit to Washington in June: that the post of leader of the free world was "vacant."[24]

The final factor, and perhaps the clincher, was the political situation in the United States. Clinton's domestic policy advisors were becoming persuaded that he had to settle Bosnia before the 1996 campaign. Anthony Lake was reported to have told him that Bosnia was a cancer threatening to devour his presidency. Once again observers complained that the president was too far removed from the intricacies of policy. The NATO council had already approved an operational plan (Op-Plan 40-104) for twenty thousand U.S. troops to support a UN withdrawal. Apparently Clinton did not realize this; the briefing he received about Bosnia just before Chirac's arrival in Washington had played down the automatic character of the NATO plan. Clinton was stunned that same evening of the state dinner for Chirac to learn from Holbrooke as well as Christopher that Europe was interpreting his various remarks as a firm commitment to use American troops to extricate the UN forces if need be.[25]

Clinton insisted on a new and "coherent" peace plan. It was reported that the administration was "frantically" working on a strategy that would permit the United States to take the lead. Lake produced a "plan" revolving around active American diplomacy to bring the three Yugoslav sides into face-to-face talks under American auspices. The president convened three meetings with his advisors in early August. Clinton's only condition was that no American combat troops were to be involved in the fighting. He decided to proceed with a two-stage strategy: (1) Lake and Tarnoff would go to Europe and Russia to present a framework; (2) Holbrooke would then begin an all-out negotiating effort. The goal was a "comprehensive peace settlement," including three-way recognition, among Bosnia, Croatia, and Yugoslavia. Economic sanctions would be lifted after a ceasefire. The territorial settlement would be based on the earlier plan of a 51/49 percent division.[26]

As Lake began his mission to Europe, attitudes in the United States were beginning to change. In particular, resistance to American intervention was weakening. A *Washington Post* editorial (May 30, 1995) asserted that "abandonment of Bosnia would rip at the threads of international order." It was another Bosnian Serb shelling of Sarajevo, killing over thirty people, that finally ignited NATO air strikes; this time they were no "pinpricks" but sustained attacks on military targets, including for the first time attacks by American cruise missiles against a Serb base. Holbrooke, who was at the beginning of his diplomatic mission, advised Washington that the Serb attack and NATO's response was the "most important test of American leadership since the end of the Cold war . . . not only in Bosnia but in Europe." He speculated that the unlike the Vietcong, the Bosnian Serbs would not stand up to NATO air attacks; moreover, he predicted Belgrade was not going to back Bosnians Serbs, and he was right.[27]

By early September 1995, therefore, the conditions were ripe for peace. Milosevic might get the sanctions lifted. The Bosnian Serbs could head off further losses on the ground. The Croatians could consolidate their new territorial gains. The Bosnians were understandably dubious, especially since their military prospects were improving. On the other hand, a cease-fire could bring in American troops as peacekeepers. The NATO allies were ready to police an agreement, especially since it would involve American troops, as Clinton had repeatedly promised.

Holbrooke was the ideal man to pull all of this together. He was highly intelligent, remarkably energetic, and a persuasive negotiator. In fact, to almost everyone's surprise he brokered not only a simple cease-fire but a more far-reaching agreement on "principles" of a final settlement. Announced on September 8, 1995, its main points were: (1) Bosnia and Herzegovina would continue a legal existence within its present borders and would consist of two entities: the Federation of Bosnia and Herzegovina, and the Republika Srpska; (2) the territorial proposal of the Contact Group, that is, the 51/49 percent split, would be the "basis" for a settlement; and (3) both Bosnian entities would have the right to establish parallel special relationships with "neighboring" countries. The results were eventually incorporated into the peace agreements, after negotiations in Dayton, Ohio, that Holbrooke would characterize as "conflict, confusion and tragedy."[28] Bosnia would be partitioned, but no one, especially the Americans, would admit it.

Commentary, however, was generally favorable, if guarded. It was the kind of agreement that the administration had refused to approve almost three years earlier, when it came into office. On September 9, the *New York Times*, however, editorialized, "The partition plan, imperfect as it is, offers the best hope for ending a war that has done grievous damage to Bosnia's people. It would be better if Bosnia were untouched and intact, but three years of vicious fighting have eliminated that possibility, and the Bosnians themselves are resigned to accepting a good deal less." Clinton announced that a cease-fire had been agreed on October 5; it went into effect on October 12. NATO approved a plan to send in troops to separate the fighting forces; the force would amount to about fifty or sixty thousand troops. The American share would be around twenty thousand.

The prospect of American combat troops going into Bosnia provoked the expected resistance in the Congress. The chief concerns were: What would be the actual mission of the American troops? When would they be withdrawn, and how? In other words what was the exit strategy?[29] While the administration announced that it would welcome congressional support, it insisted that the president did not need congressional authority to send troops. Clinton joined a long line of his predecessors who had invoked their constitutional authority as commander in chief. The administration faced a dilemma: to reassure Congress it insisted on the firmness of its commitment to a specific timetable for withdrawal, an exit strategy, but to reassure its allies the administration's position had to be flexible and subject to modification in light of events.

The administration gained support by indicating that the deployment of American forces would be limited to one year and by promising there would be no "mission creep," as had been the case in Somalia. Clinton said that "in Bosnia we can and will succeed because our mission is clear and limited." The American ambassador to NATO, Robert Hunter, explained, "This is going to be a limited duration operation, 12 months max." He explained that setting a timetable would force speedy action on reconstruction.[30] More realistic observers pointed out that these assurances of a strict deadline might undercut the mission's effectiveness. Senator Robert Dole, facing early presidential primaries, argued that since the deployment was proceeding, preserving American credibility was in the national interest; a negative vote would be a repudiation of the troops themselves. He proposed that the deployment should be supported but for "approximately" one year. The Senate acquiesced in the troop deployment, by a vote of sixty-nine to thirty and turned back a resolution opposing the dispatch of troops by fifty-two to forty-seven.

One year after the signing of the Dayton agreements, Bosnia remained a deeply divided country. Mindful of the lessons of Somalia, Washington made little effort to re-create the institutions of a single unified state; there would be no nation building. There were periodic hints that American forces might have to remain beyond the deadline of December 1996. Most commentators, diplomats, and some American officials concluded that the peace effort had failed and that war would resume if NATO forces were withdrawn. Once safely reelected, Clinton announced on November 15, 1996, that American forces would remain until July 1998! Soon however even that new deadline was being questioned.[31]

Washington had counted heavily on Milosevic to bring the Bosnian Serbs into line, but Milosevic himself came under heavy internal pressure from dissidents rebelling against his arbitrary cancellation of the results of municipal elections in Yugoslavia. Accordingly, Milosevic could not afford to offend or challenge the Serbian nationalists inside Yugoslavia. Moreover, his governing party faced a presidential election, in which the opposing candidate was Vojislav Seselj, an extreme nationalist who had led guerrilla forces in Bosnia. Radovan Karadzic and his faction were relatively free to defy the UN, NATO, and the United States.

As this stalemate became more and more apparent, American authorities switched tactics. They split the Bosnian Serbs by embracing the Serbian faction located in Banja Luka, led by the nominal president of Srpska, Biljana Plavsic.[32] She succeeded Karadzic when he was forced to step down from the presidency under American pressure, but then she broke with him. She was encouraged by American officials to rebel against the authorities in Pale, and on several occasions NATO troops intervened to help her faction in the run-up to elections for the Bosnian Serb parliament. NATO support strengthened Plavsic's faction in these elections.[33] The net result, however, was that NATO forces, including American forces, were operating increasingly as political police, drawn more deeply into domestic Bosnian politics.

The newly elected Bosnian Serb parliament chose a new prime minister, thirty-eight-year old Milorad Dodik. He immediately pledged to "follow to the dot" the Dayton peace agreements, announced a number of reforms, and promised to turn over the indicted war criminals. But he quickly explained that it would be political suicide to turn them over at that time. Milosevic endorsed Dodik's election, which gave Dodik a much needed legitimacy inside Bosnia. Milosevic told Senator Dole, then visiting Belgrade, that he believed Dodik's government would "cooperate completely" in the peace process and that he supported him.[34]

NATO intervention had succeeded in imposing order in Bosnia but not in creating unity. It was obvious that American troops had to remain; the issue was how to define their mission and accordingly, what size force should remain. Clinton finally announced on December 18 what everyone had anticipated—that American forces would indeed remain in Bosnia and without a deadline for their withdrawal.[35] He disarmed his critics by freely acknowledging his error in setting previous deadlines, but he argued that progress was "unmistakable." An American withdrawal would mean falling back into "violence, chaos and ultimately, a war." His aim, he said, was to create a "self-sustaining" peace. There were still skeptics, however.

A senior NATO commander said that in Bosnia "We are stuck in a holding pattern from which we can not escape."[36]

Hopes for a political breakthrough faded. Prior to the September 1998 Bosnian parliamentary elections, prominent American officials campaigned openly and blatantly for Plavsic. Nevertheless, she suffered a major setback; a hard-line nationalist won the Serbian seat in the three-man Bosnian presidency, and the Karadzic faction scored gains. It was a dramatic defeat for American political meddling. The net result was a further hardening of the Bosnian partition, and, consequently, an increased likelihood of an indefinite occupation by NATO troops.

KOSOVO

As American troops settled in for a prolonged occupation of Bosnia, the situation in Kosovo began to cast an ever longer shadow. Ironically, as long as the fighting continued in Bosnia, Kosovo remained quiet. The Serbs were reluctant to launch yet another war, and the Kosovars were content with the ambiguity of virtual self-rule under the guise of nominal Serbian sovereignty. Moreover, there was the Christmas warning issued by Bush on December 25, 1992, to the effect that the United States would not tolerate a Serbian crackdown in Kosovo.

Once there was peace in Bosnia, however, the calculations began to change. In 1996 a small Kosovo faction began to form armed units, known as the Kosovo Liberation Army (KLA). As the fighting intensified, the faction lead by the pacifist Ibrahim Rugova began to lose ground to the militants of the KLA, which launched small attacks on Serbian police units. The Serbs began to respond with increasingly violent crackdowns. Small villages were burned and destroyed; heavier military units were brought in; in the spring of 1998 more arms began to flow to the KLA across the Albanian border. Europe's worst nightmare, another Balkan war, seemed likely.

Europeans and Americans began to speculate about a "second Bosnia," a highly misleading comparison. There were a number of significant differences between Kosovo and Bosnia. In Bosnia the Serbs were about one-third of the population; in Kosovo they were a tiny minority. All Bosnians speak the same language, but in Kosovo the Serbs and Albanians are distinctly different ethnic groups. The fighting in Bosnia was more or less confined, while that in Kosovo threatened to spill into neighboring Albania and Macedonia. In Bosnia, in the end, Milosevic had sold out his Serbian allies in Bosnia, but he had made his reputation by a virulent nationalistic stand in Kosovo in the late 1980s, when he deprived the province of its autonomous status. Finally, outside intervention in Bosnia was welcomed by the legitimate authorities, while in Kosovo the Serbian military would almost certainly resist. The alternative for outside powers was not likely to be peacemaking or peacekeeping, but a straightforward war.

Thus, in the words of one expert observer, the former U.S. ambassador to Yugoslavia, Warren Zimmermann, "Inconceivable though it may seem, Kosovo is also a more complex problem than Bosnia."[37] Yet the United States proceeded to make every mistake that it had made in handling Bosnia.[38]

It began by denouncing the KLA as "terrorists"—probably an accurate description, but one bound to encourage Milosevic to use military force. Washington, acting through Secretary Albright, then began to draw comparisons with Bosnia and to issue vague warnings, in effect that the Serbs understood only force. However, as in the early phase of the Bosnian crisis, Washington failed to deliver on its warnings. The United States advocated economic sanctions, despite the poor record of such measures in Yugoslavia; predictably, both France and Russia resisted strong economic sanctions. Tough talk by the United States may well have encouraged the KLA, while the weakness of support for sanctions relieved pressure on Milosevic. Having proclaimed that Milosevic only understood force, the United States dispatched Richard Holbrooke to Belgrade, where he finally arranged a meeting between Milosevic and the Kosovar leader, Rugova. That meeting gained nothing, but to set it up Holbrooke convinced Washington to restrain the imposition of new sanctions—a complete reversal of the position advocated to the Contact Group by Albright. President Clinton even met with Rugova in Washington, apparently to urge him to compromise—a naive expectation of a man whose entire career had been based on his nonviolent campaign for Kosovo independence.

Within a few weeks, Washington reversed itself once again. It began to press for more forceful action, including military intervention by NATO. Clinton said that no options should be ruled out. But once again Washington had no plan, strategy, or clear objectives. Richard Holbrooke held a highly publicized meeting with one of the KLA leaders inside Kosovo; in effect, he legitimized the KLA guerrillas, who had been denounced as terrorists only a few weeks earlier by Holbrooke's colleague, the American ambassador Robert S. Gelbard, appointed to implement the Dayton agreements. Further meetings were arranged with Ambassador Gelbard to persuade the Kosovar factions to work together. The American side was frustrated, because there seemed to be no clear leader of the KLA with whom to negotiate. The Europeans were dismayed by American floundering, and some American commentators were apprehensive that the administration was drifting into an ethnic war with "slight if any relevance to American security."[39]

The NATO foreign ministers issued a statement declaring that "the status quo is unacceptable," but the joint declaration was ambiguous as to what was expected. NATO supported a "political solution" but defined it in such a way as to satisfy every party except the majority of the Kosovo Albanians, who wanted independence. The so-called political solution would provide an "enhanced status" for Kosovo but preserve "the territorial integrity of Yugoslavia" and safeguard the human and civil rights of all inhabitants of Kosovo, "whatever their ethnic origin." Finally, NATO acted as it had in Bosnia, employing a meaningless and weak military gesture, flying sixty-eight jet fighters over the border areas on June 15. It was ironic that as this demonstration took place Milosevic was in Moscow conferring with Yeltsin, who arranged for another round of negotiations. Moscow heralded Milosevic's "concession," even though he refused to withdraw his forces from Kosovo. Clinton had called Yeltsin just prior to the meeting; after it the Clinton administration called Milosevic's concession only a "first step." It was a familiar and discouraging pattern: "Small wonder Milosevic sees Western threats as empty rhetoric," commented a British specialist in military strategy at Kings College London.[40]

Indeed, despite NATO's threats, Milosevic ordered a major spring and summer offensive that reduced the Kosovar rebels forces to a tattered band in retreat but not totally defeated. The usual anonymous American officials admitted they had been hoodwinked by Milosevic. American reaction was restrained, however, to avoid challenging the Serbs before the Bosnian parliamentary elections of mid-September. Once that voting was safely over, the clamor rose once again for military action in Kosovo. But the same old questions persisted: would air strikes alone be effective? what would follow? occupation of a sovereign country by ground forces? under what international authority? Although Kosovo was still recognized as an integral part of Yugoslavia, American officials argued that NATO did not need prior UN approval; the Russians, of course, vociferously disagreed. In the fall of 1998, skeptics feared that President Clinton, caught in his own domestic political crisis, was looking for a diversion, to salvage his presidency. A familiar pattern reappeared. The United Nations' Security Council urged a cease-fire and negotiations; the United States offered a peace plan based on broad autonomy for Kosovo; Richard Holbrooke was once again dispatched to Belgrade; finally, Milosevic ordered a partial retreat; KLA forces returned in strength, but there was no political settlement.

When he came into office Clinton had faced the grim prospect of intervention in Bosnia. More than five years later he faced the same prospect in

Kosovo. Much would depend on Clinton and Milosevic, an odd couple whose destinies seemed to be intertwined.

A severe judgment of Clinton's record was pronounced by David Owen in his book dealing with his Bosnian experiences. He wrote that Clinton's failure to exercise leadership at the critical juncture in early 1993 had been a tragedy. Had Bush been reelected, Owen concluded, the war would have been settled on the basis of his plan in the spring of 1993.[41]

This was a searing indictment of the Clinton administration but not an unjustified one. Had Clinton made the kind of commitments in spring of 1993 that he did in the late summer of 1995, he could have ended the war and saved thousands of lives—and perhaps staved off a crisis in Kosovo. The difference was that in 1993 Clinton concluded that Bosnia would not determine the fate of his presidency but that a messy foreign entanglement would jeopardize his domestic agenda. Not until two years later, when he saw that Bosnia would indeed jeopardize his presidency, did he act.

NOTES

1. Warren Zimmermann, "The Last Ambassador," *Foreign Affairs*, March/April 1995.

2. Warren Zimmermann, *Origins of a Catastrophe* (New York: Random House, Times Books, 1996), p. 137; Zimmermann, "The Last Ambassador," pp. 11–12; James A. Baker, *The Politics of Diplomacy* (New York: G. P. Putnam, 1995), p. 483.

3. David Gompert, "How to Defeat Serbia," *Foreign Affairs*, July/August 1994.

4. Don Oberdorfer, "A Bloody Failure in the Balkans," *Washington Post*, February 8, 1993.

5. Zimmermann, *Origins*, pp. 170, 216.

6. Irving Kristol, "The Challenge of a Political Reversal," *Wall Street Journal*, December 17, 1990; William Safire, "NATO on the Brink," *New York Times*, January 28, 1993.

7. Richard Holbrooke, *To End a War* (New York: Random House, 1998), p. 42.

8. R. W. Apple Jr., "Mediator Is Upset," *New York Times*, February 3, 1993; David Owen, *Balkan Odyssey* (New York: Harcourt Brace, 1995), pp. 116–117.

9. Douglas Jehl, "Clinton Outlines U.S. Interest," *New York Times*, February 10, 1993; Clinton press conference, *New York Times*, February 11, 1993.

10. Steven A. Holmes, "Ex-Officials," *New York Times*, February 19, 1993.

11. Michael R. Gordon, "12 in State Department Ask Military Move," *New York Times*, April 23, 1993.

12. Secretary Christopher, "US Consultations with Allies," opening statement at a news conference, Washington, D.C., May 1, 1993, in U.S. State Department *Dispatch*, May 10, 1993.

13. Thomas L. Friedman, "Any War in Bosnia Would Carry a Domestic Price," *New York Times*, May 2, 1993.

14. Elizabeth Drew, *On the Edge* (New York: Simon and Schuster, Touchstone edition, 1995), p. 157.

15. Michael Kramer, "Drawing a Line in the Quicksand," *Time*, May 24, 1993; John Newhouse, "No Exit, No Entrance," *New Yorker*, June 28, 1993; Tom Post, "The Road to Indecision," *Newsweek*, May 24, 1993.

16. Editorial, "Requiem for a Policy," *National Review*, June 7, 1993.

17. Elaine Sciolino, *New York Times*, May 12, 1993.

18. Michael Kelly, "Surrender and Blame," *New Yorker*, December 19, 1994; Michael Gordon, Douglas Jehl, and Elaine Sciolino, *New York Times*, December 4, 1994.

19. Holbrooke, *To End a War*, p. 81.

20. Elaine Sciolino, "U.S. and NATO Say Dispute on Bosnia War Is Resolved," *New York Times*, December 2, 1994; Ivo H. Daalder, "Anthony Lake and the War in Bosnia,"in *Pew Case Studies in International Affairs*, Case 467A and 467B (Institute for the Study of Diplomacy Publications, Georgetown University School of Foreign Service, 1995).

21. David Rohde, *Endgame* (New York: Farrar, Strauss and Giroux, 1996).

22. Thomas Lippman and Ann Devroy, "Clinton's Policy Evolution," *Washington Post*, October 22, 1995.

23. Bob Woodward, *The Choice* (New York: Simon and Schuster, 1996), pp. 260–265.

24. Elaine Sciolino, "Bosnia Policy Shaped by U.S. Military Role," *New York Times*, July 29, 1996.

25. Holbrooke, *To End a War*, pp. 67–68.

26. Ibid., p. 74.

27. Ibid., pp. 92–93.

28. Ibid., p. xv.

29. Henry Kissinger, "What Is the Mission?" *Washington Post*, October 22, 1995.

30. Rick Atkinson, "NATO Seeks Limits," *Washington Post*, October 13, 1995.

31. Editorial, "Doing the Job in Bosnia," *The Weekly Standard*, December 2, 1996.

32. Elizabeth Rubin, "The Enemy of Our Enemy," *New York Times Magazine*, September 14, 1997.

33. Anna Husarska, "Polling Alone," *New Republic*, October 13, 1997.

34. Michael Kelly, "A Chance to Change History," *Washington Post*, January 21, 1998.

35. The texts of Clinton's statement and news conference were printed in the *New York Times*, December 19, 1997; for his remarks in Sarajevo, see *New York Times*, December 23, 1997.

36. Quoted in Chris Hedges, "Dayton Peace Accord," *New York Times*, December 20, 1997.

37. Warren Zimmermann, "The Demons of Kosovo," *The National Interest*, Summer 1998.

38. Ivo H. Daalder, "Kosovo: Bosnia Deja Vu," *Washington Post*, April 17, 1998.

39. Jack F. Matlock Jr., "Too Many Arms to Twist," *New York Times*, March 22, 1998.

40. Jane M. O. Sharp, "Not Another Bosnia," *Washington Post*, June 18, 1998.

41. Owen, *Balkan Odyssey*, p. 392.

4

Nation Building

Intervention in Bosnia was relevant to American national security. The Balkans were, after all, the proverbial powder keg of Europe. Observers kept pointing out that World War I had started in Sarajevo. Nevertheless, George Bush was adamantly opposed to any American military involvement without having determined in advance how to get out of a potential quagmire. It was therefore a surprise that his administration decided to intervene with military forces not in the Balkans but in a far-off country of much less consequence to Americans—Somalia. The situation there had become a humanitarian nightmare. Thousands, even millions, were starving. A civil war was raging out of control, and there was no central authority to organize the distribution of assistance from abroad. The desperately needed food supplies that did arrive were systematically looted. The horror was publicized by American television, especially NBC, which began a series of telecasts that graphically depicted the plight of starving children.

SOMALIA

Something had to be done. President Bush decided to send in American combat troops to establish order and distribute supplies of humanitarian aid. He did so without a request from any authority in Somalia or any approval from Congress. This in itself was a radical step, even if justified by the deplorable conditions. It was the first American armed intervention for humanitarian purposes.

Like many of the new nations created after World War II, Somalia was an unnatural merger of two colonies: British Somaliland in the north and the UN Trust Territory, the old Italian Somaliland, in the south. The two had been combined in 1960 as an independent state. In the Cold War, Somalia was a strategic asset, because of the potential naval base in the deep harbor of Berbera on the Horn of Africa. Indeed, Somalia *was* the very Horn of Africa.

Somalia drifted into the Soviet orbit. In October 1969 a military officer, Siad Barre, came to power and soon declared Somalia would adopt "scientific socialism." Moscow was cynical about these would-be socialists but embraced Somalia as a strategic foothold. But Moscow switched sides when a war broke out between Somalia and another new Soviet client, Ethiopia, in a conflict over the Ogaden desert. The Ethiopian military rulers were supported by Cuban troops that not only repelled the Somali army but were poised to continue military operations into Somalia. The United States, under President Carter, had to intervene against these Soviet proxies, warning against any advance beyond the Ogaden. The war ended with the superpowers having exchanged allies. In 1980 the United States and Somalia negotiated an agreement that permitted the Americans to use the Berbera naval base, in the northern part of Somalia. The United States supported Somalia with economic aid, but in July 1988 aid was suspended over human rights violations. American citizens were evacuated in 1990, and the embassy was closed. Thus, no American interest was directly represented any longer.

Siad Barre's regime was a brutal dictatorship that alienated clans in both the north and south; he was finally overthrown in January 1991. The northern region declared its independence, and in the south there was a growing conflict between the two strong political factions of the United Somalia Congress: one faction was led by the civilian businessman, Ali Mahdi, then the leader of the provisional government; his opposition was led by a chief of staff, army colonel Mohammed Farah Aideed. Each represented a different subclan. A struggle for power began; fighting broke out briefly in September 1991 and more severely in November. The conflict continued for several months through the spring, with casualties between thirty and fifty thousand, until a cease-fire was arranged by the UN in March 1992. Public order, however, had almost completely broken down.

The situation was greatly worsened by a drought, which led to widespread famine. The UN decided in the summer of 1992 to send in military personnel to help distribute aid; a small contingent of Pakistani troops was disembarked to protect the supplies at dockside in the capital, Mogadishu. It was tokenism, and the situation became more desperate. In August the

United States began participating in emergency airdrops of supplies (over forty-five thousand tons). The Pakistani troops that were to guard the food supplies were blocked initially from entering Mogadishu.

The Bush administration had come under attack for its inaction. A *New York Times* editorial in July 1992 demanded an "effective, mobile UN peacekeeping force, strong enough to quell the warlords." Another *New York Times* editorial pleaded, "Don't Forsake Somalia." Once the American presidential elections were past, Bush was free to act. On November 25 he offered American troops to the UN. On November 30 the UN Secretary-General, Boutros Boutros-Ghali, recommended the use of armed force, and on December 3 the Security Council voted unanimously to intervene. On December 9 American Marines began landing. Actually, the night before a Navy Seal team had landed to be greeted by a small army of reporters and television cameras.[1]

The purpose, the Bush administration announced, was to create a "secure environment" in which food could be distributed. When that was accomplished the United States would withdraw its troops and hand over the mission to the UN. No definite period of time was expressed, but there was talk of perhaps a two- or three-month mission. Bush said the deployment was not open ended, and even suggested the withdrawal might begin by Inauguration Day (January 20). More important was his statement that the intervention was not intended "to dictate a political solution." Answering critics who asked why Somalia and not Bosnia, Secretary of State Lawrence Eagleburger made a frank admission: in Somalia the United States could do something about the problem at low risk. It was hoped that the intervention would serve as political catalyst; a former American ambassador, Robert Oakley, was sent to Mogadishu to establish contact with the warring factions. In a statement he would later regret, the Secretary-General of the UN declared that Somalia would make or break the United Nations.

It was a major intervention, undertaken by a lame-duck president, without congressional authority, and not in response to a local invitation. It was bound to raise some serious questions. There had been no public preparation for the use of troops; indeed, in some measure the intervention was a response to the media focus and the emotional outrage generated by television coverage. This was a dangerous precedent. There was no television coverage in the Sudan and little in Rwanda, and therefore there was no international reaction, even though the situations in both places were tragic. George Kennan commented that if the basis of American policy was to be an emotional reaction created by TV, then there was little room for thoughtful reflection or deliberative organs.[2]

Moreover, the intervention was not related to the root causes of the disaster, that is, to the internal disputes, which were bound to affect the humanitarian effort. The situation demanded establishment of a governing authority. The UN Secretary-General announced that it was crucial to disarm the various factions—an ominous portent of trouble. General Aideed proclaimed that rather than surrender their weapons his forces would fight to the last man. According to Bush officials, there was no intention of disarming the various clans or building a new political structure; the operation would be limited in its mandate, duration, and scope. In any case, given Somalia's recent history, creating a governing power could be a dubious enterprise. Even assuming some central authority could be patched together, it surely would not be democratic or sensitive to human rights.

The Somalia intervention was a unique geopolitical event. American troops were dispatched for a police action in an area where no American security interests were involved; that in itself was a serious departure. Even if justified on humanitarian grounds, it was not likely that the political mission could be accomplished quickly: Somali guerrillas would go to ground, but sooner or later the U.S. or UN troops would have to disarm them. When they did, they would become involved in a civil conflict. This was a risk inherent in the American role, which was mistakenly conceived and portrayed as a limited military effort that could be divorced from political realities.[3]

In sum, Bush's intervention in Somalia contained the seeds of a new doctrine: that Americans would fight for human and moral values, in contrast to the Cold War, when it was willing to fight only for its strategic interests. Defenders of the Somali intervention went quite far in their arguments. In their view the new international situation in the 1990s demanded a new definition of vital interests. Step by step the United States had to move toward the position that moral or human values had to be defended, and with force if necessary; protection of the Kurds in northern Iraq was cited as an example. Critics replied that in the end, this new doctrine of humanitarian intervention, because of its abstract nature, would necessarily lead to overextension, and that the United States risked becoming the world's policeman.

The president-elect sided with Bush. Clinton had, after all, implied a new emphasis on humanitarian concerns during his campaign. The Somali operation was in many respects more compatible with the Clinton administration's philosophy than with Bush's. During the campaign Clinton had praised the idea of multilateral actions. In April 1993 the new secretary of state said that the Clinton administration would emphasize multilateral peacekeeping and "peacemaking." This view was echoed in the Pentagon;

the Under Secretary of Defense, Frank Wisner, said that peacekeeping would "lie right at the core" of the Defense Department's activities.[4]

These embryonic twin doctrines of multilateralism and humanitarian interventionism were spelled out more extensively by the new ambassador to the UN, Madeleine Albright. It was she who coined the rubric "assertive multilateralism." In her confirmation hearings she emphasized the importance of "a new beginning" for the United Nations. According to her, the UN was on the verge of becoming the institution that its founders had foreseen in 1945. (She did not add, of course, that what Franklin Roosevelt had foreseen for the UN was a role as the world's policeman.) In June 1993 Albright expanded on her views: assertive multilateralism, she explained, rested on preventive diplomacy. Americans would have to "open [their] minds to broader strategies in multilateral forums." She concluded that "peacekeeping and the modern responsibilities of collective security are essential to our security."[5]

Soon after taking office, the president issued a directive ordering a study of the broad subject of peacekeeping. Rumors soon indicated that in this study the new team was prepared to go quite far toward internationalism. Early drafts reportedly advocated a rapid expansion of UN operations; the United States would be committed to support such operations in all dimensions—military, economic, and political. These versions also flirted with supporting a standing UN army and, in any case, permitting putting U.S. forces under various UN commands. Rather amazingly, such prospects provoked little debate.

At first, the UN operation in Somalia proceeded without much controversy. By March officials had concluded that the initial mission of averting mass starvation had been achieved. Congress had chosen not to challenge the constitutionality of the deployment of U.S. forces; it did not get around to approving the Bush decision until early February, in a routine voice vote. The size of the U.S. force was rapidly drawn down; from the maximum level of about twenty-eight thousand, the force was pared back by June to about four thousand, including about four hundred Rangers. The apparent success led some observers to cite Somalia as the model of humanitarian intervention, a "moral advance," as *The New Yorker* put it (March 8, 1993), which would lead to other, similar actions. In May the command of the forces in Somalia quietly passed from the United States to the UN. There were no congressional complaints.

UN forces were not engaged in Somali politics, but almost imperceptibly the mission had changed from the initial Bush objective of restoring order: under Clinton the UN forces engaged in "total pacification and nation building." One American diplomat declared that they were "recreating a

country." Ambassador Albright said, "We will embark on the unprecedented enterprise aimed at nothing less than the restoration of an entire
country as a proud, functioning and viable member of the community of
nations."[6] Obviously, this would be a vast undertaking, perhaps lasting decades. It was being launched in the name of a controversial theory by officials who had little or no experience with the area.

This new, more aggressive approach led at first only to small incidents,
but in time the clashes escalated. Nation building, as it was called, was opposed by the faction of Mohammed Farah Aideed, whose clan dominated
parts of Mogadishu. He insisted that the UN favored his opponent, Ali
Mahdi, and that therefore his forces would not give up their arms. If he was
to be disarmed, American forces would be required to mount a version of
"search and destroy."

The shift in the mission's objective was scarcely noticed. Later it would
be called "mission creep," a term used by Marine General Samuel P. Hoar
in arguing against State Department proposals for expanding the mission.
Attention was not focused on Somalia until a serious incident on June 5,
when a UN force of Pakistani soldiers was ambushed by Aideed's forces,
leaving twenty-three Pakistani dead. Immediately there were calls for drastic action. The UN Security Council demanded the "arrest and detention
for prosecution, trial and punishment," of the transgressors. The UN command on June 11 retaliated with a barrage by gunships and attack helicop-
ters against six "strategic" installations of Aideed's forces. The UN forces
were then under the overall command of a retired American admiral, Jonathan Howe. Acting on the UN resolution he issued an order for the arrest
of Aideed and later posted a twenty-five-thousand-dollar bounty. Clinton,
speaking at a news conference, denounced Aideed's attack as the worst attack on peacekeepers in three decades that could not go unpunished.

This was an extraordinary turn of policy. Aideed was cast as the villain, a
thug, even a terrorist. Capturing him would simply be "bringing him to justice." U.S. and UN forces undertook a major campaign against Aideed and
his forces, in an unsuccessful attempt to capture him.

In July the situation turned for the worse. U.S. and UN raids and air
attacks produced heavy Somali casualties. An anonymous Pentagon official was quoted saying that UN strategy was still to "trim General Aideed
down to size"; but in Washington voices were finally questioning the UN's
role. Senator Robert Byrd of West Virginia said on July 14 that it was time
for the Americans to "pack up and go home." Nevertheless, Congress did
little more than pass a resolution asking that the president make a report
by October 15.

Peacekeeping was falling apart. An internal UN report (never published) criticized U.S. air strikes and concluded that the UN mission had degenerated into a traditional military campaign. The Chairman of the Joint Chiefs of Staff, General Powell, was skeptical of the plan to capture Aideed. The Clinton administration, however, amplified its rhetoric, defending the expansive mission against Aideed. The opposing forces had to be disarmed, retrained, and "reemployed," according to Ambassador Albright. She advanced the seemingly reasonable concept that it would simply take time for people who had been shooting each other to begin trusting each other. (That guerrillas would permit themselves to be disarmed and "reemployed" and even begin trusting their enemies was dubious.) Nevertheless, the ambassador argued that UN forces had to disarm Aideed because the humanitarian and political goals could not be achieved without a secure environment. In this she was probably right, but she went too far in insisting that failure to disarm Aideed's forces would be "appeasement." She posed a choice: either pulling up stakes and allowing Somalia to fall back into chaos or "staying the course" in order to "lift" Somalia from a "failed state to an emerging democracy."[7]

This was the rhetorical high point of the administration's commitment to the bewildering strategy of pursuing a guerrilla war against Aideed and his clan in order to "lift" Somalia into democracy. The administration's extravagant ambition was vigorously challenged. One columnist, Charles Krauthammer, commented that "famine relief is one thing, nation-building another."[8] Secretary of Defense Aspin entered the fray in a major speech of August 27, in which he reasserted the aim of nation building and declared that President Clinton had given clear direction to "stay the course."[9]

In reality, the White House was beginning to question the policy of nation building. Clinton was reported to be upset over a U.S./UN gunship attack on September 9 that had killed civilians. Troubles in foreign policy were threatening the president's domestic agenda. At the very time that the White House wanted to launch its major health care initiative, events abroad were becoming serious diversions. Ex-president Jimmy Carter warned Clinton that there could be no end to the U.S. mission in Somalia unless there was some reconciliation with Aideed.

On October 3 a Black Hawk assault helicopter carrying a contingent of American troops was shot down. The survivors were trapped on the ground and badly shot up by Aideed's forces in Mogadishu; eighteen Marines were killed, seventy-five wounded, and a helicopter pilot, Warrant Officer Michael Durant, was captured alive. The body of an American Marine was scourged and dragged through the streets as Somalis celebrated, events recorded by CNN cameras.

The president, in California, was reported to have been angry that the anti-Aideed campaign was still being pursued. His aides insisted that he had been led to believe that the policy had been moderated, looking toward "reconciliation."[10] At first the administration argued that the United States could not simply "cut and run." Senator Byrd, however, now went on the attack in earnest, threatening to cut off all funding for the operation. Taking direct aim at Clinton's policy, he charged that "Americans by the dozens are paying with their lives and limbs for a misplaced policy on the altar of some fuzzy multilateralism."[11] Given Byrd's stature, this was a serious threat to the president's authority. Clinton devised a three-point plan: to establish a firm timetable for withdrawal by March 31, 1994; to send in five thousand more troops to protect the American forces already there; and to "reinvigorate" the political process, sending former Ambassador Robert Oakley back to establish contact with Aideed.[12] Some commentators were positive, declaring that the president had chosen a "sensible middle course."[13] Critics, however, attacked not only Clinton's Somalia policy but his general conduct of foreign affairs. A "pattern of incompetence" was the judgment of the London *Economist*. Columnist Anthony Lewis of the *New York Times* contrasted Clinton's advocacy of health care with his defense of his Somali policy: on health care Clinton was confident and enthusiastic, but on Somalia he was "tentative, fuzzy, unconvincing."[14] The overall burden of the commentaries was that the United States had to withdraw from Somalia. Concern about the damage to American credibility was brushed aside as a relic of the Cold War. There were no clarion calls for retaliation against Aideed, who was responsible for the deaths of eighteen American soldiers.

The White House staff defended the president by turning on his advisors, who dutifully accepted blame. Clinton's minions said that the effort to seize Aideed should never have been allowed to supplant the original mission, that it had been the American military who kept insisting on more troops to pursue Aideed. President Clinton made a much more relevant and telling point in a formal statement on October 7: "We have obligations elsewhere," he said. It was not America's job to "rebuild Somalia society."[15] This repudiated not only the UN Security Council resolutions, which his administration had promoted, but disavowed explicit pronouncements of his own cabinet members. He thus rejected his own policies—multilateral peacekeeping and support for humanitarian goals, which had been the thrust of his own election campaign.

It could have been worse. The issue was not when to get out, but who would decide, the president or the Congress. The Senate defeated a resolution demanding an earlier withdrawal than Clinton had proposed. A resolution drafted by Senator Byrd passed easily. "We put an end to this business of the appearance of the UN leading us around by the nose," Byrd said in an interview with *Congressional Quarterly* (October 16, 1993). For Clinton it was a narrow escape and a Pyrrhic victory. He had preserved his own authority, but as a Republican senator Mitch McConnell, said, "Creeping multilateralism died on the streets of Mogadishu." The administration was in full retreat.

Ambassador Oakley openly met with the infamous Aideed; the captured American Marine was released, the American Ranger contingent was withdrawn, and the remaining forces stopped patrolling. Aideed agreed to accept an impartial investigation of the incident of July 12 in which the Pakistani soldiers had been killed. In the spring a peace agreement was signed; in effect, it returned Aideed to power. American forces pulled out on schedule. There was relief at avoiding another "quagmire."

The consequences of the debacle in Somalia were not as damaging as they might have been. The temper of public opinion had never been enthusiastic about keeping troops in Somalia after the famine was overcome; pulling out was what the public wanted. The failure in Somalia obviously hurt the cause of humanitarian intervention and may well have strengthened anti-UN sentiment. There were serious questions raised about whether U.S. forces could or should operate under UN command. "Peace-keeping is not at the center of our foreign or defense policies," Lake asserted the following February.[16]

The Somali adventure was not an "abject failure"—it saved thousands of lives—yet it lacked a clear objective beyond the initial intervention.[17] Despite Bush's protestations that the mission would be limited, the original commitment was too vague and the exit strategy too indefinite. As the mission changed under Clinton, there was less and less chance of success. The fatal mistake was to have been carried away by theories of rebuilding failed states. For Clinton, Somalia greatly increased criticism of his policies, especially since in the midst of the Somalia crisis there was still another failure, this time in Haiti.

HAITI

For decades Haiti had been ignored by policy makers in Washington. The wretched dictatorships of two generations of Duvaliers, Francois ("Papa Doc") and his son, Jean-Claude ("Baby Doc") were tolerated in

Washington; they could not be easily overthrown, and the alternative was never clear. As long as the dictators seemed impervious to radical leftists, the United States did little more than dispense occasional dollops of aid and lectures about freedom and democracy. A miserable country sank deeper into despair, until riots broke out in the mid-1980s. Baby Doc saw the handwriting on the wall and decided to leave, on an aircraft provided by the Reagan administration. A military junta then took over. Elections were eventually held, and in December 1990 a Catholic priest, Jean-Bertrand Aristide, was elected president. He was overthrown within a year by another military junta.

None of this seemed to matter much to the United States. Haiti was, after all, outside the Cold War, as Secretary of State George Schultz had once said. The Bush administration was upset over Haiti but not enough to do anything beyond an embargo on trade.[18] According to Secretary of State James Baker, the administration believed that while there was a national interest in restoring democracy, it was not a sufficiently vital interest to warrant using military force.[19]

In his election campaign Clinton pledged to restore Father Aristide to office. There was no particular political pressure on Clinton to do so, except for that generated by the tides of Haitian refugees fleeing from Haiti to Florida as "boat people." The Bush administration had adopted the harsh policy of turning them back without allowing them to make a case for political asylum. This has been challenged in court, and a Supreme Court review was pending. During the campaign Clinton said he would repudiate the "cruel" policy and would grant fleeing Haitians refuge and consideration for political asylum until democracy could be restored in Haiti. But he never elaborated as to how this restoration would be accomplished.

Once in office, to the dismay of many of his supporters Clinton continued to turn back refugees. That policy was even argued successfully (March 2, 1993) before the Supreme Court, which confirmed by a vote of eight to one the government's right to intercept refugees on the high seas and return them without an asylum hearing.[20] To accusations that Clinton was breaking a campaign promise, Warren Christopher responded that it was unsound policy to accept them. The new administration, however, increased the pressure on Haiti by promoting an international embargo of trade and a freeze of Haitian assets. The Clinton rationale was that this pressure on the military leaders would eventually lead to a return to democracy, thereby ending the refugee problem. The U.S. Navy was patrolling Haitian waters to enforce the embargo, but also to intercept refugees. The potential stalemate was broken when the UN helped to negotiate an agreement, called the Governors Island Accord, under which Aristide would be returned to power, not immediately but step by step.

The prospects for the restoration of democracy looked good in the summer of 1993. President Clinton announced on July 4, 1993, that it was a historic moment for Haiti, for the hemisphere, and for the "principle of democratic rule." The Haitian military leader, General Raul Cedras, accepted the Governors Island compromise, which included assurances of the safety of Aristide and his colleagues; Aristide in turn relented on his demands that the military be brought to trial and punishment. In late August, the UN voted to suspend some aspects of the embargo. A supporter of Aristide, Robert Malval, became prime minister, but the military prevented him from assuming any real authority. Then one of Aristide's financial advisors was murdered in Port-au-Prince in September, and later his designated justice minister was shot. The country was being terrorized. In retrospect, it seems clear that the Haitian military was simply shadow boxing with the Clinton administration, hoping to relieve American economic sanctions but also testing how far it could press the Clinton administration. It was naive of Clinton to have believed otherwise.

Prior to the return of Aristide on October 30 preliminary arrangements were made to implement the Governors Island agreement. In early October some American and Canadian engineers and specialists landed, wearing UN blue helmets. Part of their mission was to retrain the police forces. The bubble burst on October 11, when a shipload of military engineers, American and Canadian, were unable to go ashore because they were confronted by violent mobs at dockside shouting "Somalia! Somalia!" The following morning the American vessel, the USS *Harlan County*, turned around and sailed away to the U.S. naval base in Guantanamo, Cuba. It was reported that there was dancing and singing at dockside as the ship pulled out.

This was a humiliation, and it was the end of the Governors Island Accord. The American retreat emboldened the military in Haiti to dig in, according to the chief American negotiator, Lawrence Pezzullo.[21] But no Americans were killed, unlike in Somalia, which was still commanding most public attention that week. President Clinton insisted that he was "dead serious" about enforcing the Haitian agreement, but another ship scheduled for Haiti was canceled. Rather than confront the military regime, Clinton turned to the United Nations. The UN Security Council passed a resolution ordering a tightening of the embargo and naval blockade of Haiti. Virtually no one, however, insisted that the United States should dispatch major military forces in order to restore Aristide. Ambassador Albright, speaking at the UN, said that in order to bring pressure on

Cedras the UN and the United States intended to do everything short of "an armed intervention that nobody wants." She added that "this has never been, nor should it be, some kind of gunboat diplomacy." Haiti was no longer on the "A-list" of crises, a White House aide callously remarked at the end of November.

Nevertheless, Haiti was a bitter setback, more so than Bosnia or Somalia. It deeply offended the moralists in the administration, who believed that Haiti was a test case for an American policy of defending human rights and advancing democracy. Haiti was, after all, in the backyard of the United States. Opinion polls showed that the public thought the United States had a more vital interest in Haiti than in Bosnia. In a poll asking whether the United States should take all action necessary, including military intervention, in Haiti, the split was 50 percent against but a surprising 45 percent in favor; in the same ABC–*Washington Post* poll 45 percent disapproved of Clinton's handling of Haiti.[22]

The real catalyst for action was pressure from inside the Clinton administration, from a group that became known as the "Haiti hawks," led by Anthony Lake. As described by *Newsweek,*

Clinton's zig zag policy came to be dominated by a group of moralists who form a liberal web knotted together during the administration of President Jimmy Carter. They all speak the same language, the Carteresque "human rights first" policy. All hated the Central American policy of the 1980s. And they have no real feel for politics. . . . And because Clinton eventually got the Pentagon he wanted—led by technocrats with no powerful say in policy—nobody was there to counterbalance the Haiti hawks.[23]

On May 8, 1994, it was announced that the administration had completed a "comprehensive review" of policy toward Haiti. There would be a "new emphasis" on comprehensive sanctions and on improved enforcement of the sanctions that had been adopted by the UN Security Council on May 6. Clinton sought to increase the pressure by new and tougher rhetoric; a campaign of psychological warfare followed, but without much success. The Security Council passed a resolution authorizing the use of force if necessary.

It was never clear whether the administration thought that Cedras and the junta would collapse and flee or stand and fight. The administration was split. One news story reported that at a high-level meeting on August 2 Strobe Talbott favored an early invasion, within weeks, but that William Perry was strongly opposed, arguing for more diplomacy, including guarantees to Cedras of his personal safety. The particulars of this debate leaked to the press. The writer Richard Reeves just happened to be visiting in the White House on the morning this story broke (August 4, 1994), and Anthony Lake complained bitterly about the leaks. Months later, both President Clinton and Vice President Gore were still talking about the leak, according to Reeves. As a consequence, the dialogue inside the White House became "more and more distorted," as the meetings became smaller and less was put in writing.[24]

The arguments against using armed force, especially from Republicans, became quite vociferous. Former secretary of state James Baker was opposed, as was former secretary of defense Dick Cheney. In effect they argued that restoring Aristide was not worth a single American life. The whole thing "smells like Somalia," Baker said: "It could easily be another open-ended operation."[25] Others concluded the intervention defied almost every rule of political prudence that the government supposedly had learned in Vietnam.

On September 15, Clinton addressed the nation and issued a dramatic but simple warning to the Haitian military regime: "Your time is up. Leave now or we will force you from power." Even as he spoke, however, Clinton was preparing to authorize a last-minute maneuver proposed by former president Jimmy Carter, who urged that he be allowed to go to Haiti and talk with Cedras. At first Clinton was reluctant, fearing that Carter would become embroiled in a long negotiation. Clinton finally agreed but insisted that his deadline for the invasion was nonnegotiable. With this leverage, Carter, accompanied by Senator Sam Nunn and General Colin Powell, negotiated an agreement in which Cedras and his entourage agreed to transfer power and leave. American troops landed unopposed, Cedras left, and Aristide returned triumphantly.

Why did the Haitian operation succeed and Somalia fail? Haitians had a national consciousness dating back for over a century, whereas in Somalia, a new country, there was no such national feeling. Haiti had not "failed," in the sense that Somalia had failed, as a state. Haiti had established institutions, a parliament, and a constitution, even if they were brushed aside by the military. Finally, the opposition in Haiti had a rallying point, Aristide, and the United States was aligned with him, whereas in Somalia the rallying point, General Aideed, was in the opposition. In Haiti the combination of power and diplomacy, which the administration had talked about on many occasions, worked and worked rather well.

Some American commentators, still fearing another nation-building exercise as in Somalia, urged a quick exit. Clinton was careful to spell out an exit strategy: the American deployment of troops would not be "open ended." American troops, which numbered over twenty thousand at the high point, were reduced and then withdrawn in April 1996, turning their mission over to the UN. Clinton officials rebutted their critics with the usual epithets that the critics were isolationists or playing partisan politics.

Haiti had been delivered from a ruthless dictatorship, but the outlook for building a genuine democracy was not bright.[26] When Madeleine Albright visited Port-au-Prince in April 1998, after she became secretary of state, she was disappointed that there had been no progress in resolving the political deadlock that had paralyzed the country for over a year. Such a resolution was not something that the Americans could provide, however, she said—a fitting epitaph for nation building.[27]

Haiti became part of an anti-Clinton litany, along with Bosnia and Somalia, a three-part indictment of his mismanagement of foreign affairs. While each was different, there was also a common thread.

In each situation the administration's approach was flawed, but not hopelessly. In Bosnia, "lift and strike," if pressed vigorously, might have precipitated a political settlement. In Somalia there was nothing intrinsically wrong in "nation building"; some sort of political solution was implied in the original intervention. However, it was arrogant to believe that nation building could be accomplished within a few months in a land as ravished and divided as Somalia. Returning the legitimate president to power in Haiti was also a worthy objective, but it required a consistent follow-up from Washington, which was never organized once the troop landings redeemed Clinton's reputation.

What linked these diverse situations was the personal failure of Bill Clinton. He refused to pay enough attention until it was too late. Critics believed that Clinton and Christopher shared one crucial characteristic: neither displayed strong convictions about what American foreign policy should accomplish, "except to please voters." In trying to find his way through Bosnia and Somalia, one critic suggested, Clinton was a president whose interest "lagged at the water's edge," a "slave to public and congressional opinion when he lacks his own clear bearings."[28]

Nation building and humanitarian intervention faded. The much-debated presidential study of peacekeeping operations had to be drastically revised yet again; as finally published as a Presidential Decision Directive (PDD 25) in May 1994, it merely restated a version of traditional foreign policy.[29] Peacekeeping would henceforth be measured by American interests. For operations involving substantial use of force, U.S. participation would require (1) that vital national or allied interest be at stake, and (2) a clear commitment to win. Clinton's advisors quietly pointed out that this was very close to the Weinberger Doctrine enunciated under Reagan.

Haiti also marked a step in Clinton's disengagement from his Wilsonian rhetoric. His rationale for occupying Haiti had reflected less of the human-rights and democracy-building ethic of his aides and more of a traditional geopolitical framework. In a letter to Congress on September 18 announcing the troop landing, for example, he wrote, "The United States has a particular interest in responding to gross abuses of human rights when they occur *so close to our shores.*" In his earlier speech (September 15) he took a similar line: "When brutality occurs *close to our shore*, it affects our national interests, and we have a responsibility to act."[30] Indeed, his remarks had the quaint aura of the Monroe Doctrine.

NOTES

1. Ken Menkhaus and Louis Ortmayer, "Key Decisions in the Somalia Intervention," in *Pew Case Studies in International Affairs*, Case 464, 1995.

2. George F. Kennan, "Somalia, through a Glass Darkly," *New York Times*, September 30, 1993.

3. Henry Kissinger, "Somalia: Reservations," *Washington Post*, December 13, 1993.

4. Ivo H. Daalder, "The Clinton Administration and Multilateral Peace Operations," in *Pew Case Studies in International Affairs*, Case 462A, 1994, p. 3.

5. Ibid., p. 3, n. 11.

6. Quoted in John R. Bolton, "Wrong Turn in Somalia," *Foreign Affairs*, January/February 1994.

7. Madeleine K. Albright, "Yes, There Is a Reason to Be in Somalia," *New York Times*, August 10, 1993.

8. Charles Krauthammer, "Playing God in Somalia," *Washington Post*, August 13, 1993.

9. Barton Gellman, "U.S. Rhetoric Changed," *Washington Post*, October 7, 1993.

10. Ibid.

11. Helen Dewar and Kevin Merida, "From Congress, More Questions," *Washington Post*, October 5, 1993.

12. *New York Times*, October 8, 1993.

13. Editorial, "Middle Course in Somalia," *Washington Post*, October 8, 1993.

14. George F. Will, "When to Fold," and Charles Krauthammer, "When To Hold," *Washington Post*, October 8, 1993; Anthony Lewis, "Foreign Policy Morass," *New York Times*, October 11, 1993.

15. "Clinton's Words on Somalia," *New York Times*, October 8, 1993.

16. Anthony Lake, "The Limits of Peacekeeping," *New York Times*, February 6, 1994.

17. Walter Clarke and Jeffrey Herbst, "Somalia and the Future of Humanitarian Intervention," in Walter Clarke and Jeffrey Herbst, eds., *Learning from Somalia* (Boulder Colo.: Westview Press, 1997), chap. 14, pp. 239–253.

18. Louis Ortmayer and Joanna Flinn, "Hamstrung over Haiti: Returning the Refugees," in *Pew Case Studies in International Affairs*, Case 355, 1993.

19. James A. Baker, *The Politics of Diplomacy* (New York: G. P. Putnam's Sons, 1995), p. 60.

20. Ortmayer and Flinn, "Hamstrung over Haiti," p. 1.

21. Lawrence A. Pezzullo, "Our Haiti Fiasco," *Washington Post*, May 3, 1994.

22. U.S. State Department *Dispatch*, August 15, 1994.

23. "How Did We Get Here?" *Newsweek*, September 26, 1994.

24. Elaine Sciolino, "Top U.S. Officials," *New York Times*, August 4, 1994; Richard Reeves, *Running in Place* (Kansas City, Mo.: Andrews and McNeel, 1996), pp. 57–58.

25. Michael Kramer, "The Carter Connection," *Time*, October 3, 1994.

26. "The Wonders of Haitian Democracy," *Economist*, February 28, 1998.

27. Mark Falcoff, "What 'Operation Restore Democracy' Restored," *Commentary*, May 1996; Georges A. Fauriol and Michael N. Zarin, "Three Years after the 'Rescue' Haiti Still Floundering," *Wall Street Journal*, July 18, 1997; Michael Norton, "Get House in Order," *Washington Post*, April 5, 1998.

28. Michael Kramer, "It's All Foreign to Clinton," *Time*, October 18, 1993.

29. Daalder, "The Clinton Administration and Multilateral Peace Operations."

30. The texts of Clinton's remarks and letter to Congress are printed in *Dispatch*, Vol. 5, No. 38, September 19, 1994.

5

South of the Border

Clinton's inner circle freely admitted that he had little interest or experience in foreign affairs, but they insisted that he was quite knowledgeable about and involved with international economic policy. He demonstrated this in the fall of 1993, when he won a strong victory in the contest over the North American Free Trade Agreement (NAFTA) with Mexico and Canada. It was in quite a different category from Bosnia, Somalia, or Haiti. It was relatively easy to walk away from crises in distant areas, but trade directly affected domestic interests and politics. And this was Clinton's strength.

NAFTA

To be sure, NAFTA was also an issue inherited from Bush. The treaty had been initialed and then signed by his administration during the election campaign. It was crystalized as a political issue during the campaign by the colorful comments of H. Ross Perot who said that if NAFTA were approved it would be followed by a "giant sucking sound" of American jobs going south to Mexico. Perot reflected the popular notion that NAFTA was a favor to Mexico, would cost American jobs, and eventually force down American wages. This turned out not to be true, and for a time it seemed that President Clinton was vindicated.[1] But NAFTA turned out to be a Pyrrhic victory; it was buried by a severe financial crisis in Mexico that forced a huge American bailout.

NAFTA represented a new direction in Mexico's economic policy. The tradition in Mexican politics had been anti-Yankee. Throughout the Cold

War Mexico had engaged in a foreign policy that badgered the United States on virtually every issue. Mexico could be counted on to stand to the left, whether the issue was Castro or nuclear testing. In Mexican domestic politics the dominant political party, the Institutional Revolutionary Party (PRI), was instinctively anti-American; it was perhaps less blatantly so in the 1980s, but that was its leadership's basic orientation.

What changed was Mexico's economic condition. Oil was Mexico's main export, and Mexico had benefited from the sharp rise in oil prices in the 1970s. This windfall, however, was squandered by a political system that was increasingly corrupt. In the mid-1980s oil prices fell, and as a result the Mexican economy was plagued by a large foreign debt, growing unemployment, inflation, and stagnated growth. It was an increasingly unattractive place for investors; in 1987 its stock market suffered a crisis. All of this was reflected in domestic politics, and the governing PRI almost lost the presidential election of 1988. President Miguel de la Madrid was replaced by Carlos Salinas de Gortari, but his victory over Cuauhtemoc Cardenas was a thin one and, some argued, a corrupt one.

Once in office, Salinas surprised his party by deciding to gamble on a program of economic liberalization, opening Mexico to foreign investment and expanding foreign trade. He cut down restrictions on imports, joined the General Agreement on Tariffs and Trade (GATT), and negotiated debt relief with investors from the United States. His most radical step, however, was to propose a free trade agreement with the United States and Canada.

Although the Republicans had been for such an agreement since the Reagan administration, George Bush was wary. He had just signed a free trade agreement with Canada. To expand it to include Mexico, a much shakier economy, was risky, even though by the time of Salinas's proposal the Mexican economy had improved, if not much.

On the political side, however, NAFTA offered some advantages. Illegal Mexican immigration was a growing issue in American politics. Nearly everyone agreed that its root cause was poverty and lack of opportunity in Mexico. If Mexican conditions could be alleviated, perhaps illegal immigration would start to dry up and eventually end altogether. Some experts even predicted that NAFTA would reduce illegal immigration by six hundred thousand over ten years.

Free trade was part of the American tradition. Until the 1980s, the United States had enjoyed favorable trade balances; lower tariffs seemed to benefit the United States. During the late 1980s, however, attitudes had begun to change. Free trade began to come under attack as trade imbalances turned unfavorable, and the trade deficit seemed destined to become a permanent ailment. Opening foreign markets was increasingly difficult and frustrating. Questions were being raised within the United States as to whether America could compete with subsidized, lower-wage economies. The dollar was in constant trouble. Negotiations over a new round of tariff reductions under GATT were stalled, in part over American demands for better access to markets. There was even some revisionism about the value of tariffs: historians pointed out that for most of its history the United States economy had expanded behind very high tariffs.

Bush decided to work for a Mexican agreement. Negotiations began in 1991, but they were slow. It took a high-level meeting between Bush and Salinas to break out of the negotiating bog. An agreement was signed in August 1992, and all three countries signed their implementing agreements in December 1992.

Clinton's position, of course, would be critical. At first, there was reason to believe that he would oppose NAFTA—at least as written. Political constituents, the AFL–CIO and the environmentalists, were against it. During the election campaign Clinton sidestepped the issue: he praised the "concept" but insisted that there be new side agreements to protect the concerns of American labor and the environmentalists. Clinton, however, was enough of a New Deal Democrat to advocate free trade and good relations with America's two immediate neighbors. The insistence on the "side agreements" was therefore more of a finesse than a deal breaker. He could drag out the new negotiations or speed them up. Meanwhile, he had a relatively free hand.[2]

At first the debate over NAFTA was waged largely in terms of economics. Proponents argued that NAFTA would create a net of 170,000 new jobs in the United States. American companies would find a new market in Mexico as tariffs were lowered. As the Mexican economy improved because of access to markets in the United States, the resulting prosperity should reduce illegal emigration. Opponents followed Perot's lead, predicting that American manufactures would move south to exploit the low cost of labor in Mexico.[3]

There were also geopolitical arguments, though they were not prominent at first. Regional trading arrangements were increasingly attractive as a form of protective insurance to protect domestic economies. In both Europe and the Asia-Pacific region the trend was toward regional blocs. A North American bloc therefore made political sense. Thus NAFTA was increasingly portrayed as a move toward a larger association: NAFTA would expand, first to the south to embrace Latin America, and then to the west to join the Asian economies of the Pacific Rim.[4]

Henry Kissinger argued that NAFTA was about not only free trade but foreign policy architecture as well. He had written on the eve of the voting:

> This country has an opportunity in foreign policy to do something defining, something that establishes the structure for decades to come. . . . We live in a world in which the ideological challenge has disintegrated and a new architecture needs to be created, and NAFTA is the first and crucial step in that direction.[5]

Economist Paul Krugman concluded that rejecting NAFTA would return the United States to the "bad old days." The treaty was not about jobs, or economic efficiency and growth, but about helping a friendly government succeed. He wrote, "It will be a monument to our foolishness if our almost wholly irrational fears about NAFTA end up producing an alienated or even hostile nation on our southern borders."[6]

These geopolitical arguments were never given their appropriate weight, because the debate degenerated into a political battle. The AFL–CIO was not satisfied with the side agreements Clinton had negotiated with Mexico. The Democratic Party was split; a favorable vote in the House would clearly require major Republican assistance. On the right wing of the Republican Party there was strong resistance, led by Patrick Buchanan. The majority of Republicans in the House, however, were for the treaty. Some of Clinton's aides saw the prospect of a bipartisan coalition as a good omen for his presidency. A victory for NAFTA might be a defining moment, establishing the president firmly in the center.

Opinion polls showed surprising public support (76 percent), mainly because the public concluded that good relations with Mexico were a "vital interest." Negative opinion was relatively weak. This reflection of public attitudes may have tilted President Clinton in favor of the treaty. While the administration argued that NAFTA would mean more jobs and less illegal immigration, what worked better for Clinton was good old-fashioned politics. This was his field, and he relished it. He made numerous deals in the Congress to line up votes. There was scarcely a subject that was not open for bargaining. His campaign was so blatant that it infuriated some of his supporters. "It's obscene, this horse trading of votes," complained Congressman John Lewis, a Democrat from Georgia.[7]

Clinton's victory was a victory not for a new foreign policy but of petty politics. The turning point may have been the live television debate between Ross Perot and Vice President Albert Gore. All observers concluded that Gore had won, hands down: "Perot Gored" read one headline the following morning. The final vote in the House was a strong win for Clinton,

234 to 200. He got 132 Republicans in favor but gained only 102 Democrats. His staff thought that his victory was proof that he was indeed a "New Democrat" and would pave the way for other successes based on the new bipartisanship. Secretary of Labor Robert Reich commented to his diary: "It's a well-kept secret: American taxpayers will shell out much more to pay for NAFTA than for getting people into new jobs—including, of course, people who might lose their jobs because of NAFTA."[8]

In the wake of his victory, at a summit meeting in Miami with the leaders of the Americas, Clinton spoke glowing about the prospects for a free trade agreement for the Americas by the year 2005. NAFTA was a step in this direction. Shortly after this summit, however, a crisis blew up in Mexico. First, a peasant revolt began in the remote Mexican state of Chiapas. Then the presidential election campaign to replace Salinas took a drastic turn. The PRI's candidate was Luis Donald Colosio, a government minister and a graduate of the University of Pennsylvania. Observers interpreted his choice as a signal that the party would continue on Salinas's course of reform; American officials were particularly pleased. On March 23, Colosio was murdered. He was replaced as the PRI candidate by Ernesto Zedillo, minister of education.

Investors began to lose confidence and to pull out. At first it was believed that it was foreign investors who were withdrawing, but in fact Mexican investors were selling pesos for dollars; there was a massive run on the dollar reserves of the government. Zedillo had not yet been inaugurated, and it was a tradition that the outgoing government devalue the peso to give its successor a breather. Salinas, however, refused, leaving the decision to Zedillo. Once in power, after first claiming that no devaluation was contemplated, Zedillo's government announced a devaluation; in a fatal move, he then decided to allow the peso to float freely. Inflation exploded, and the Mexican stock market went into free fall.

The Clinton administration faced a major crisis. At first Clinton issued pious reassurances that there was only a short-term "liquidity" crisis (January 11, 1995). Technically he may have been right, but he sounded like Herbert Hoover. Robert Rubin was replacing Lloyd Bentsen, who was leaving his office as secretary of the treasury. This turned out to be a stroke of good luck: Bentsen had been a plodder, whereas Rubin took charge. Under Rubin's plan the United States would rush to Mexico's rescue; he proposed a forty-billion-dollar loan "guarantee" program.[9] Rubin warned that the risks were not only economic: a protracted crisis, he said, would increase illegal immigration by as much as 30 percent.

The size of the bailout, however, stunned Washington; there was a virtual congressional revolt against such a huge sum. Clinton argued that it was not a bailout, or foreign aid, or even a genuine loan, but only the equivalent of "co-signing" a note. Alan Greenspan of the Federal Reserve was skeptical; he preferred to let Mexico and its investors suffer whatever consequences were dictated by the play of market forces. But he had no choice but to support a bailout as the crisis deepened and the administration unveiled its plan. Faced with opposition to the size of the financial package, Clinton had to retreat; he withdrew his original proposal and announced that the United States would supply twenty billion dollars, to be taken from an emergency account known as the Exchange Stabilization Fund.[10]

Congressional critics were not placated; there was even resistance in the Federal Reserve Board. Congressmen claimed that the president's use of the Exchange Stabilization Fund was not only unprecedented but of dubious legality. Meanwhile, Secretary Rubin negotiated several agreements to salvage the Mexican economy. The total package was estimated at about fifty billion dollars, including about twenty billion from the International Monetary Fund (IMF) and ten billion from the Bank of International Settlements.

The Clinton rescue was effective: the situation in Mexico stabilized. It was Bill Clinton's "finest moment," one Wall Street banker said. Had Clinton not acted the contagion would have spread rapidly. Nevertheless, Republicans in Congress charged that the administration had known that the trouble was coming and had covered it up. In congressional hearings documents were produced that in fact did show growing worries inside the Treasury Department about the stability of the Mexican currency. There was even evidence that as early as the NAFTA debate in 1993 American officials had been concerned about state of the Mexican economy. Moreover, warnings to Mexico City had been ignored.[11]

The financial crisis had an obvious effect on trade. Imports from Mexico grew to record levels. By 1996, the unfavorable balance of trade with Mexico had spiraled to a record $16.2 billion deficit. It had been argued that NAFTA would lead to 130,000 new American jobs by 1995, but despite the booming American economy the loss of jobs directly related to NAFTA was estimated to be on the order of 125,000.[12] More importantly, illegal immigration was unaffected, and the drug traffic through Mexico significantly worsened.

Drugs, rather than trade, became the central contentious issue between the two countries. In spring 1997 and again in 1998 the administration narrowly averted a congressional vote to decertify Mexico as an "ally" in fighting drugs.[13] During his official visit to Mexico (May 1997) Clinton acknowledged that American demand for drugs was the key element in the illegal drug traffic. But American officials were increasingly suspicious of Mexico's anti-drug efforts, which were infested with corruption at all levels. In May 1998 officials of the Drug Enforcement Agency and the Customs Service revealed an undercover "sting" operation that resulted in indictments against three leading Mexican banks and their officials. It was variously described as the "largest, most comprehensive drug money laundering case in the history of U.S. law enforcement." The operation recovered only a small fraction of the forty to sixty billion dollars in profits from drug trafficking (roughly two to three times the U.S. financial bailout of 1995). Mexican officials were outraged at the clandestine American actions inside Mexico and protested vigorously. It seems that the secretary of state had not been informed of the entire operation and was reported to be angry that she had been "left in the dark." She apologized in a private meeting with the Mexican foreign minister.[14] But the real lack of control was at the White House. Not surprisingly, relations deteriorated badly. At an international conference about drug trafficking, Clinton and Zedillo were virtually antagonists.[15]

In retrospect, NAFTA had little impact. Mexico remained a very poor country; the gap between the very rich and the poor was enormous; its economy was backward, its society badly divided, and its leadership was corrupt. None of this was affected by NAFTA. In May 1997 Clinton finally visited Mexico and ostentatiously met with opposition party leaders, albeit quite briefly. One American journalist compared Clinton's policy toward Mexico with his policy toward Boris Yeltsin: the government was corrupt, incompetent, and politically feeble, but the man at the top meant well, and all the alternatives appeared worse.[16]

In the summer of 1997, the administration produced a report on NAFTA, as required by law. It was at best a tepid claim of success; NAFTA was a "modest, positive contribution." White House aides conceded that NAFTA had been oversold and that the cause of free trade had suffered as a result. Moreover, the public regarded NAFTA as a failure.[17] The disillusionment with NAFTA and Mexico cast a long shadow. Four years after his victory over NAFTA, Clinton faced another congressional test of his foreign trade policy. The issue was the so-called "fast track." This time, he lost.

FAST TRACK

The basic idea of a "fast track" is relatively simple. Congress grants to the president the authority to negotiate trade agreements that have to be voted up or down without any amendments and within a specified time limit (ninety days). Clinton inherited the authority given to Bush, and under it

both NAFTA and the Uruguay Round of talks to revise GATT were negotiated. In 1994, Clinton linked the new GATT agreement, which was before the Senate for approval, to an extension of fast track for seven years. To
placate the anti-NAFTA Democrats, the Clinton administration had
added two provisions committing the administration to secure protection
for the environment and for foreign workers' rights in any new fast-track
agreements. By the summer of 1994 the political weight of this package had
become too much, especially in the face of the coming midterm congressional elections. The administration scuttled fast track altogether.

After his reelection in 1996 Clinton decided to make another try. While
originally giving it a top priority, the White House delayed specific legislation. Memories of the Mexican bailout were still relatively fresh. The
administration report on NAFTA was so weak that it added to the arguments against fast track. Trade imbalances through the summer of 1997
were exceedingly bad, and most analysts expected the totals for 1997 to
create new records. The administration's fast-track campaign did not begin
until early September.

Once again the debate was politicized. The opponents of NAFTA in
1993 were still strong and active. The AFL–CIO immediately announced a
million-dollar advertising campaign against fast track. Representatives
Richard Gephardt and David Bonior, the Democratic leaders in the House,
were still opposed. This time Gephardt's opposition was much more significant, because he was thought of as a rival to Vice President Gore for the
Democratic nomination in 2000. On the other hand, the Republicans,
though vigorous advocates of free trade, were still sharply opposed to link-
ing the issues of environmental protection and foreign workers' rights. The
Speaker of the House, Newt Gingrich, warned that the Republicans would
not commit to more than 150 House Republicans, out of the 218 votes
needed for approval.

The administration's strategy was murky and confusing. Given the sour
taste left by the Mexican bailout, the administration decided to occupy
higher ground in the debate. Fast track was not to be about the extension of
NAFTA but about the leadership of the global economy. This was confusing, because one of the immediate aims of fast track was to start negotiations to expand NAFTA to include Chile. In any case, Clinton's tactical
arguments were becoming shopworn. Like his predecessors, Clinton argued that no country would commit itself unless assured that the agreements were amendment-proof. Bush had made these identical arguments,
but the Clinton team was more apocalyptic—failure of fast track would
condemn the global trading system to limbo: compete or retreat, was the
administration's slogan.[18]

As for geopolitics, the administration no longer held out the promise of a new foreign policy architecture. Instead, President Clinton and Secretary Albright warned that other countries would move into the lucrative Latin markets; since 1992, in both Latin America and Asia, more than twenty trade agreements had been negotiated that excluded the United States.

The debate became more and more political. Senator Dole and former treasury secretary Lloyd Bentsen teamed up to write an op-ed article for the *New York Times* supporting fast track. Nevertheless, the bipartisan coalition was coming apart. Gingrich publicly doubted that the votes were there for approval. In the NAFTA debate four years earlier, the Democrats had been in the majority and reluctant to repudiate their newly elected president. Four years later he was a lame duck, who many Democrats thought had abandoned them in the 1996 elections. The media was also framing the issues as a referendum on NAFTA, a viewpoint sure to lose votes. The political clock was also ticking. Ramming through fast track in 1998, a midterm election year, would be more difficult than adopting it in 1997.

Shortly before Clinton's departure for a visit to Latin America, the House Ways and Means Committee approved fast track, twenty-four to fourteen, but only four of sixteen Democrats voted for it. During the president's trip to Venezuela, Brazil, and Argentina he was forced to soft-pedal fast track. His staff stressed that the importance of the visit was his "presence." In Argentina he went so far as to proclaim that Argentina was a non-NATO ally of the United States—whatever that meant.

Ironically, it turned out that Clinton's vagueness was an asset. The major Latin countries, except for Chile, were reluctant to move further toward the Miami summit's goal of establishing the Free Trade Area of the Americas (FTAA) by 2005. Brazil in particular, facing another internal economic crisis, was relieved to pass over the question of the FTAA.[19] The trip was successful as a personal venture in "catch up" diplomacy, but strategically it was irrelevant. It changed no votes at home and made little impression abroad. Clinton had spent the week "preaching a sunny vision," wrote one reporter.[20]

Upon returning home, at a news conference on November 7 Clinton commented with some irritation that on its merits fast track was a "no brainer," but he acknowledged that politics was in command. Despite a favorable vote in the Senate, sixty-nine to thirty-one against invoking cloture, the outlook in the House was doubtful. A vote was scheduled, then postponed and rescheduled. Finally, rather than face an outright defeat in the House, the president withdrew the proposed legislation altogether. At a press conference on November 10 he delivered a statement vowing to fight again after the new year, but, in a sign of the times, the first reporter's question was about Iraq.[21]

Why had the controversial NAFTA passed, while the vague fast track failed? The *Washington Post* editorialized (November 11, 1997) that Clinton's "inconstancy over the years left many members of Congress unwilling to put faith in his promises and assurances."[22] Other Democratic analysts blamed Clinton for making fast-track authority "sound like a trivial, technical matter."[23]

In the NAFTA contest Clinton had chosen to live by politics; in the fast-track conflict he died by politics. Conditions had obviously changed since the first NAFTA votes. The reluctant Democratic congressmen earned the lion's share of the blame for the failure of fast track; Clinton's defeat was more complicated, however. Democrats had not forgiven Clinton for moving toward the "third way" in the 1996 elections. The estrangement between Clinton and the Democratic rank and file had obviously grown. Congressmen were miffed by the president's remark that the vote would have been favorable if taken in secret, implying crass motives on the part of the opponents.[24]

The failure of fast track reflected deeper changes. Clinton had failed to embed his trade policy in any longer-term strategy. In 1993 NAFTA had been held up as a precursor of a new foreign policy directed toward a broad free-trade area for the Americas. At the Summit of the Americas in Miami in December 1994 he not only linked NAFTA to the broader Free Trade Area of the Americas but set forth a vision of the "spirit of Miami." At that summit (December 11, 1994) he said,

> In the last two weeks the United States has concluded agreements to push for regional free trade in the two fastest growing areas in the world—first, at Bogor in Indonesia with the Asian Pacific economies, and now here with the free trade agreement at the Summit of the Americas. These things—along with the implementation of GATT and the expansion of the NAFTA arrangement—will set the agenda for world trade for years to come. . . . Our goal is to create a whole new architecture for the relationship of the nations and the peoples of the Americas. . . . There is truly a spirit of Miami.[25]

The Mexican crisis effectively killed this "new era for the Americas." In the 1997 debate over fast track the administration never really tried to spell out the geopolitical virtues of free trade for the hemisphere. The arguments used were altogether different: cutting out competitors, especially the Europeans, from the Latin American market was cited far more often as an incentive for fast-track trade agreements.

Free trade was no longer the icon it had been, as mounting trade deficits soured the atmosphere. Some observers began to question the very concept of a free trade area for the Americas, on the grounds that it was not really a "natural market" for the United States.[26] Moreover, a new economic nationalism, espoused at first by Perot and Buchanan, had seeped into the Republican Congress; many of the new members were skeptical on all foreign economic issues. Finally, in an economy near full employment, the promise of new jobs from increased trade seemed less urgent and attractive than it would otherwise have. Thus, ironically, President Clinton was a victim of his own economic success. In a larger sense, however, he once again could not disentangle his foreign policy strategy from his preoccupation with domestic politics. His decision to postpone the fast-track vote was read as a defeat, not a defeat for his foreign policy but confirmation of his lame-duck status: "Clinton Bruised" read one typical headline.

To be sure, the failure of fast track was a serious political setback that might someday be recouped (it was voted down 242–180 in September 1998). But the broader message was the confirmation that the Clinton administration would not, or could not, reorient American foreign policy toward the Western Hemisphere. The vaunted second Summit of the Americas in Chile in April 1998 provided little more than "smiling and backslapping," according to one Latin minister. Several new bureaucratic committees were set up, but there was skepticism among Latin participants about whether the United States was really committed to free trade.[27] Moreover, the dream of an FTAA that would be linked to the Pacific basin was already undermined, if not killed, by the severe financial crisis in Asia. In this sense the post–Cold War transition ended in Santiago, Chile. American foreign policy would remain Eurocentric, as it had for over two hundred years.

NOTES

1. For background see *Congressional Quarterly*, November 20, 1993, pp. 3174–3186.

2. Tim Golden, "In Mexico, NAFTA Isn't Just about Trade," *New York Times*, August 22, 1993.

3. *Congressional Quarterly*, October 16, 1993; Jeff Faux, "NAFTA Delusions," *Washington Post*, September 3, 1993.

4. Warren Christopher, "U.S.-Mexican Relations and NAFTA," statement at the U.S.-Mexican Bilateral Commission Meeting, Washington, D.C., June 21, 1993.

5. Henry Kissinger, "NAFTA: Clinton's Defining Task," *Washington Post*, July 20, 1993.

6. Paul Krugman, "The Uncomfortable Truth about NAFTA," *Foreign Affairs*, November/December 1993; Gary Clyde Hufbauer and Jeffrey Schott, *NAFTA: An Assessment* (rev. ed.) (Washington, D.C.: Institute for International Economics, 1993).

7. Stanley Komarow, "Wheeling, Dealing to Assure a Victory," *USA Today*, November 18, 1993; *Congressional Quarterly*, November 20, 1993, p. 3179.

8. Robert Reich, *Locked in the Cabinet* (New York: Alfred A. Knopf, 1997), p. 132.

9. Statement of Robert Rubin, House Committee on Banking, January 25, 1995.

10. A. M. Rosenthal, "$40 Billion Questions," *New York Times*, January 27, 1995; Editorial, "The Yeas and Nays on Mexico," *Washington Post*, January 27, 1995.

11. "Report on the Mexican Economic Crisis," Senate Banking Committee, presented by Senator Alfonse D'Amato, June 29, 1995; Edwin M. Truman, "The Mexican Peso Crisis: Implications for International Finance," U.S. *Federal Reserve Bulletin*, March 1996, p. 199.

12. Donald Lambro, "NAFTA Success Saga beyond Expectations," *Washington Times*, June 2, 1997.

13. Helen Dewar, "Senate Passes," *Washington Post*, March 21, 1997.

14. Julia Preston, "Mexico to Prosecute U.S. Agents," *New York Times*, June 4, 1998.

15. M. Delal Baer, "The U.S. at Odds with Itself on Mexico," *Washington Post*, June 1, 1998.

16. Thomas W. Lippman, "Political Necessity," *Washington Post*, May 4, 1997; Sam Dillon, "Opposition in Mexico," *New York Times*, May 7, 1997.

17. Paul Blustein, "White House Subdued on NAFTA's Impact," *Washington Post*, July 11, 1997.

18. C. Fred Bergsten, "American Politics, Global Trade," *Economist*, September 27, 1997; a rebuttal by Jagdish Bhagwati, professor of economics at Columbia University, appeared in the *Economist*, October 18, 1997.

19. David E. Sanger, "A Handicap," *New York Times*, November 11, 1997; "The Free Trade Winds Die Away," *Economist*, November 22, 1997.

20. John F. Harris, "Clinton Sees Two Sides," *Washington Post*, October 16, 1997.

21. *Congressional Quarterly*, November 15, 1997, p. 2751.

22. Editorial, *Washington Post*, November 11, 1997.

23. Ted Van Dyck, "Off Track on Trade," *New York Times*, November 7, 1997.

24. Sander M. Levin, "Why Fast Track Failed," *Washington Post*, November 24, 1997.

25. Department of State *Dispatch, Supplement*, May 1995.

26. Bernard K. Gordon, "The Natural Market Fallacy," *Foreign Affairs*, May/June 1998.

27. Calvin Sims, "Latin America Fears Stagnation," *New York Times*, April 19, 1998.

6

Russia

The Clinton administration paid a political price for its early mistakes. The president had managed to provoke serious questions about his competence in foreign affairs. Although the situations in Somalia and Haiti had little impact on national security, Clinton's credibility was damaged. After the 1996 elections were safely over, Christopher and others admitted to mishandling Somalia, Haiti, and Bosnia. By that time Haiti and Somalia were only painful memories, and the administration had reversed course in Bosnia. On balance, they were secondary problems. Even the situation in Bosnia did not constitute a threat to American security—at least not directly. What would matter was how the new administration dealt with the great power centers—Russia, China, Japan, and Europe. Mistakes in Bosnian policy could be repaired, but a confrontation with Russia or China, or a serious split with NATO, would have long-term strategic consequences. On the other hand, putting these great-power relationships on a firm foundation would be a durable accomplishment.

The new administration was probably better prepared to deal with Russian issues than, say, with Bosnia. The Soviet Union had been familiar terrain. The State and Defense departments were staffed with officials with long experience in Soviet-Russian relations. But they would soon learn that their experience was now less relevant: circumstances were radically different from the Cold War years.

The dissolution of the USSR had been greeted with a strange mixture—euphoria that a new age had begun, certainly in Europe and perhaps even in the world, and skepticism. Russian democracy seemed a historical oxymoron. Autocrats and dictators had ruled Russia and the Soviet Union for centuries; why should the leader of the new Russia be an exception? After all, Boris Yeltsin had spent decades as a communist apparatchik. Nothing in his background or experience suited him for the role of a democrat. At the age of sixty, however, he was suddenly the successor not only to Gorbachev but to Nicholas II as well. For a few months at least, he was potentially as powerful as any of his predecessors.

The former Soviet lands presented a maze, with no guideposts. There were now fifteen independent states, including Russia, that varied greatly in history, character, size, wealth, and strategic importance. Two were obviously critical for the United States—Russia and the "Ukraine" (now to be known only as Ukraine, without the definite article). The United States, of course, had never had a Ukrainian policy, per se—or, for that matter, a Kazakh or Kyrgyz policy, in fact any policies toward the constituent republics of the USSR, except perhaps for the Baltic States.

The central reality was the economic crisis. The situation in Russia as well in the other independent areas was on the brink of catastrophe. The links that had tied together the central economy of the USSR were broken. Gorbachev's reforms had failed, but the centralized economy and bureaucracy were still limping along as they had for decades. However, while a large cadre of communist bureaucrats were still running the Russian government and the economy, central plans were no longer forthcoming from Moscow. Grain deliveries to feed the cities were not assured. The ruble was virtually worthless. Foreign markets were questionable. Inflation, unemployment, corruption—all the vices of a market economy—were suddenly threatening. The compensation—political freedom—had yet to be savored. The omnipotent Communist Party apparatus was diminished but not eliminated. Extremists on the right were in the ascendance.

The Russian leaders, including Boris Yeltsin, had calculated that they would have a grace period of perhaps several years to experiment with a new order of their own, while still retaining a tentative alliance with the USSR. But the abortive August coup against Mikhail Gorbachev and the collapse of the USSR had accelerated every timetable. Yeltsin and his aides now had to cope with devising a new economy, for an independent Russia, a new political order, and a new foreign policy, and to start immediately.

The Bush administration was guarded. It had taken some time to warm up to Gorbachev. After Reagan's ebullient embrace of the Soviet leader, Bush had been cooler for a time, mindful of the criticism that he should not invest too much in one man. After the collapse of the Soviet empire in Eastern Europe, however, Bush had also enthusiastically embraced Gorbachev. Bush's investment paid off handsomely during the Gulf War and the negotiations for the reunification of Germany. Now in Gorbachev's place came Boris Yeltsin—a man whose emotional and personal stability was suspect and whose political future was uncertain.

For decades American statesmen had been conditioned to deal with a few Soviet leaders at the top of the communist power structure. Yeltsin was viewed more as Gorbachev's successor than as the president of a democratic republic. But they were quite different personalities. Gorbachev had been a visionary who believed that the Soviet system he inherited could be reformed and redeemed. Yeltsin was animated by no great vision, but he believed the Soviet system was not worth saving. On the other hand, both men were egoists, bordering on arrogance; they suffered from an excessive preoccupation with tactical maneuvers, and both lacked a firm strategic grasp on how to implement their ideas. Gorbachev tried to use the communist bureaucracy, which eventually betrayed him. He brashly dismissed his opponents as pygmies too weak to challenge him, a mindset that led to his downfall. Yeltsin sought to dispense with the old-guard bureaucracy but failed to develop an alternative. He dealt with opposition ruthlessly, crushing opponents.

Finally, the international situation was different. Gorbachev had presided over a vast empire of over 250 million, feared if not respected throughout the globe. He was well regarded as a statesman. Yeltsin sought to govern a country reduced to less than 150 million, widely believed to be weak and clearly no longer a superpower. Gorbachev had sought peace abroad in order to concentrate on his domestic revolution; no one could say how Yeltsin would deal with the disastrous decline of Russia.

In the West, and especially in Washington, there was a strong residual distrust of Russian intentions. Would the new Russia give up Soviet pretensions to a global role? Could Russia become a state like any other state? If so, what would be the interests of this new state? Would Russia join the West and become a cooperative partner in building a new regime of European and international security? Or would it relapse into a new Russian imperialism?

The initial answers were both troubling and reassuring. For example, Yeltsin's earlier statement that Russia's borders were subject to renegotiation had been alarming[1] but had come at a time when Gorbachev was still in power and had probably been needling the USSR rather than expressing Russian aims. Moreover, Yeltsin's foreign minister, Andrei Kozyrev, was well known in the West and generally regarded as a sympathetic partner. He had a history of advocating a reorientation of Russian policy toward friendlier relations with the West, especially with the United States. Even before the collapse of the Soviet Union, Kozyrev had said that Russia would have to abandon its messianism and set a course of pragmatism; geo-politics would replace ideology. Yeltsin also made it clear that Russia had no aspiration to be "the center of some sort of new empire." Rather, he would anchor his foreign policy in relations with the United States, and this called for a friendly American response.[2]

The Bush administration, however, was ambivalent about Yeltsin. Some officials privately criticized him as a "demagogue." As long as Gorbachev was in power, Washington kept Yeltsin at arm's length. The Bush admini-stration encouraged Gorbachev to work closely with Yeltsin, but this was more for the record than a serious policy. Later it was reported that Bush had felt during the anti-Gorbachev coup that Yeltsin had humiliated Gor-bachev in a way that violated Bush's sense of personal honor.

The Bush administration had considerable room to create a new struc-ture of relations with Russia. But what to do and how to do it were by no means simple. Attitudes in the United States toward Russia were funda-mentally divided. For decades American statesmen had debated the mo-tives and intentions of the Soviet Union. Many had preached that antagonism toward the USSR was an inevitable result of the dictatorship of the Communist Party. There might be periods of coexistence, but there could be no permanent settlement with the Soviet Union as long as the communist regime remained in power. There was another school of thought that held that expansionist Soviet foreign policy was in reality his-torical Russian imperialism in a different ideological guise. Even if the communist structure were to collapse, it would merely uncover the hard core of Russian expansionism.

This debate, long considered merely academic, now was a central reality. The corollary debate was the Western response. Should the West address Soviet foreign policy or seek to go beyond interstate relations and influ-ence the internal order of the Soviet Union itself? That debate had swung back and forth for years. Now that issue too was part of the new reality.

Bush adopted a policy that in effect argued both ways. On the one hand, Russian internal policies and the views of its leaders were still critical; in-deed, for outside powers to influence the domestic order was now more fea-sible and therefore vastly more important than when outside powers had confronted an impervious communist monolith. The key to Russia policy therefore was to encourage and support democracy inside Russia. Russian democracy, it was believed, would tame Russian imperialism.

There was a strong dissent, especially in Eastern Europe, from this American policy. Eastern Europeans found it naive: Yeltsin was no demo-crat but a Russian feudal lord. American critics also found it naive to be-lieve that Russia, even if gravely weakened, would give up its centuries-old interest in dominating its surrounding territories. Inside the new Russia there were strong nationalist voices urging Russia to reestablish its hegemony over the former Soviet republics. Such views came not only from the extremes but from moderate segments of the Russian hierarchy. Yeltsin's ambassador to the United States, for example, argued that Russia's role as "defender of its smaller neighbors and as guarantor of stability and security of their borders" were roles compatible with a democratic foreign policy.[3]

Bush pursued three objectives: to encourage economic reforms and tailor American assistance toward that end; to further limit Russian military power through new arms control agreements; and to build up Ukraine as a counterweight to Russian domination.

American preoccupation with nuclear weapons was clearly justified. During the coup against Gorbachev there had been a gnawing question of who controlled the nuclear release authentication codes (no one, it turned out). Now that problem was multiplied by potential missile command centers in the new states of Belarus, Ukraine, and Kazakhstan. Who owned these nuclear arsenals? Were they still Russian missiles? If not, would Washington have to negotiate treaties to limit and control the weapons of all those nations?

The Bush administration set to work almost at once to sort out this tangle, and by the time it left office there was in place a new treaty reducing strategic armaments even further (START II). The groundwork was also laid for the three new nuclear states to abandon their weapons, transferring them to the Russian republic or destroying them.[4]

Under some prodding from Richard Nixon, the Bush administration also devised an economic assistance program for Russia. Nixon argued that there was no better alternative to Yeltsin and that the reform of Russia was the key to the reform of the other formerly Soviet states.[5] The Bush administration did push through a small program of assistance, including a package devised by Senators Sam Nunn and Richard Lugar to appropriate money to assist with the dismantling of the strategic arsenal. Led by the United States, the Group of Seven (G-7) announced a package of twenty-four billion dollars in aid, but it was largely smoke and mirrors. A standby loan from the IMF was also heavily conditioned, and the various bilateral assistance programs were mainly in credits for exports.

In the campaign of 1992, candidate Clinton attacked the administration's record as overly cautious. Nevertheless, once in office Clinton followed a policy not greatly different than that of Bush. Even the overblown rhetoric was much the same. The chief architect of Clinton's Russia policy was Strobe Talbott, ambassador at large and later deputy secretary of state. He put the issues in nearly apocalyptic terms:

There have been three great struggles in this century. The first was World War I, a conflagration that ignited the Russian Revolution of 1917; the second was the World War against fascism and imperialism of 1939–1945; the third was the Cold War against Soviet communism and expansionism. Now a fourth great struggle is underway in Eurasia. It pits those who brought down the Soviet communist system against those who would like to preserve its vestiges if not restore its essence. It pits those who are determined to build a proud future against those who are clinging to a cruel and shameful past. In short, it pits reform against reaction. We have a stake in the outcome of that struggle.[6]

Talbott argued that Americans saw the stakes too much in terms of what the United States wanted to prevent, that is, political turmoil that could trigger a civil war. He urged Americans to adopt a more "positive" attitude: "An investment now in the heroic effort of these new democracies to re-structure their economies will pay dividends down the road." Russia would be a reliable source for raw materials, a reliable market for American goods, and a reliable partner in diplomacy. Just as Russia was undergoing a historic transformation, Talbott argued, the United States also should undertake a corresponding transformation in its role: "We must now lead a strategic alliance with post-Soviet reform." This prescription was probably right, even if Talbott had gone too far comparing World War I and II with the struggle over reform in Russia.

Warren Christopher also made a strong case for the priority of Russian policy. In a speech only three months after taking office, Christopher laid down the administration's basic approach:

One of the highest foreign policy priorities [is] helping the Russian people to build a free society and a market economy. This in my judgement is the greatest strategic challenge of our time. Bringing Russia—one of history's most powerful nations—into the family of peaceful nations will serve our highest security, economic and moral interests. For America and the world the stakes are just monumental. If we succeed, we will have established the foundation for our lasting security into the next century. But if Russia falls into anarchy or lurches back to despotism, the price we pay could be frightening.[7]

In effect, Clinton's team turned around the old Cold War priorities. Previous administrations, including that of Bush, had scrupulously avoided tailoring policies to help this or that Soviet leader. This had changed somewhat under Reagan with respect to Gorbachev. Under Clinton relations would not be determined by the traditional interaction of American and Russian foreign policies but would be governed by the state of Russian internal affairs. In other words, Russia would be granted a certain latitude in its foreign policy as long as its domestic order was evolving in the right direction. The Clinton administration never went this far in public, but that was the gist of its policies, as would later become clear in the debates over expanding NATO.

In moving toward this approach Clinton was privately encouraged by conversations with Richard Nixon. It was shrewd of Clinton to consult Nixon about Russia; it gave his policies a protective cover against right-wing criticism. Clinton telephoned Nixon and then invited him to the White House, where they discussed Russia. Clinton was mainly interested in whether Yeltsin would survive; Nixon responded that he would not without American aid. With Yeltsin, "what you see is what you get," Nixon said. Nixon rather enthusiastically told his young assistant Monica Crowley that it was the best conversation with a president that he had experienced since he had left office.[8]

Few could quarrel with the administration's according high importance to Russian policy. The stakes were indeed "monumental," as Christopher said. But the administration's proposed prescription was at least open to question. To promote a "free society and a market economy" were both legitimate objectives, but to make the creation of a free society and a market economy the tests for American policy risked setbacks, if not major failures. These objectives, however laudable in theory, were well beyond the capacity of any outside force, even the powerful United States. George Kennan pointed out that it was unlikely that Russia would ever achieve democracy in the sense of institutions similar to America's.[9]

Moreover, it turned out that the Russian government was quite capable of pursuing reform at home while conducting an increasingly nationalistic, if not expansionist, foreign policy. The assumption that a democratic evolution would encourage a benign foreign policy was Clinton's major error; it ignored the realities of Russian domestic politics. To stay in power Yeltsin would have to oscillate between his right and left, much as Clinton and other Western politicians did.

The hardening of Russian policy, however, would not become clear for some years. At least in some part, that hardening came to pass because American policy became condescending. The idea of a partnership, but an unequal one, was finally rejected, and Kozyrev was eventually replaced by Yevgeny Primakov, whose reputation as anti-American was well founded. In any event, Clinton's policy was deliberately mortgaged to internal Russian forces and volatile personalities beyond its control, in a quest for an elusive goal.

As Clinton took office, events inside Russia demonstrated the difficulties the two new governments had to face. Like any new democracy, Russia had to redefine its power structure. The struggle for power between the president and the Russian parliament had become much sharper by the early spring of 1993. The lower house of parliament (the Duma) was still heavily influenced by ex-communists and right-wing extremists; they were determined to tie down Yeltsin and reduce him to a figurehead. He was equally determined to fight back. Yeltsin had even threatened to do away with the parliament altogether—an event that would have confronted Washington with a new nightmare. Could the United States support a democratically elected president of Russia who was eliminating the very institutions of parliamentary democracy? On the other hand, why should Washington support the sanctity of a parliament loaded with communists?

The intensification of the clash in Moscow was unfortunate for Clinton. Nixon had urged him to meet Yeltsin before the G-7 summit in Tokyo, which was to consider aid to Russia. Clinton agreed to meet Yeltsin in early April in Vancouver, British Columbia, a convenient stopover on Clinton's way to the G-7 meeting. For Clinton it would be embarrassing if Yeltsin had already routed the Russian parliament, especially since Clinton's team had fashioned a new aid package that needed congressional support. Initially, an interagency team had proposed about a billion dollars, on the grounds that Congress would not approve more, but Clinton rejected this as too mild. He wanted more; he urged his staff to be "bold." His aides then developed a new package totalling $2.5 billion. Beyond that, Clinton was prepared to seek an international package that would total about twenty billion dollars. Before the Vancouver summit Yeltsin was quick to reassure Clinton that he would not move against the parliament. Oddly enough, the effect of the growing constitutional crisis in Russia was to increase congressional support for a Russian aid package, apparently on the grounds that the alternative to Yeltsin was chaos or despotism.

In defending his aid plan, Clinton coined a phrase that would sum up his Russian policy: his aim was to forge a "strategic alliance with Russian reform." When Yeltsin had first met George Bush he asked, rather plaintively, whether the two countries were still adversaries. Bush had said they were not adversaries, they were friends and partners. Yeltsin suggested saying in their formal statement that they were "allies," but Bush balked at going that far. In their 1992 summit meeting the two had issued a communiqué announcing a "strategic partnership." Two years later, in their Moscow Declaration (January 14, 1994), Clinton and Yeltsin not only proclaimed their "mature strategic partnership," but Clinton went so far as to tie the success of his own domestic programs to his Russian policy: "Our ability to put people first at home requires that we put Russia and its neighbors first on our agenda abroad." Apparently what he meant was that a failure of Russian policy might bring back the Cold War and jeopardize any hopes of domestic progress. If a little vague, it was still a persuasive argument, if a risky linkage.

The first Clinton-Yeltsin summit (April 3–4) in Vancouver was the beginning of a serious attempt to reconstruct Russian-American relations. The two leaders established some overriding themes. They declared

> their firm commitment to a dynamic and effective U.S.-Russian partnership that strengthens international stability. . . . President Yeltsin stressed his firm commitment to fostering democratization, the rule of law, and a market economy. . . . President Clinton assured President Yeltsin of active American support for the Russian people as they pursue their own chosen course of political and economic reform.[10]

This was not very different from Bush's summit with Yeltsin. Clinton, however, made it clear how concerned he was with Russian internal developments. He said (April 4, 1993) that the United States would not "stand on the sidelines" when it concerned democracy in Russia:

> We know where we stand. We are with Russian democracy. We are with Russian reforms. We are with Russian markets. We support freedom of conscience and speech and religion. We support respect for ethnic minorities. We actively support reform and reformers and you [Yeltsin] in Russia.[11]

In short, Clinton and Yeltsin struck a bargain: in return for progress toward democracy the United States would extend economic assistance. Such assistance was justified as not merely helping the Russian economy but buttressing the new commitment to reforms and reformers in Russia. More worrisome was Clinton's ambitious characterization of what he expected and would support in Russia; reform and free markets were understandable, but Clinton added a throwback to the Cold War—"freedom of conscience."

The idea of a partnership sounded good, but it was questionable. The gap between American power and Soviet weakness was large and growing. Russia clearly would have to be the junior partner; many in Russia saw the partnership as only a mechanism for commanding Russian support for American global ambitions. On the other hand, partnership with real content would smack of a condominium. This had been the European nightmare during the Cold War; it would be ironic if it developed with a democratic Russia.

Clinton did not really keep his part of the bargain, except superficially. After Vancouver, Clinton flew on to Tokyo for the G-7 summit, where all the participants, including the Japanese, paid lip service to helping Russia. The amount of concrete help was impressive on paper, but the G-7 was playing a shell game: it was offering the same monies that had been agreed with Bush. Much of it was in the form of credits for the Russians to buy the exports of the donor countries. Secretary Christopher announced that the United States was increasing its own commitment to $2.8 billion. This too was disingenuous: Washington had all along planned for a total package of $2.5 billion, but Christopher made it seem that the G-7's cooperation had stimulated an even greater American effort. It was good gamesmanship. Subsequently, Clinton was able to get an aid program through Congress. It was finally passed in September 1993 with a Senate vote of eighty-eight to ten, including a Republican split of thirty-six to seven in favor. In subsequent years, however, Clinton would relinquish control of his economic relations with Russia to the bureaucrats of the IMF. They in turn were particularly uninformed and myopic; in effect, they would help to drive Russia's economy into worse crises.[12]

Nevertheless, these problems were yet to come, and at the time Clinton's Russian policy seemed on course. It would soon be badly buffeted by new political crises that erupted in Moscow. The basic issue was still the same: a struggle for power between Yeltsin and his opponents in the parliament. On September 21, the Russian congress locked itself in the parliament building, known in Moscow as the "White House." The parliament then proceeded to "impeach" Yeltsin and elect Alexander Rutskoi as the new president. Rutskoi was a general, a hero from the war in Afghanistan, and the vice president of the Russian Federation. He was an avowed Russian imperialist who kept a map of the czarist empire prominently displayed on the wall of his office.

The Clinton administration supported Yeltsin throughout. Clinton talked with Yeltsin on the telephone and assured him that history was on his side. Nothing much happened for several days, but on Sunday evening, October 3, a mob of several thousand attacked the government television station. Fighting broke out, and Yeltsin declared a state of emergency. The army and Yeltsin's defense minister, General Pavel Grachev, swung their support decisively to the government. On Monday, October 4, Russian tanks pounded the White House, forcing the rebels to surrender.

An anonymous "senior" American official said that they wanted to see the crisis end quickly and for Yeltsin to "prevail." Clinton's support for Yeltsin was generally approved in the United States. James Baker in a *Newsweek* article, strongly endorsed Clinton's handling of the crisis. Other commentators went quite far in their assessments of the significance of the coup's failure: it was the "last gasp" of communism, the historian and Sovietologist Richard Pipes concluded. "Western statesmen have acquitted themselves splendidly in this crisis," he wrote, "In coming months, Western government should continue to extend unstinting support—moral, diplomatic, economic—to those who have just brought Russia back from the brink of disaster."[13] Such comments from diverse sources, such as Baker and Pipes, must have gladdened the hearts of Clinton's advisors. Pipes was known as a leading "hawk." A dedicated critic of detente, he had served in the Reagan National Security Council. Warren Christopher, visiting Moscow, defended Yeltsin vehemently. The "defenders of the old order" were defeated, he said:

> When those demagogues at your White House waved the hammer and sickle, in the name of democracy, you [the Russians] saw the hypocrisy. . . . We are truly proud to stand with you and to call Russia our friend and partner. . . . What America and Russia share is not merely friendship. What our two nations are building is a strategic partnership.[14]

There were, of course, skeptics. In the wake of the episode of the Russian White House there was a surprising amount of hand-wringing. Many observers thought that the army would now become dominant. Others predicted increasing domestic disorder. No one, at least no one in Washington, foresaw what happened next in the elections for a new parliament. The elections, held on December 14, 1993, were an implicit referendum on Yeltsin. The political battle would be over the control of the democratic center. Yeltsin had no organized party, however. On the radical fringes were the communists and the national socialists of Vladimir Zhirinovsky. The Communist Party was once again legal, having defeated Yeltsin's ban in the Russian courts. Zhirinovsky had run third in the presidential elections of 1991, behind Yeltsin. In one of his more unfortunate gaffes, Warren Christopher said shortly before the elections that the Russian people had chosen "reform over reaction."

The outcome of the vote was stunning. Zhirinovsky's extreme right-wing "Liberal Democratic Party" won a major victory—32 percent for his party, well ahead of his closest competitor "Russia's Choice," the reformist party. The former Communist Party registered 12 percent of the vote, and a front group of communists called the Agrarian Party got 8 percent. Thus the extremists, left and right, had won the majority of the popular vote. Two years after the dissolution of the USSR, Russian democracy had been dealt a blistering defeat.

Largely overlooked because of the extremists' gains was a significant turning point—the approval of the new constitution (known as the Basic Law). It had been pushed through by Yeltsin and narrowly endorsed in the voting. It became the legal basis for the beginning of a strong presidential system coupled with a weakened parliament.

After the elections, rethinking Russian policy was the new order of the day. Strobe Talbott commented, too caustically, that the time had come for less shock and more therapy.[15] This enraged the Russian reformers, especially those who had pushed the so-called shock therapy and had suffered badly in the elections. Talbott tried to take back his unfortunate words, but the Russian reformers blamed the United States for "stabbing them in the back" and failing to give them wholehearted support. It was an unfounded and unfair charge, but the Russian political climate was becoming more and more anti-American. As the internal situation failed to show any real improvement, the United States was a convenient scapegoat for the failure and fumbling incoherence of the Russian reformers' own programs.

Clinton had tied himself to reform as he had been urged to do by the experts; he had even gone further, tying himself to the person of Boris Yeltsin. At the beginning of 1994, Clinton's second year in office, it seemed more and more likely that neither reform nor Yeltsin would survive. If they went down they would sink Clinton's policies as well. This was the uneasy situation that confronted Clinton when he left Washington for his first visit to Europe and Russia in January 1994.

NOTES

1. Andrew Rosenthal, "Farewell Red Menace," *New York Times*, September 1, 1991.

2. Stephen Sestanovich, "Andrei the Giant," *The New Republic*, April 11, 1994.

3. Vladimir P. Lukin, "Our Security Predicament," *Foreign Policy*, Fall 1992, p. 68.

4. The START II treaty was not ratified by the U.S. Senate until January 1996. U.S. Department of State *Dispatch*, January 19, 1996.

5. Richard Nixon, "The Time Has Come to Help," *Time*, January 13, 1992.

6. Statement before the Subcommittee on Foreign Operations of the House Appropriations Committee, Washington, D.C., April 19, 1993.

7. Warren Christopher, "The Three Pillars of U.S. Foreign Policy and Support for Reform in Russia," address before the Chicago Council on Foreign Relations, March 22, 1993.

8. Monica Crowley, *Nixon Off the Record* (New York: Random House, 1996), pp. 170–177.

9. George F. Kennan, *At a Century's Ending* (New York: W. W. Norton, 1996), pp. 332–333.

10. U.S. Department of State *Dispatch, Supplement*, Vol. 4, No. 2, May 1993.

11. Ibid.

12. Jeffrey Sachs, "Betrayal," *The New Republic*, January 3, 1994.

13. Richard Pipes, "The Last Gasp of Russia's Communists," *New York Times*, October 5, 1993.

14. Warren Christopher, "A New Generation of Russian Democrats," address at the Academy of the National Economy, Moscow, October 23, 1993, in *Dispatch*, Vol. 4, No. 43.

15. Bruce W. Nelan, "Clinton's Obstacle," *Time*, January 17, 1994.

7

European Security

A trip to Europe is usually good for a president. A carefully arranged grand tour almost always means crowds, receptions, honors, photo opportunities, and even some serious business. Clinton enjoyed the public side and could charm his various hosts. But it was the business side of his first venture into Europe—the enlargement of the NATO alliance—that would have the more lasting effect. Indeed, with his trip in January 1994 to Europe and Russia Clinton would embark on a project that was most likely to define his foreign policy.

Clinton delayed his trip until almost a year after his inauguration. There was the inevitable speculation that the delay was calculated. It was no secret that the British prime minister, John Major, had supported Bush's reelection. Clinton's decision to start his trip in Brussels, at NATO headquarters, skipping London altogether, seemed a spiteful choice (denied, of course). Other European leaders had been sympathetic to Bush, if for no other reason that he was a known quantity. Helmut Kohl, the German chancellor, obviously owed Bush a huge debt for his role in securing the unification of Germany. The French were more cynical; a new, inexperienced president might provide some maneuvering room to advance France's ambitions in Europe and around the globe.

The general posture of the Clinton administration worried some Europeans. Rarely has a president been subjected to more skeptical scrutiny in Europe than was Bill Clinton in January 1994. R. W. Apple Jr., writing in the *New York Times*, set the stage for the visit:

Europeans have been watching, trying to take his measure from afar, studying his policies (or what many see as the lack thereof) and wondering why he had waited so long to come. Their anxious mood is compounded of many things: an apprehension about the unknown, an unsettling generational change, a sense that history may be flowing away from them.[1]

The fact that Clinton had visited Tokyo and had met with the Asian leaders in Seattle was cited as evidence that America was turning away from its European vocation. Christopher's offhand comment that American policy was too "Eurocentric" was widely quoted. In an interview he refused to repudiate this remark, only explaining that he had meant to say that more attention had to be paid to Asia and Latin America. Margaret Thatcher's former special assistant, Sir Charles Powell, was quoted as saying, "There always used to be someone we knew to go to for a clear reading on where you [Americans] were heading. . . . To put it mildly that has not been the case in recent months."[2] Other news accounts contained many similar quotes.

A year into office, therefore, Clinton was still on trial in Europe. The alliance was "in danger of drifting slowly apart," wrote the *Economist*. Such pessimism reflected the plague of Bosnia, as well as the growing feeling that after the Cold War the Western alliance had no real mission. Many feared that the United States would disengage from Europe. With the signing of the German treaty, the central confrontation of the Cold War in Europe had been settled. But there was no broad European settlement. What had emerged was not Europe "whole and free," as Western leaders hoped, but a fragmented conglomeration of unstable states. East Europe was once again a grey area lodged between rising German power and declining Russian power.

The solution to this age-old European dilemma was to unfold the umbrella of American protection over this benighted area. In Brussels Clinton sought NATO's endorsement of an American plan for opening the alliance to the states of Eastern Europe. The plan was already public, but the meeting was to be at the summit level, so a NATO endorsement would take on added weight.

Not surprisingly, the new, free states of Eastern Europe had no confidence that they could remain outside the Russian orbit unless they were brought into NATO. Three of them—Poland, Hungary, and Czechoslovakia (before it broke apart)—had met and agreed to press for NATO membership. Whether and how to expand NATO were becoming the most critical tests of European security, rivaling if not overshadowing Bosnia.

Critics of NATO expansion argued that the immediate problem in Eastern Europe was not a threat from Russia but the weaknesses of the economies and political structures of the states freed from Soviet domination. If the aim was to ensure their security, the first and most vital step, it was argued, should be to strengthen their economies and solidify democratic processes, as a prelude to their membership not in NATO but in the European Union. The Western European members of the EU, however, were not yet prepared to dilute their own political and economic institutions by expanding to the east. This left NATO as the only means of assurance. The Bush administration sought a vague compromise, inviting former members of the Warsaw Pact to send official emissaries to NATO, thus creating a measure of association but one well short of membership. A special North Atlantic Cooperation Council (NACC) was created that included these new associates and NATO's permanent members. Prospective members were becoming impatient and apprehensive, however, and were pressing for outright membership.

The Clinton administration simply dodged. Rather than choosing immediate expansion for Poland, Hungary, and after the split, the Czech Republic, Clinton's team created a halfway house: before outright membership there would be a trial arrangement called the Partnership for Peace (PFP). The new members were neither in nor out; no timetable was announced, and various conditions for membership were suggested. Since the Clinton administration had not decided what role NATO should play in the future, it was not surprising that it waffled on including new members.[3]

Nevertheless, the immediate reaction was that Clinton had retreated in the face of the Russian nationalist threat reflected in Zhirinovsky's surprising election success. The rationale for the PFP, especially its conditional nature, did indeed reflect concerns about Russia's future. Refusing to "draw a line" between East and West was the contribution of Strobe Talbott, the administration's leading specialist on Russia. Inside the administration he had vigorously argued against immediate NATO expansion. He had finally carried the day, on the grounds that "drawing a new line" between East and West could become a self-fulfilling prophecy of a future confrontation with Russia. For example, an unnamed "senior" Clinton official told *Time* columnist Michael Kramer that after the shock of the Russian election

we're more gun-shy than ever about substituting our judgement for [Yeltsin's]. He's our guy. We're not going to undermine him with a policy of neocontainment that boosts the hard-line empire builders. Yeltsin says drawing a new line in Europe that shifts the Iron Curtain

back to Russia's border could do just that. And we're going with his
instincts. End of story.[4]

That the administration had once again flinched is probably too harsh a
judgment, but there was a good deal of confusion about Clinton's new Partnership for Peace. It was becoming typical of Clinton's administration that
even before his trip to Europe began it was surrounded by press accounts of
internal bickering. It was reported that the administration had still been
groping for a strategy on the very eve of his departure. With some glee reporters noted that the State Department and the White House had given
competing and conflicting background briefings. The Chairman of the
Joint Chiefs, General John M. Shalikashvilli, said that while it was hoped
the PFP would lead to an extension of the alliance, the "who, when and
how" were premature issues. Anthony Lake, however, said that the administration was setting in motion a dynamic process that was "explicitly opening the door."[5] This description went well beyond the secretary of state's
version of the plan. At a preliminary NATO meeting on December 2,
1993, Christopher had emphasized that membership would depend on the
ability of each state to meet certain conditions: consolidate democratic institutions, respect human rights, and sustain the "hard march" of economic
reform. "Each of these must advance or none of them will," he told the
NATO ministers.[6]

At bottom, there was no real American commitment, which caused
concern in Eastern Europe but private relief in Western Europe. The
former members of the Warsaw Pact saw an opportunity rare in European
history: Russia was weakened and Germany was restrained by its Western
allies. Thus, such countries as Poland and the Czech Republic could reach
out for a pan-European security guarantee backed by the nuclear power of
the United States. Such a historic opportunity might well be a fleeting moment, before Russia revived or Germany broke free of its restraints. This
was the reasoning throughout the area. There was also the psychological
advantage of being admitted as a partner of the West.

Clinton had scheduled a second stop in Prague to meet with the leaders
of the three most likely candidates for NATO membership, the Czech
president, the Polish president, and the Hungarian prime minister. In these
meetings Clinton would try to explain why his plan for NATO was conditional rather than an outright invitation for membership, and he would
seek their acquiescence.

NATO governments were more or less supportive of Clinton's plan. The
British and French liked its noncommittal tenor. The French were preoccupied by Bosnia as were the British. In talks in Washington the British for-

eign secretary, Douglas Hurd, had indicated his desire to go slowly. Mitterand also supported expansion at a "measured" pace but wanted NATO first to strengthen its European "pillar" of Western defense (in other words, give France a stronger role). John Major noted that the prospective candidates had much "work" to do to prepare for membership. The Germans favored NATO expansion, indeed they were eager to relinquish Germany's role as a frontline state; Poland and others would become buffers for Germany against Russia. At the same time, Bonn was reluctant to create a new confrontation with Moscow. Of course, an unstated reason for NATO expansion was to tie down Germany. Involving Germany in a wider framework, Zbigniew Brzezinski said, would be a means for dealing with Europe's central security problem, "how to cope with the reality of Germany's power."[7]

Approval of Clinton's plan was a foregone conclusion. NATO's official decision, however, was generally interpreted as putting off membership rather than opening the door. An "informed" British reporter claimed that the final stage would be delayed for five years. This turned out to be about right.

What mattered for Clinton was not what the formal governmental statements said but how his performance was read in Europe and at home. His relaxed style was well received; both the European and American media concluded that the president's first outing in Europe could be considered a success. American commentators were upbeat as he prepared for his next stop, his Yeltsin summit in Moscow.

Clinton's administration had backed away from offering NATO membership outright to the former Warsaw Pact countries, mainly out of deference to Russia. Also out of self-interest, but of clear benefit to Russia, Washington had badgered Ukraine into adopting a nonnuclear status. On both of these points Clinton should have earned some good will in Moscow, but Russian foreign policy was becoming more nationalistic and assertive. The American honeymoon of 1992–1993 was almost over. Foreign aid to Russia had come in dollops. It had been administered by the IMF, which treated Russia with near contempt; its prescriptions for the Russian economy were ludicrous. American aid, in any case, was a small part of the total—a "drop in the bucket," former Secretary of State Baker said. Russia was becoming disenchanted. To many Russian observers there the benefits of the Western option had turned out to be minimal. Moreover, as the new Russian state recovered its bearings, it asserted a special role in the "near abroad," neighboring states that had been parts of the former USSR. It proposed that the international community recognize these special rights, including the right of Russian intervention if necessary. As for Eastern

Europe, it had never ceased to be an "area of interest for Russia," Foreign Minister Kozyrev said in September 1993.[8] It was even rumored that Yeltsin had concluded that Clinton was weak and could be easily managed.

Nevertheless, Clinton's visit was a replay of the Vancouver summit. Only a month had passed since the disastrous Russian elections; reassurances were in order on both sides. The two leaders continued to talk of "a new stage of mature strategic partnership." Yeltsin reaffirmed the irreversibility of Russia's transition to a market economy and his promotion of further reforms. This was what the Clinton party wanted to hear; there was an "audible sigh of relief" from the Clinton entourage. Clinton, in turn, expressed strong support for Russian reform. He walked the streets of Moscow, in his familiar campaign mode, and took questions at a townmeeting forum.

There was a dramatic announcement that after May 30, 1994, Russian and American intercontinental ballistic missiles (ICBMs) would not be targeted against each other. Experts quickly pointed out that this was meaningless: missiles could be retargeted within minutes. Clinton, however, would cite this new symbol of trust time after time in his subsequent speeches. More surprisingly, Yeltsin claimed that Russia would participate actively in NATO's new Partnership for Peace and might even join NATO. Several commentators suggested that Russian membership in NATO would mark the end of any effective alliance. At the time it seemed a sign of reassurance, however, that Russia would not conduct a campaign against NATO enlargement. (A few months later Yeltsin would say that he would not object to Polish membership in NATO.) In retrospect, the United States probably should have pushed hard for NATO expansion after this Clinton summit, rather than dragging out the affair with the weird arrangement of the PFP.

It was becoming clear, however, that if Washington wanted a good working relationship with Yeltsin it would have to accede to his new, assertive posture. Yeltsin seemed to be proposing to Clinton an implicit agreement on spheres of influence. Russia would have a relatively free hand in the former Soviet states. This meant turning a blind eye to his political and military intervention around the Russian periphery—in Moldova, in Georgia, in the Armenian-Azerbaijani conflict, and in Tajikistan. As for Eastern Europe, Yeltsin implied he would settle for a condominium with the United States. No American government could go that far. Conceding a Russian sphere in its neighboring areas was conceivable, provided the Baltic States and Ukraine were excluded. In effect, that was happening in practice. But acquiescing in a Russian veto in Eastern Europe was too sensitive an area for explicit bargaining, a reminder of Yalta.[9]

Nevertheless, soon after the summit the impression began to circulate that Clinton had made an unsavory deal with Yeltsin. If Russia would play the role of stabilizer in the areas surrounding the Russian Federation, Washington would ignore its more flagrant interventions. That the United States had not complained of Russian military intervention in the newly independent Republic of Moldova, formerly Moldavia (an intervention led by General Alexander Lebed), was cited as evidence of a bargain. Moreover, Washington and its allies approved of Russian military intervention in Tajikistan, which was threatened by an Islamic fundamentalist revolt. Six months after the Clinton-Yeltsin summit, Secretary Christopher, speaking of the states that had emerged from the Soviet empire, even said, "We recognize Russia's legitimate concerns in this region."[10]

NATO expansion was still an unsettled issue. American critics were beginning to express doubts. How far would NATO expansion go? Would states left out be open to Russian pressure? Would the American nuclear guarantee apply to new members? Most critics concentrated on the effect on Russia: would the expansion of NATO lead to a major split with Russia? As these questions were pressed, defenders of NATO expansion insisted that the Clinton administration stop wasting time with the PFP and move to outright NATO membership for Poland, Hungary, and the Czech Republic. Clinton reversed his original position: without abandoning the PFP, his administration adopted a schedule for formal membership. In September 1994, NATO published some details on the plans for bringing in new members.

Yeltsin immediately stunned Clinton by going over to a slashing counterattack, during a meeting in Budapest of the Conference (now Organization) on Security and Cooperation in Europe (then CSCE, now OSCE). Yeltsin warned that Europe was in danger of plunging into a "cold peace." He said that if the purpose of NATO's expansion was to guard against fears of "undesirable" developments in Russia, "it's too early to bury democracy in Russia."[11]

Clinton attended the Budapest meeting for a few hours but made no effort to meet with Yeltsin. American officials tried to brush off Yeltsin's attack as a sop to internal Russian opinion. As usual, "senior" American officials also claimed that Yeltsin's outburst reflected a misunderstanding of NATO's plan, but some commentators concluded that the "romance" with Russia was over.[12]

Relations degenerated, not only because of the conflict over NATO but also over a more immediate crisis. Russia launched an attack on the tiny separatist area of Chechnya and for eighteen months was bogged down in a bloody conflict. At first the Chechen affair was treated coolly by Washington: it was an internal Russian matter, and the United States would stay on the sidelines. As gory pictures and reports began to accumulate, the Clinton administration become more critical. Critics advocated distancing the United States from Yeltsin. The United States, a *New York Times* editorial (January 9, 1995) stated, needed a Russia policy, not a Yeltsin policy; accordingly, Washington should be reaching out for other democratic leaders.

The Clinton administration was thrown into disarray, and understandably so. The Chechen crisis created an agonizing dilemma. On the one hand, the United States could not afford to urge the breakup of the Russian state into ethnic components. Time and again the United States had argued for the inviolability of borders and of national sovereignty in Europe as a deterrent against Soviet-style intervention; this could not be suddenly reversed. Moreover, encouraging secession could lead to a bloody civil war that might end in a dictatorship in Moscow, which in turn would surely revive threats against the neighboring new republics. On the other hand, a long, costly struggle would undercut democratic tendencies in Moscow, inflame nationalism, and strengthen the influence of the military.

A quick, effective, and efficient military campaign to restore Russian authority might have satisfied Washington, but this was not to be. Gradually, Clinton's position became more critical, and, somewhat incongruously, he gave stronger support for expanding NATO, regardless of Russian objections. Yeltsin in turn hardened his opposition to NATO expansion. Official relations between Clinton and Yeltsin reached a low point in May 1995, the fiftieth anniversary of the end of World War II. Clinton's visit to Moscow for the occasion was a failure; his performance was clumsy and unnatural. To offset charges that he was too pro-Yeltsin, he met with opposition leaders, including, of all people, the leader of the communists, Gennady Zyuganov. This was a stupid blunder, which gave Zyuganov international legitimacy. Nevertheless, Clinton and Yeltsin continued to meet, and their personal relationship seemed cordial enough.

More shocks came in December 1995, when the Russian parliamentary elections returned a clear majority for the communists. "Who lost Russia?" suddenly became a significant political issue. Only Yeltsin and a handful of ineffective reformers seemed to stand in the way of a return of the communists to power.

American policy had been based on gaining time for Russian opinion to settle down, for the reformers to take hold, for their policies to yield results, and for the old days to recede in people's memories. Supporting Yeltsin, a strong man in his own right, seemed the most effective approach. By the spring of 1996 this strategy seemed highly questionable. Backbiting began at once, with the blame focusing on Strobe Talbott as the architect of a failed policy. Instability, which both Bush and Clinton had warned was the main threat, now seemed more likely than ever, seven years after the fall of the Berlin Wall.

The danger of new instability was compounded by the forthcoming Russian presidential elections, scheduled for June 1996. Yeltsin was running well behind in early opinion polls. There was increasing speculation that he would postpone the elections. Some observers thought that even if the elections were held they would be badly rigged in Yeltsin's favor. Others countered that it was the communists, not Yeltsin, that had the most potent organization at the grass roots, where fraud was most likely. There were palpable fears that the communist candidate, Zyuganov, might win in any case. The handful of other candidates included Zhirinovsky, whose star was beginning to fade, and Mikhail Gorbachev, who was given no chance at all. General Alexander Lebed, who had been dismissed from his post in Moldova by Yeltsin, was making his first entry into politics.

To everyone's surprise, Yeltsin conducted an old-fashioned American whistle-stop, barnstorming campaign. He traveled widely, dancing, singing, kissing babies, and disbursing large grants and subsidies from the Russian treasury. He used his official position to dominate the television newscasts, shutting out his opponents. He eventually negotiated a cease-fire in Chechnya, and his popularity began to rise, though Zyuganov remained the front runner. The communists' strength was among the elderly and in the rural areas; they could not expand their appeal without undercutting their basic nostalgia for the "good old days." Yeltsin was strong among the younger citizens and in the larger cities. As the communists' strength declined and Yeltsin's position grew stronger, the communists began to complain that the elections would be unfair and dishonest, an irony not lost on Western observers.

The United States tried to stay neutral, but its hands-off posture led to some foolish remarks. The administration was ready for "any conceivable outcome," Strobe Talbott reassured reporters. Secretary Perry said that no matter what the outcome, the good military relationship would continue. Such statements, implying an evenhandedness and even complacency about the outcome, finally provoked critical comments from outside the administration to the effect that the stakes were enormous and there was little to gain from pretending that America's interest was only in whether the elections were "free."[13]

Yeltsin won the first round of voting, but by only a few percentage points over Zyuganov. Since neither candidate had scored 50 percent, a runoff was necessary. The great surprise was the strong third-place showing of General

Lebed, who had won 15 percent of the votes (Gorbachev received 1 percent). Lebed quickly announced that he would not support the communists, as some had feared. Yeltsin, in a display of crude power politics, then named Lebed to the post of his national security advisor. This went a long way toward assuring Yeltsin's victory in the second round of voting.

Clinton, still maintaining the fiction of evenhandedness, called Yeltsin to congratulate him, not on his victory but for holding a free election. Since the runoff on July 3 would be between Yeltsin and Zyuganov, this ostensible neutrality was a pretense. As the second round approached, Yeltsin more or less withdrew from public appearances; there was widespread speculation that he was ill. David Remnick, an American writer and a longtime observer of Soviet and Russian affairs, commented that Yeltsin's strategy was simple: "Get out the vote, hide the President, and scare the hell out of the population."[14] It worked. Yeltsin won a clear victory, 54 to 40 percent, over Zyuganov.

Suddenly, everyone realized that Russia had turned an important corner. It had conducted three major national elections. For the first time in its history it had a freely elected president, an elected parliament, a constitution, and the beginnings of a political system. Its chances of becoming a genuine democracy were much brighter on July 4, 1996, American Independence Day.[15]

The pessimists would not be silenced. They continued to cry wolf: the elections had been unfair, because the government had dominated the television coverage; Yeltsin was too sick to govern; the economy was on the verge of catastrophe; Yeltsin had no plan; the economy was so bad that after the elections the government's task was more, not less, difficult; his advisors, Lebed and Viktor Chernomyrdin, would be locked in a vicious power struggle; and the war in Chechnya was by no means over. Yeltsin's second term, editorialized the *New York Times*, was "clouded in doubt." A different assessment came from the Harvard historian Richard Pipes, who concluded that the "cause of democracy appears strengthened" and that the prospects for a restoration of communism were "dimmer than ever."[16]

After his formal inauguration in early August, Yeltsin disappeared again. It turned out that he had a serious heart problem and had to undergo bypass surgery. This provoked a new rash of pessimism in the United States. Yeltsin had won four more years, *Newsweek* wrote, "if he can live that long." For a time it seemed that the Yeltsin era was drawing to a close, with no clear heir apparent and no political party that represented his position.

Nevertheless, a new institutional order was emerging—very slowly and hesitantly, to be sure. Gradually, Yeltsin began to take hold again; his health improved, and his old vigor reemerged. He split with Lebed and later replaced his entire cabinet, but kept Chernomyrdin as prime minister and Primakov as foreign minister. He pulled in important reformers. By the time he met Clinton at a summit in Helsinki in March 1997 he was in top form, while the American president had to appear in a wheelchair as a result of an accident to his knee. Russian commentators relished the contrast, especially in light of the remarks by many Americans who had dismissed Yeltsin only a few months earlier.

By this time Clinton had decided to adopt the enlargement of NATO as the emblem of his foreign policy. In effect, he would stake his place in history on reconstructing Europe, "whole and free." Before the final NATO decision Clinton had to try to make a deal with Yeltsin. Clinton's new secretary of state, Ambassador Madeleine Albright, traveled to Russia, where she made the rather amazing claim that United States and Russia were "on the same side." Soon thereafter, in his March 1997 summit meeting at Helsinki, Clinton made two important concessions: that no nuclear weapons or large contingents of "foreign troops" would be stationed on the territory of new NATO members. In addition, it was agreed that Russia would become a member of a special NATO consultative council. Clinton officials insisted that Russia would have "a voice but not a veto," a slogan critics found somewhat naive. These concessions were then embodied in the new Russian-NATO Founding Act, signed in Paris in May. The great irony was that the only country that could conceivably pose a threat to NATO would henceforth participate at least nominally in the alliance's military planning.[17]

Criticism of NATO enlargement had grown since the first year of Clinton's presidency, when he had offered the timid Partnership for Peace.[18] As it became clearer that he intended to push through NATO enlargement, influential voices were raised against the idea: it was "a gratuitous risk," according to a *New York Times* editorial (July 6, 1997). The administration seemed at times to undercut its own arguments. A new document on national strategy, for example, reportedly indicated that the American military command viewed the period through 2010 as a "strategic pause," during which no challenge of the magnitude of the Cold War would be likely.[19] Gaining Senate ratification, therefore, would be no "slam dunk," as his aides kept repeating. In fact, opponents included not only professional and academic experts but a number of influential congressmen.

The NATO summit at Madrid in early July was a celebration for Clinton. The formal invitations to Poland, the Czech Republic, and Hungary were agreed upon. Clinton took a quick tour of Poland, where he was welcomed as a virtual savior. Joining NATO, he said, would be history's most precious gift, "a second chance." Denouncing the infamous Yalta agreement of 1945, Clinton administration officials sounded like 1950 Republicans. Clinton had now put history right: "Poland is coming home."[20]

The irony was the fate of the Baltic republics. They had common borders with Russia, and in Estonia there was a large Russian minority. Unlike Poland, Hungary, and Czechoslovakia, for centuries the three Baltic countries had been part of the Russian empire. If any European states deserved protection against Russia, it was they. But despite some anodyne declarations of support for the Baltic countries, these states in fact were shunted aside by Clinton, out of deference to Yeltsin. In a speech at Stanford the previous September Talbott had said the United States was trying to balance Baltic "anxieties about Russian motivations and their legitimate desire to join western institutions" with "Russia's fear and loathing at the prospects of the Balts fulfilling those aspirations." The three Baltic countries signed a Charter of Partnership with the United States in Washington on January 16, 1998; President Guntis Ulmanis of Latvia declared that the charter "makes us allies."[21]

After several false starts, the debate over NATO expansion finally began in the Senate on April 27, 1998. The debate produced some strange alignments between extreme conservatives and liberals. At the outset, Senator Richard Lugar, Republican of Indiana, a well regarded expert in foreign affairs, advanced the main arguments of the advocates: (1) American interests were involved, because the stakes were order and stability in Europe; (2) accession of three new democracies would eliminate the immoral and destabilizing dividing lines in Europe; and (3) expanding peace and stability in Europe would lessen the chances that the United States would be pulled into conflicts there. The opponents countered that expansion would antagonize Russia and thereby destabilize Europe. Even before the debate the columnist Charles Krauthammer had cut through the miasma by posing and answering the question that was the essence of the issue: "Is NATO expansion directed against Russia? Of course it is."[22] In a powerful speech, Senator Dale Bumpers of Arkansas, normally a supporter of Clinton, cited this article to good effect: "The Russians would have to be naive beyond all imagination to believe that Dr. Krauthammer wasn't saying it exactly right. NATO enlargement is designed to hem Russia in."[23] As the debate was ending, a *New York Times* editorial (April 29, 1998) stated, "It is delusional to believe that NATO expansion is not at its core an act that Russia will regard as hostile."

The Senate rejected amendments intended to limit American costs and link NATO membership to membership in the European Union, and finally it rejected (fifty-nine to forty-one) a bid to mandate a three-year pause before admitting any more new members. Voting for this amendment, however, were the chairman of the Foreign Relations Committee, Senator Jesse Helms; the chairman of the Armed Services Committee, Senator Strom Thurmond; and that committee's ranking member, Senator John Warner. The final vote (eighty to nineteen), however, was well over the sixty-six required votes for ratification. The anti-expansion vote had included senators from fifteen different states, ten of them west of the Mississippi. The pro-NATO votes included thirty-five Democrats and forty-five Republicans. NATO's supporters were hinting that an enlarged alliance would be the basis of a military coalition acting beyond the confines of NATO territory, as in Bosnia or Kosovo. An obvious new area was the Middle East.[24] Almost immediately the proponents of expansion began to backtrack, urging conciliatory overtures to Russia to either join in an expanded alliance system or associate itself with NATO more deeply. Zbigniew Brzezinski urged the United States to slow down expansion, giving Russia time to digest the admission of the three new members, while still making it clear that expansion would continue: "Even Russia's membership in NATO might make sense both for NATO and Russia."[25]

The NATO debate was overshadowed by a new Russian political crisis. Yeltsin fired his entire cabinet and, under the threat of dissolving the parliament, forced the Duma to accept a young reformer, Sergei Kiriyenko, as premier. Nevertheless, the economic crisis worsened in the late spring and summer of 1998, partly in reaction to the Asian financial debacle. Inevitably, Russia turned to the IMF and the Western powers for new loans. At first the IMF dismissed the gravity of the crisis; the chief IMF negotiator was openly skeptical. Predictably, the IMF laid down demands that were absurd for a government whose very survival was in doubt. The IMF did "everything possible to accelerate the crisis," said one former Russian official, Andrei Illiarnov.[26] The Clinton administration dithered once again. There were strong voices urging new assistance, as well as others dissenting.[27] Finally, as the atmosphere turned ominous in Moscow, with warnings from Yeltsin and others of a coup against the government, Washington overrode the IMF objections and insisted on a sizeable new package of loans—eventually totalling over twenty-two billion dollars.[28]

The Russian parliament, however, refused to accept the IMF's stringent conditions; Kiriyenko announced a disastrous devaluation of the ruble and a moratorium on paying foreign debts; on August 23 Yeltsin once again fired his entire cabinet. At first he tried to bring back Viktor Chernomyrdin as prime minister but failed to overcome the Duma's strong opposition. Finally, Yeltsin retreated and turned to his foreign minister Yevgeny Primakov as the new prime minister. Primakov admitted he had no economic plan, but ideologically he was quite acceptable to the communists and nationalists and was easily approved by the Duma. His accession was a sharp turn away from reform. The communists and nationalists had demonstrated their political power. Russia seemed to be imitating the disaster of the interwar Weimer Republic, with Yeltsin playing the role of Hindenburg and the communists and nationalists in the role of Hitler.

President Clinton visited Moscow during this crisis but brought no new economic assistance and little more than sympathy. His demeanor was reserved, at least in part because it was widely predicted that Yeltsin would not survive, but also because the meeting occurred when Clinton himself was deeply wounded by a climax of his own investigation by independent counsel Kenneth Starr. Clinton was urged to cancel the summit, but others argued that he had to go, if only not to undercut Yeltsin at a critical moment. By the fall of 1998, the prospects for Russian democracy and economic reform were once again increasingly gloomy. This time Yeltsin was probably a spent force, and the succession to his post was wide open.[29] The crisis in Russia produced a shift in American policy, as the administration began to distance itself from the Primakov government.

Thus, reconstructing the security of Europe was still a gamble. The success of NATO expansion depended heavily on the continuing acquiescence of Yeltsin and especially the evolution of post-Yeltsin Russia. The enlargement of NATO would probably be Clinton's most significant geopolitical accomplishment. Nevertheless, building European security without, or against, Russia has not worked for four centuries.

NOTES

1. R. W. Apple Jr., "On Eve of NATO Talks," *New York Times*, January 10, 1994.

2. R. W. Apple Jr., "New Kid on the Block," *New York Times*, January 9, 1994.

3. Both Henry Kissinger and Zbigniew Brzezinski argued in favor of NATO expansion: see Brzezinski, "A Bigger—and Safer—Europe," *New York Times*, December 4, 1993, and Kissinger, "Be Realistic about Russia," *Washington Post*, January 25, 1994.

4. Michael Kramer, "The Case for a Bigger NATO," *Time*, January 10, 1994.

5. Elaine Sciolino, "U.S. Scrambling for a Strategy," *New York Times*, January 5, 1994.

6. Secretary Christopher's explanation of the PFP is contained in his speech to the NATO Ministerial Meeting, December 2, 1993: "Strengthening the Atlantic Alliance through a Partnership for Peace," U.S. Department of State *Dispatch*, December 13, 1993. See also Christopher's article "NATO Plus," in the *Washington Post*, January 9, 1994.

7. Jane Perlez, "Blunt Reason for Enlarging NATO: Curbs on Germany," *New York Times*, December 7, 1998.

8. Kozyrev's comments are quoted in Allen Lynch, "After Empire: Russia and Its Western Neighbors," *RFE/RL Research Report*, March 25, 1994. See also in the same *Report*, Michael Miahalka, "Squaring the Circle: NATO's Offer to the East."

9. William Drozdiak, "Summit Shows U.S. Easing Grip," *Washington Post*, January 12, 1994; Jim Hoagland, "Europe's Fear," *Washington Post*, January 11, 1994; John Goshko, "Yeltsin Claims Russian Sphere of Influence," *Washington Post*, September 27, 1994.

10. Warren Christopher, "Transforming the NATO Alliance to Meet New Security Needs," speech before the Ministerial Meeting of the North Atlantic Council, Istanbul, Turkey, June 9, 1994, in *Dispatch*, Vol. 5, No. 24.

11. Daniel Williams, "Yeltsin, Clinton Clash," *Washington Post*, December 6, 1994.

12. Charles Krauthammer, "The Romance with Russia Is Over," *Washington Post*, December 16, 1994.

13. Steven Erlanger, "For U.S. Russia-Watchers Bipartisan Fear over Future," *New York Times*, June 17, 1996; A. M. Rosenthal, "Why Should We Care?" *New York Times*, June 14, 1996.

14. David Remnick, "The War for the Kremlin," *New Yorker*, July 22, 1996; Lee Hockstader and David Hoffman, "Yeltsin Campaign Rose from Tears to Triumph," *Washington Post*, July 7, 1996.

15. Angela Stent and Lilia Shevstova, "Russia's Elections: No Turning Back," *Foreign Policy*, Summer 1996.

16. Richard Pipes, "Yeltsin's Edge: Fear of the Past," *New York Times*, June 19, 1996. Negative comments were summarized in Robert Kagan, "The New Russophobes Are Here," *The Weekly Standard*, July 1, 1996, and also Peter Reddaway, "Russia Heads for Trouble," *New York Times*, July 2, 1996.

17. Henry Kissinger, "Helsinki Fiasco," *Washington Post*, March 30, 1997.

18. Irving Kristol, "Who Now Cares about NATO?" *Wall Street Journal*, February 6, 1995.

19. William Drozdiak, "Pentagon Assesses Future Demands on a Smaller Military Force," *Washington Post*, April 2, 1997.

20. Christine Spolar, "Noting Poland's Past," *Washington Post*, July 11, 1997.

21. Steven Erlanger, "Clinton and 3 Baltic Leaders," *New York Times*, January 17, 1998.

22. Charles Krauthammer, "Good Geopolitics," *Washington Post*, April 17, 1998.

23. *Congressional Record*, April 29, 1998, p. S3777.

24. Warren Christopher and William J. Perry, "NATO's True Mission," *New York Times*, October 21, 1997.

25. Zbigniew Brzezinski, "On to Russia," *Washington Post*, May 3, 1998; Brzezinski, "What Next for NATO?" *The National Interest*, Fall 1998.

26. Arnaud de Borchgrave, "IMF Is Given Blame for Economic Chaos Bedeviling Russia," *Washington Times*, September 9, 1998.

27. Jeffrey D. Sachs, "Rule of the Ruble," *New York Times*, June 4, 1998; Benjamin A. Gilman, "Stop Coddling Yeltsin," *Washington Post*, June 19, 1998.

28. Michael R. Gordon, "Yielding to West, I.M.F. Will Double Russia Loan Offer," *New York Times*, July 12, 1998.

29. Editorial, "The Price of an Icon," *Economist*, July 11, 1998.

8

Asian Tangles

The end of the Cold War was less important in Asia than in Europe. In Europe the United States had to build new and different relationships not only with Moscow but all of Eastern Europe. In Asia this was not the case. Most of America's longer-established relationships were unaffected. The United States and China had enjoyed a rapprochement for two decades. The American alliance with Japan was fundamentally sound. Except for the worrisome prospect presented by North Korea's ever-unpredictable policies, the broad Asian security issues could be dealt with less urgently than those of Europe.

Since Nixon's opening to China in 1971–1972, American policy had rested on certain fundamentals. At the core was the alliance with Japan. It was a limited partnership, however; Japan's role had never been well defined, especially after the end of the Cold War. A natural complement to the American-Japanese alliance was continuing engagement with China. America sought to occupy a pivotal position, to be able to reassure both Japan and China about the other's intentions. Also complementary was the enduring American commitment to defend South Korea—one of the few nations still threatened after the end of the Cold War. Both China and Japan had come to share a common interest in stability on the Korean Peninsula. Finally, America remained involved in Southeast Asia, not only for commercial advantage but also as an instrument of reassurance against Japanese or Chinese hegemony.

This juggling of China and Japan, however, was not a role the Clinton administration relished playing. Changes in America's Asian policy there-

fore began to accumulate, until they reached a point where both key relationships, with China as well as Japan, had deteriorated. As geopolitical
imperatives receded, secondary issues—trade and human rights—came to
the fore. American complaints about human rights came to dominate the
relationship with China, while the imbalance in trade came to dominate
the relationship with Japan.

The deterioration in relations with Japan was the result of a nearly fa-
natical assault on Japan's trade policies by Clinton administration officials
who knew next to nothing about Japan or Asia. The turnaround in China
policy, on the other hand, was not intentional, at least not at first; rather, it
was a reflection of diminishing security requirements on both sides. The
collapse of the USSR had removed a major threat to Europe and to the
United States, but it had also removed a threat to China and had given Beijing new freedom of action.

When George Bush left office, his China policy was in deep trouble. It
was ironic. As a former ambassador to China and to the UN, Bush should
have enjoyed a successful relationship with China; instead, after 1989 he
had found himself in a protracted struggle with Congress over human rights
violations in China. The Democrats were determined to punish China for
the "massacre" in Tiananmen Square in June 1989. At a minimum they
wanted to withdraw the tariff privileges of the most-favored-nation (MFN)
status that China held, along with more than a hundred other countries.
Bush had vetoed each congressional attempt to revoke MFN. The unfortunate result, however, was that he appeared to be defending China's brutal
internal regime. After Tiananmen, American China policy was essentially
"treading water," according to Secretary of State James Baker.

During the election campaign of 1992, Clinton singled out China policy
as one of the few specific charges to be leveled against Bush. He criticized
Bush for secretly rushing envoys to resume a cordial relationship with
China barely a month after the massacre in Tiananmen Square. Clinton
strongly implied that there was no longer any geopolitical dimension to
America's relations with China. According to Clinton, speaking at
Georgetown University on December 12, 1991,

> The administration continues to coddle China, despite its continu-
> ing crackdown on democratic reforms, its brutal subjugation of Tibet,
> its irresponsible exports of nuclear and missiles technology, its sup-
> port of the homicidal Khmer Rouge in Cambodia and its abusive
> trade practices. Such forbearance on our part might have made sense
> during the Cold War, when China was a counterweight to Soviet

power. But it makes no sense to play the China card now, when our opponents have thrown in their hand.[1]

Dismissing the China card was amateurish, as the Clinton administration's subsequent reversals would soon demonstrate. Despite his election rhetoric, President Clinton brought into office no clear concept of a China policy. He had had no experience with the Far East. The top levels of the State and Defense departments tended to be Europeanists. The strongest voice was that of the new assistant secretary of state for the Far East, Winston Lord, who had been a member of the Kissinger entourage on the secretary's famous secret trip to China in 1971. He had later served Reagan as ambassador to China but had become alienated from the Bush administration.

Virtually everyone admitted that China was the rising new power, not just in Asia but globally. Long lists of statistics about its economic growth, population, and military strength were frequently cited. The issue therefore was a classic one: how to deal with an emerging power. The choices were usually simplistically described as either containment or engagement. The conventional wisdom was that China was still worried about both a revival of Russian power and the growth of Japanese influence; hence Beijing still looked to the United States as a counterweight to Russia and a regulator on Japan. Winston Lord felt the United States indeed had a major role to play balancing China and Japan, and he shared the views of most China experts—that China and the United States had overlapping interests. This was a valid analysis, but it underrated the growth of Chinese nationalism, which was filling the vacuum created by the decline of Maoist ideology.

The new administration's first step was to back away from Clinton's flamboyant campaign criticisms. In the Senate hearings for his confirmation Winston Lord advocated a "nuanced" policy toward Beijing until a more humane system emerged there. Lord did not say so, but this implied a very long-term approach. He argued that the Chinese leaders were gambling that they could conduct a liberalized economic policy while maintaining a closed political system. This gamble, Lord concluded, would eventually fail: economic reform would produce political reform. This was quite different from the election campaign's implication that China ought to be punished, not coddled. While Lord did not advocate "coddling," his approach was closer to the Bush program than to Clinton's election campaign.[2]

Critics still wanted to repeal the annual grant of most-favored-nation treatment to Chinese trade. Democrats in particular hoped that the new administration would adopt revocation as a punishment for human rights abuses. As the deadline approached for the annual renewal, Clinton began to retreat. He was willing to extend MFN, but he needed the cover of a bargain with the congressional critics who eventually agreed to a conditional extension. After announcing that he had studied the issues, Clinton concluded that revoking MFN might cause serious economic damage, that it would not only not help the cause of human rights but would risk a "long-term fissure" with a country that the United States still had a chance to influence. Using MFN as a blunt instrument would have "serious long term adverse consequences."

This change of heart was not the result of Clinton's "study"; the potentially damaging long-term consequences of using MFN revocation as a punishment was already a shopworn argument in Washington. It is more likely that Clinton had found the China card a good argument to play against Bush but of no political value once in office. Three years later, musing over his China policy, Clinton admitted that his campaign views had been "simply not right."

In May 1993 he decided on a conditional approach: he would extend MFN for one more year but make its subsequent renewal conditional on the performance of China in human rights over that year. His decision was announced as a new executive order of May 28, 1993. The question, Clinton declared, was how to cultivate the "hopeful seeds of change" in China while expressing the clear disapproval of the United States of China's repressive policies. The core of his policy, he explained, would be a "resolute insistence upon significant progress on human rights." Extending MFN in 1994 would therefore depend upon whether China made "significant progress in improving its human rights record."[3]

The administration had dodged a confrontation, but it was naive to believe that China would make "significant" progress in human rights within a year of Clinton's new executive order. The effect of Clinton's approach was to increase the burden on Chinese behavior. China now had to meet specified conditions set down in writing in an executive order. If the Chinese leaders had not made concessions to Bush, an acknowledged friend, why would they make them to Clinton? No one seemed to ponder this. The new linkage was made explicit by Winston Lord, in explaining the policy to the Congress: China could not expect the full benefits of membership in the international community unless it abided by recognized international standards regarding treatment of its citizens, the rules of global commerce, and the prohibition against transfer of weapons of mass destruction and of sensitive technologies. What Clinton offered in return was relief from the annual fight over MFN—not much, considering the sweeping demands on Beijing.

Clinton rather shrewdly justified his turnabout as an element of a broader Asia-Pacific strategy. At the G-7 summit meeting in Tokyo in July

1993 Clinton stressed his new Asian strategy. He cited with approval an article by Henry Kissinger.[4] In that essay Kissinger argued that America could not withdraw from Asia, for several reasons. In Asia the rise of nationalism was particularly virulent, because Asia had no institutions like Europe's to contain it; America's purpose therefore was to mitigate the rivalries produced by resurgent nationalism. Moreover, in Kissinger's view, engagement with China was necessary as a reassurance of Japan; without the American influence over China, Japan would try to play the role of mediator, which would imply disassociation from the United States. Kissinger had concluded that nearly all of Asia looked to the United States to create a "framework in which neither China nor Japan dominates."

Despite Clinton's favorable reference, the Kissinger prescription was not the policy carried out by the president's team. To be sure, the official policy was "comprehensive engagement." It was intended to broaden the dialogue and designed to give China an incentive to move forward on a number of contentious issues. The badgering of China, however, never really stopped. China was subjected to periodic criticism for its human rights violations, and the battles over human rights continued every year in the congressional debates over MFN. Moreover, China was publicly challenged over several security issues. Chinese nuclear tests were condemned. It was charged that China had shipped missile parts to Pakistan, violating an international agreement, the Missile Technology Control Regime (MTCR). Later the same charge was made over Chinese missile shipments to Iran. Even Winston Lord doubted that the Chinese were taking the administration's concerns seriously: "Overall, significant progress on human rights [was] necessary to sustain and strengthen the relationship," he said. An American official, the assistant secretary of state for human rights, John Shattuck, went to China, where he met with dissidents, to the outrage of the Chinese officials.[5] There were several severe disputes over trade and the pirating of American technology, especially by clandestine compact discs.

American policy was obviously undisciplined. In effect, the policy was reverting to the campaign rhetoric. There were periodic diplomatic contacts to improve the atmosphere; each failed. Warren Christopher traveled to China for the first time in March 1994. His visit was doomed in advance: his mission, Christopher said, was to inform the Chinese of the "urgent need" to make further progress on human rights. The character of the relationship depended "significantly on how the Chinese government treats its people."[6]

With this simple, straightforward statement, Christopher threw over two decades of American policy. In return he got what he asked for: a sharp rebuff from the Chinese leaders. He was treated with disdain. His visit was a major debacle; it was an amateurish performance from the start. He had scheduled his visit for March 10 but had been asked to defer it because the Chinese were holding a National People's Congress; he had "obliged" them by postponing it one day! The Chinese retaliated by downgrading the visit, making a point of the fact that Deng Xiaoping, who did not receive Christopher, was in excellent health and walked three kilometers a day.

At the end of the visit the two sides gave parallel, rather than the customary joint, press conferences. The Chinese foreign minister, Qian Qichen, declared that the United States was responsible for all of the "consequences" of the visit; he added that the two sides would have different concepts of human rights "for a long time to come." The premier, Li Peng, brushed aside threatened trade sanctions: "China relies mainly on its own market, but the U.S. will lose its share of the big China market." Christopher's cabled report of his visit described his reception as "rough, somber, sometimes bordering on insolent." Christopher remained indignant, and thereafter he advised against any major visits to Beijing by anyone in the administration.[7]

At home Christopher was criticized not for bungling but for "flinching" in the face of Chinese arrogance. He was attacked for signaling a retreat on human rights even before his departure from China. Others felt that his rejection was proof that the Chinese were contemptuous of American resolve—what was required, therefore, was a toughening of the American position. Christopher's defenders insisted that Christopher had laid out what the Chinese needed to hear from a high-level spokesman. Unnamed aides insisted that he had delivered a "tough message." Perhaps the most telling statement was from a "senior official" who said that "human rights goes to the heart of the political struggle in China." In other words, the United States saw its policy as an element in Beijing's power struggle, not a commitment to high moral principle. This, of course, is what the Chinese suspected.[8]

The rough treatment accorded Christopher led not to a toughening of policy but to the opposite. In May 1994, President Clinton formally announced that he would henceforth "delink" human rights and MFN. A policy of linkages had reached the end of its usefulness, he explained. He proposed to take a new path, which turned out to be the old path of engagement. The United States would do more to advance the cause of human rights by staying engaged in a growing web of political and economic contacts. The administration's objectives would be best served, he asserted, by not conditioning MFN eligibility on the issue of human rights. This was the exact opposite of what Christopher had argued in Beijing. Christopher himself made a major speech emphasizing the importance of stability in the Asia-Pacific region. For fifty years, he said, the United States had understood that "the emergence of a dominant hostile power in Asia would threaten important US allies and, ultimately, America itself." This was very close to the policy that candidate Clinton had dismissed with disdain eighteen months earlier.[9] On the other hand, Clinton's aides said, he had treated China primarily as a matter of domestic politics; at one point during a White House meeting he had exploded: "I hate our China policy!" he exclaimed. "I wish I was running against our China policy. I mean we give them MFN and we change our commercial policy and what has it changed?"[10]

Not surprisingly, Clinton's retreats on MFN were supported by the "Eastern Establishment." Presumably unaware of Clinton's outbursts against his own policy, former secretaries of state Henry Kissinger and Cyrus Vance wrote a joint letter to Clinton applauding his effort to define a new, sustainable stance toward China. They praised Clinton's "courageous" decision to delink human rights and MFN.[11] The Kissinger-Vance argument was that America needed China's cooperation on a number of issues, such as dealing with the North Korean nuclear challenge. To be sure, there were critics who insisted that Clinton's surrender made it impossible for friend or foe to trust his word on foreign policy.

Clinton nevertheless stuck to his new policy: indeed, as the post–Deng Xiaoping era drew nearer it was even more important that Washington maintain broad links to China. For some years there had been speculation about China's future after Deng Xiaoping. He was holding on tenaciously, much as Mao had done, but his influence had declined. Some of his partisans began to lose ground in the inevitable power struggles. Policy toward American had been swept into this struggle.

When a harder-line faction seemed to be gaining ground in Beijing, Clinton's policy of engagement was jeopardized. Many American analysts believed that China was embarking on a hegemonic policy in Asia. They believed that the Chinese leaders had concluded that trade was so important to Washington that it gave Beijing a free hand. Beijing was increasing its defense spending and laying claim to territories throughout the South China Sea (such as to the Spratly Islands), and American critics concluded that these trends demonstrated that the Clinton administration was locked in to the wrong approach: conciliation was increasingly irrelevant and even dangerous.[12]

Always lurking in the background of Sino-American relations was the anomaly of Taiwan. For over twenty years, through six administrations of both political parties, the United States had pursued a "one-China" policy, that Taiwan was part of China. The threat of American support for two Chinas or for Taiwan's independence had been quiescent since the American normalization of relations with the mainland in 1979, negotiated by Jimmy Carter and approved by Congress. From time to time there had even been tentative contacts between the mainland communists and the Taiwan government.

It was odd that the Clinton administration decided to undertake a review of Taiwan policy, the first since 1979. It turned out to be a time bomb. Testifying about this review Winston Lord noted that "our bonds with Taiwan are robust, friendly, growing, and complex."[13] The operative word was "growing," and the administration did in fact strengthen relations with Taiwan. For example, the Taiwanese mission in Washington was upgraded, becoming the "Taipei Economic and Cultural Representative Office." Clinton was trying to appease critics in Congress who still wanted to repeal MFN. Congress, however, urged that Washington should go further and relax restrictions on visits to America by high-level Taiwanese officials.

Sooner or later the mainland Chinese leaders, who were jockeying for position in the struggle to succeed Deng Xiaoping, had to react. No potential successor wanted to look soft or weak on such issues as Tibet, Taiwan, Hong Kong, or trade with America. Some American observers predicted increased tensions with China, because the Chinese leaders were becoming convinced that a new American strategy of containment was emerging, one reflected in a new military arrangement with Japan, arms sales to Taiwan, and the potential deployment of a new theater missile defense system under development for the Pacific.

A serious confrontation was provoked by the visit to the United States of the president of Taiwan, Lee Teng-hui. His visit had been turned down by the administration, and Secretary Christopher is alleged to have reassured the Chinese ambassador that it would not take place. But the visit was warmly encouraged by massive votes in both the Senate and the House, and the administration then agreed to a compromise: Lee would come to the United States on an ostensibly "private" visit to receive a degree at his alma mater, Cornell University. The mainland Chinese, however, saw it as a "betrayal" and still another sign of a new American policy of containment.[14]

Beyond Chinese "gong-banging," as one observer put it, at first there was no particular reaction to Lee Teng-hui's visit. It still rankled the Chinese communists, however, and as the Taiwanese presidential elections approached (scheduled for March 23, 1996) tensions rose further. There was a great deal of speculation that Lee, if reelected, would move toward independence for Taiwan. Another candidate was campaigning openly for independence. These harbingers, of course, were unacceptable to Beijing, and the Chinese started a campaign of intimidation, including military maneuvers and missile firings into the waters around Taiwan; one missile even passed over Taipei, landing on the other side of the island. This blatant crudeness made China's actions even more ominous.

No one expected a military clash, unless by accident, but matters were sufficiently worrisome that the United States had to react. Consequently, a flotilla of warships was redirected to the Taiwan straits. This deployment of two carrier battle groups (those of both the USS *Nimitz* and *Independence*) was the most formidable American force assembled since the Gulf War. Neither carrier entered the Taiwan Straits, but the United States announced that it regarded the Straits as international waters and of "great strategic interest." Clinton was supported by two strong congressional resolutions; nonetheless, a key supporter, congressman Lee Hamilton, the ranking member of the House Foreign Affairs Committee, said that the administration and the Congress were drifting apart and that the long-standing consensus on China policy was eroding.

In the end, the crisis dissipated without major incident. There were diplomatic conversations, including secret contacts between Anthony Lake and his counterpart, Liu Huaqui, the director of the State Council's Foreign Affairs Office. Lake had been pressing to open such a private channel, but it had been months before Christopher was won over. It so happened that Liu was in Washington as the missile crisis broke; he was sternly warned by Secretary Perry. On Taiwan, Lee was reelected and quickly made conciliatory gestures. (Lee and his opponent, Peng Ming-min, who favored independence, had collected about 75 percent of the vote.) Clinton announced a new policy review to "reinvigorate" the policy of engagement.

Clinton claimed credit for a tough response in the confrontation, but the crisis also provoked some stinging attacks on his China policy, which some believed had failed altogether. One of the main charges was that engagement had deprived the reformers in Beijing of any ammunition to ward off the hard-liners. Beijing was free to escalate its aggressive behavior.

The policy of engagement had not completely failed, but it was close to doing so. Clinton again refused to suspend MFN, and he was able to avoid the annual congressional fight only because the Republican presidential candidate, Senator Robert Dole, supported him. Dole needled Clinton for his "long silence and history of zigzags on China," but in the end he supported extension of MFN. The House voted by 286 to 141 to defeat the resolution that would have overridden the president's extension of MFN.

Having opened the private channel between Liu Huaqui and Anthony Lake, Clinton decided in July 196 to send Lake to China. It was an interesting move on the international chessboard: Yeltsin had visited China in April, and now Lake, Kissinger's successor, would go there. There were no breakthroughs reported during Lake's trip, and differences over the main issues—human rights, nonproliferation, trade, and Taiwan—did not change in any essential way. Nevertheless, it was the beginning of a new "strategic dialogue." Over the next year, however, that dialogue produced mainly atmospherics.[15] It was announced that if reelected President Clinton would visit China in 1997 (he did not) and that the Chinese president, Jiang Zemin, would visit the United States (he did).

Deng Xiaoping died in February 1997, and Jiang seemed likely to prevail in the succession struggle. There was concern in Washington over the fate of the reformers, but some commentators thought a much larger issue was at stake. Was China to remain the invincible "oriental despotism" that had created the "most thoroughly totalitarian system" in the twentieth century, or would modernization lurch China into the "democratic denouement sought by Sun Yat-Sen?"[16]

Another round of the debate in the United States began almost immediately. Conservatives now argued that China was emerging as a genuine threat to America: it was naive to expect to coax the Chinese into becoming a responsible member of the international community. Proponents of engagement cited a historical parallel: the failure of the British vigorously to pursue engagement with Whilhelmine Germany, thus propelling a world war. The critics answered that Germany had wanted predominance, not integration into the international system, and that the Chinese leaders were also seeking hegemony. Engagement would only encourage Beijing to believe America would acquiesce.[17] The critics, however, failed to advance an alternative policy other than confrontation or sustained harassment.

Nevertheless, the debate put the Clinton administration on the defensive and led to some exaggerated claims and murky arguments. Opposition to Clinton's China policy seemed to be growing, especially as religious groups joined the anti-China coalition. Liberal Democrats as well as moderate Republicans were keenly sensitive to charges of softness on human rights. While arguing for continuing engagement with China they invariably insisted that the cause of human rights not be abandoned. The overall effect was a confusing policy. For example, Clinton's new secretary of state, Madeleine Albright, said that "the fundamental challenge for U.S. policy is to persuade China to define its own national interests in a manner compatible with ours. That's why we are working to encourage China's development as a secure, prosperous, and open society as well as its integration as full and responsible member of the international community."[18] To persuade the communist leaders that it was in their interest to create an "open society" was tantamount to asking them to commit political suicide. Jiang Zemin knew it, of course. Indeed, the drumbeat of criticism about human rights had provoked the Chinese leaders into mobilizing Chinese opinion against the United States with appeals to national pride and to the fear of chaos. It was a vicious circle: the rising nationalism was grist for the administration's critics, who cited it as proof that engagement was not working.[19]

The debate sputtered along, growing more strident as the visit of Jiang Zemin to the United States drew nearer. He had emerged as the dominant leader at the Fifteenth Party Congress in September. He had announced a rather grandiose plan for privatization of state-owned enterprises and proclaimed a "fundamental shift of the economic system." What this meant in practice was vague, however. In any case, he had also said that it was imperative to uphold and improve the political system.

As a backdrop to Jiang's visit, several events demonstrated how far international politics had changed since the Cold War. In the spring of 1996, Boris Yeltsin had visited China. The visit had been cynically dismissed at the time as a ploy in his campaign for reelection as president. China, however, had expressed sympathy for Yeltsin's campaign against Chechnya, on the grounds that Russia was safeguarding its national unity. Jiang had also supported Yeltsin's opposition to NATO expansion. In turn, Yeltsin said that Russia recognized Tibet and Taiwan as "inseparable" and "inalienable" parts of China. In Shanghai, Yeltsin and Jiang signed a nonaggression treaty with three Central Asian republics—Kazakhstan, Kyrgyzstan, and Tajikistan. Shanghai, of course, was the site of the first Nixon–Chou Enlai statement of principles of relations, signed in 1972. Some observers concluded that the selection of Shanghai for the Yeltsin-Jiang bargain had been a deliberate affront to the United States.[20]

The game continued. In the spring of 1997 Yeltsin, Jiang, and the leaders of three Central Asian republics met again in the Kremlin to sign another agreement, this time confirming all of their existing borders, thereby ending disputes of almost four hundred years. Yeltsin gave the occasion an anti-American twist: he said (April 23) that while some wanted to dictate a new unipolar world, "we want a multipolar world." Jiang was more circumspect, but he did say that his agreement with Yeltsin was of "enormous historic importance"; he borrowed Clinton's phraseology to describe his relations with Russia as a "strategic partnership."[21] Two months later Russia and China joined forces in the UN to rebuff the United States in a crisis over Iraq.

The United States countered by upgrading its alliance with Japan; a new agreement called for a larger Japanese military contribution in the event of a new crisis "in areas surrounding Japan." Earlier in September, Prime Minister Ryutaro Hashimoto had gone to China to reassure Beijing's leaders. While China was not specifically singled out, the Chinese understood the game and issued a formal protest warning against including Taiwan within the scope of the new U.S.-Japanese cooperation.[22] The thrust and parry continued. In November 1997, just after Jiang's visit to Washington, Yeltsin and the Japanese prime minister agreed to work for a World War II peace treaty by the year 2000. In April 1998 Yeltsin visited Japan for a twenty-four-hour summit. The Japanese presented their draft of a peace treaty and offered six hundred million dollars in commercial assistance, the first tranche of an anticipated two billion dollars.

In the United States the great debate over MFN once again flamed up. In June Congress rejected a new challenge, but the margin of favorable votes was smaller than the previous year; the number of anti-Chinese votes (173) was the highest since 1992, when Bush had vetoed the resolution. Charges that the Chinese communists had interfered with the funding of the American presidential elections did some additional damage; these charges would grow into a significant political issue in 1998.

Jiang's visit was the first summit in eight years. He was shrewd enough to put on something of a show, much as Deng had done in 1979. However, visiting Colonial Williamsburg, with its Jeffersonian aura, and traveling to Independence Hall in Philadelphia turned out not to be so shrewd. The sites were reminders of the festering dispute over human rights. Clinton's performance was typically schizophrenic. In a joint press conference, he rudely contradicted Jiang, asserting that China was on the wrong side of "history." On the other hand, he hosted a grand dinner in the White House in which he toasted the Chinese leaders. The substantive outcome of the visit was vapid, but the Clinton administration had weathered another mini-storm.

The persistent difficulties besetting Clinton's China policy were baffling. The basic concept of engagement was sound enough: buying time made sense, given China's internal turmoil. But too often Washington portrayed engagement as a tool to reform Chinese institutions. Moreover, its implementation was ragged and inconsistent. It is doubtful that Clinton was ever enthusiastic about it. His own participation was minimal; he did not schedule a visit to China until June 1998. The administration was too undisciplined to conduct the kind of patient policy that was required. After his reelection, Clinton had admitted that engagement had no impact on China's internal repression.

Before his own visit to China in June 1998, Clinton was still fumbling for a policy. He found himself in the odd position of defending the essence of the very China policy he had attacked in 1992, while his Republican opponents were adopting his own charge that he was kowtowing to China's dictators.[23] His metamorphosis was completed in the spring of 1998. First came the announcement that the president's visit to China would be advanced from November to late June (after, that is, the June 4 anniversary of Tiananmen). Cynics observed that this new date would put the president in China just after the opening of the sexual harassment court case brought by Paula Jones; that case was dismissed by the judge, but the visit to China remained on schedule.

Shortly after the announcement of the visit, American policy reached a major turning point. Every year since 1990 the United States had sponsored in the United Nations a resolution of the Human Rights Commission condemning China's human rights record. Every year it was defeated. The Chinese had been shrewd in splitting first the Asians and then the Europeans from the United States. In 1997 France, Germany, Italy, and Japan had refused to cosponsor the American resolution; in 1998 the situation had worsened, when the entire EU went on record against an anticipated American resolution of condemnation. Whereas in 1997 Secretary Albright had vowed to continue the fight against egregious violations of internationally recognized human rights in China, one year later the United States threw in the towel. At the meeting of the UN Commission in Geneva, the United States ostentatiously dropped its prospective resolution. The usual "senior official" said that while China still had an "enormous way to go," and while Washington intended to press them at every opportunity, the new U.S. action was a "calculation," not a reward. China reciprocated by releasing some prominent political dissidents. The Washington director of Human Rights Watch Asia, Mike Jendrzejczyk, perhaps summed it up best: "They've caved."[24]

China became the administration's most intricate intellectual challenge. And this is likely to be true for some years, for Clinton's successor as well. After all, no country has had any experience with the transformation the Chinese want to accomplish—shifting to a liberal economic order while maintaining an authoritarian political regime. The role of outside powers in such a situation is also unprecedented. An American commentator summarized things, the China of "nice fuzzy Panda bears" was gone; henceforth the United States would be confronted by a "big developing garrison state, with few redeeming qualities other that the fact that it sits next to the Soviet Union."[25]

Gradually the internal American debate over China policy reverted to the stridency of the sharp disagreements that had characterized it during the 1940s and 1950s. In preparation for the president's trip in June, Secretary Albright visited Beijing in late April, carrying a letter from Clinton to Jiang calling for a new momentum in Sino-American relations; surprisingly, Clinton agreed to start his formal visit in Tiananmen. This gesture was widely interpreted as an effort to put human rights issues to the side and to emphasize the economic and strategic interests of the two countries in Asia. The symbolism of a ceremony in Tiananmen was widely and sharply criticized. There were demands that Clinton cancel the visit, or refuse to arrive at Tiananmen, or use the occasion for an all-out attack on China's human rights record.

On April 29, at the end of her pre-summit visit, Secretary Albright said that the United States and China had moved "well down the road toward building a constructive, strategic partnership." The public controversy surrounding China relations belied this Pollyannish conclusion. President Clinton's China policy was in deep trouble. There were scandals involving transfers of sensitive American technology to the Chinese missile program, claims that technology transfer had been permitted because of large campaign contributions, and new charges of Chinese interference in campaign financing. Documents released under congressional pressure demonstrated that the administration had shifted the authority for approval of foreign sales of sensitive equipment from the State Department to the Department of Commerce; for several years, it turned out, the president had routinely approved every transfer of technology by American companies, despite objections from the State and Justice departments. His willingness to schedule his arrival at Tiananmen Square was being constantly attacked.

Clinton defended his policy as both "principled and pragmatic." He described the choice as between his policy of expanding areas of cooperation while dealing "forthrightly" with differences, and one of seeking to contain and isolate China. Nevertheless, he also said the Chinese leaders had to recognize the reality that what they had done in Tiananmen was "wrong." Once in China, he repeated it in a widely televised joint press conference with Jiang Zemin.

It was naive to expect or even ask the communist leaders to "recognize" they were "wrong"; it would mean disavowing Deng Xiaoping and his colleagues, many of whom still occupied high places in the political hierarchy. It might lead to the end of the current leadership and its replacement by the leaders purged in 1989 (including Zhao Ziyang); it might even be a critical step toward the downfall of the communist regime altogether. Prior to Clinton's arrival in China, a letter from Zhao

Ziyang to the leadership had been leaked to the Western press: he called for resolving the Tiananmen issue "voluntarily ourselves" rather than letting it grow as an international issue.

So the issue of right or wrong in Tiananmen was not merely bickering with Clinton but a major issue for the political survival of the Chinese regime. At the joint press conference Jiang reiterated his defense of Tiananmen. Nevertheless, given the wide publicity during Clinton's visit, including live coverage of the press conference, the issue had not been put to rest. Some observers began to see Jiang Zemin in the role of Gorbachev—who, ironically, had visited China only a few days before the disaster at Tiananmen.

Clinton's visit was a personal success, especially if measured by opinion polls that indicated support of his decision to make the trip and approval of his conduct during it.[26] Not surprisingly, there was also sharp criticism, to the effect that Clinton had not changed China but that China had changed him: "We will express our disagreements, and then move on," was how an American critic interpreted Clinton's new policy.[27] The visit was probably the high point of his policy. The very fact of the visit was important in light of the growing criticism of China's human rights record and investigations of Chinese access to high technology. He also disarmed his critics by speaking out on human rights. His remarks reiterating American policy on one China—the so-called "three noes": no Taiwanese independence, no recognition of a separate Taiwanese government, and no admission of Taiwan to international organizations—drew predictable heavy fire from Republicans.

Clinton had come into office sharply critical of Bush's "coddling" of China and appeasement of Japan's unbalanced trade polices. By 1997, Clinton had reversed himself almost completely: he had become an ardent defender of engagement with China. His China policy was a risky adventure. It involved brushing aside evidence of China's hegemonic ambitions in Asia and tolerating China's radically different view of the requirements for international stability (as evidenced by missile sales to Pakistan and Iran). Yet the alternative, containment, amounted to little more than moralistic posturing. Bush had been right in defending his post-Tiananmen overtures as a way of keeping contact with China and avoiding its isolation. The foes of engagement, however, did have one telling point—the importance of strengthening the Japanese alliance, a dictum the Clinton administration could never quite accept, for it was an example of the balance-of-power politics that Bill Clinton had so vigorously denounced when he first sought the presidency.

NOTES

1. Address by Governor Clinton, "A New Covenant for American Security," Georgetown University, December 12, 1991.

2. Winston Lord, testimony in his Senate confirmation hearings, in U.S. Department of State *Dispatch*, April 5, 1993.

3. "China: Most Favored Nation Status," *Dispatch*, June 14, 1993.

4. Henry Kissinger, "Why We Can't Withdraw from Asia," *Washington Post*, June 15, 1993.

5. Winston Lord, "Statement before the House Ways and Means Committee," *Dispatch*, March 7, 1994.

6. Warren Christopher, "My Trip to Beijing Was Necessary," *Washington Post*, March 22, 1994.

7. Barton Gellman, "U.S. and China Nearly Came to Blows," *Washington Post*, June 21, 1998.

8. Christopher, "My Trip to Beijing Was Necessary"; Daniel Williams, "Chinese Rebuff Christopher on Human Rights," *Washington Post*, March 13, 1994, and "U.S. Disappointed as Christopher Leaves China," *Washington Post*, March 15, 1994.

9. Secretary Christopher's text in *Dispatch*, March 28, 1994.

10. Gellman, "U.S. and China Nearly Came to Blows."

11. Letter to the president, May 6, 1994, released by the Council on Foreign Relations, New York; also, Council on Foreign Relations, Policy Impact Panel, "On the Future of U.S.-China Relations," Henry A. Kissinger and Cyrus R. Vance, cochairmen, May 11, 1994.

12. Arthur Waldron, "Deterring China," *Commentary*, October 1995.

13. Winston Lord, testimony of September 27, 1994, before the Senate Foreign Relations Committee, in *Dispatch*, October 17, 1994.

14. Michel Oksenberg, "Heading Off a New Cold War with China," *Washington Post*, September 3, 1995; Jim Hoagland, "China: Before There Is a War," *Washington Post*, February 11, 1996.

15. Barton Gellman, "Reappraisal Led to New China Policy," *Washington Post*, June 22, 1998.

16. Roderick MacFarquhar, "Demolition Man," *New York Review of Books*, March 27, 1997.

17. Robert Kagan, "What China Knows That We Don't," *The Weekly Standard*, January 20, 1997; "China the Issues," *The Weekly Standard*, February 24, 1997 (several articles were grouped under this heading). See also editorial, "No Favors for China," *The Weekly Standard*, April 27, 1997; for a different assessment see Arthur Waldron, "How Not to Deal with China," *Commentary*, March 1997.

18. Secretary Albright, "Maintaining Normal Trade Relations with China," June 19, 1997 in *Dispatch*, June 1997.

19. At one extreme was the claim that war with China was inevitable, a view subsumed in the title of a new book, *The Coming Conflict with China*, by Richard

Bernstein and Ross H. Munro, both journalists who had served in China (New York: Alfred A. Knopf, 1997). An excerpt was published as "PLA Incorporated," *The Weekly Standard*, February 24, 1997.

20. Henry Kissinger, "Moscow and Beijing: A Declaration of Independence," *Washington Post*, May 14, 1996.

21. Lee Hockstader, "Russia, China Sign New Friendship Pact," *Washington Post*, April 24, 1997.

22. Kevin Sullivan and John Goshko, "U.S., Japan Expand Pact," *Washington Post*, September 24, 1997.

23. Robert Kagan, "Most Favored Nation—Or Most Appeased," *The Weekly Standard*, June 3, 1996; editorial, "Kowtowing to Beijing," *The Weekly Standard*, December 9, 1996. For a more balanced assessment see Patrick E. Tyler, "Why China Has No Ears for American Demands," *New York Times*, November 3, 1996.

24. Philip Shenon, "Annual U.N. Ritual," *New York Times*, March 14, 1998.

25. Thomas L. Friedman, "For the U.S. and China, a Rocky Period Ahead," *New York Times*, June 10, 1989, quoted in Vincent A. Auger, "Human Rights and Trade: The Clinton Administration and China," *Pew Case Studies in International Affairs*, Case 168, published by The Institute for the Study of Diplomacy, Georgetown University, 1995.

26. Jonathan Alter, "Don't Break the China," *Newsweek*, July 6, 1998.

27. Michael Kelly, "A New China Policy Is Born," *Washington Post*, July 1, 1998.

9

Unsinkable Japan

Despite the end of the Cold War there was no reason to reexamine the relationship with Japan. The security relationship was still important to both sides, even if somewhat less critical. The economic relationship, however, was badly out of balance. Friction over trade gradually escalated into antagonism. The United States was inclined to insist more vigorously on better terms in trade with Japan. The old priorities, security first and trade second, were still evident in American rhetoric as the Clinton administration took office. But there was already a different and disturbing change in the psychological climate. A quip by Senator Paul Tsongas during the 1992 primary campaign summed up American frustrations: the Cold War was over and Japan had won. The Japanese, on the other hand, believed that they were not treated as full security partners.

The Clinton administration, in particular the new assistant secretary of state, Winston Lord, and Secretary Christopher, acknowledged the need for changes in policy, but they were careful to describe the changes in traditional geopolitical terms: Japan would remain the highest priority in American strategy in Asia; the Asia-Pacific region would receive even greater attention; and, above all, the United States would continue to remain "engaged," as betokened by the presence of about a hundred thousand American troops stationed in Asia. This military presence would shore up political stability, which in turn would ensure the continued growth of the Asian economies. In the Lord/Christopher view, resolving the perennial disputes over trade would be balanced by the continuing requirements of a solid security partnership.[1]

It turned out that the Lord/Christopher policy was not the one adopted by the administration. A more aggressive view emerged from Clinton's new economic team. The Special Trade Representative was Mickey Kantor, a lawyer from Los Angeles and chairman of the Clinton election campaign. His lack of experience proved to be no bar to his influence over trade matters. He established himself immediately as a "no-nonsense" pragmatist, uninterested in ideology but determined to produce "results."[2] In effect, he turned the old formula of "security first" on its head: "Gone are the days when this nation could subordinate trade concerns to national security in the traditional sense of that term." In a statement before the Senate Finance Committee, on March 9, 1993, he elaborated:

> Past Administrations have often neglected US economic and trading interests because of foreign policy and defense concerns. The days when we could afford to do so are long past. In the post–Cold War world, our national security depends on our economic strength. . . . When all is said and done, opening foreign markets is our main objective.[3]

Kantor's economic hawkishness was shared by the new chairperson of the Council of Economic Advisors, Laura D'Andrea Tyson. She was a well known and respected professor of economics at the University of California who had written a book advocating a more rigorous line on trade issues. When told that the Japanese seemed to be worried by the administration's tougher line, she commented, "That's good. It shows they fear that we're on to something that will get results."[4] The third member of the triumvirate was the new Secretary of the Treasury, Lloyd Bentsen. His attitude toward trade was a typical senator's attitude: the Clinton administration was going to promote exports because exports were the path to economic growth and the creation of new jobs ("That is what nine million Americans want—jobs"). Too many American plants had closed and too many high-paying jobs had disappeared, Bentsen told the Trilateral Commission annual meeting in Washington. While America enjoyed somewhat better balances with Europe and Mexico (in 1992), the deficit with Japan had scarcely changed since the high point of 1987: "So America needs to look at opening foreign markets." In short, the Clinton team meant to put pressure on its trading partners. The strategy was summed up by the new under secretary in the Commerce Department, Jeffrey Garten. He wrote that "commercial diplomacy must become more central to overall foreign policy, more expansive and more aggressive."[5]

The new team was critical of the Reagan-Bush efforts to talk the Japanese into restricting exports to the United States or to redress trade imbalances by monetary policies that manipulated the price of the yen and the dollar. Many businessmen and economists also believed that these policies had failed. Trade deficits with Japan, which had reached an all-time high in 1987 (about $57 billion), continued to run between forty and fifty billion dollars. Confronted with the reality of Japan's trade and industrial policies, Kantor said, the Reagan administration's initial response had been laissez faire and, after the 1985 Plaza Accord, a policy of dollar devaluation. Both policies, Kantor claimed, "saddled our companies with every conceivable burden."[6]

The Japanese argued that the trade imbalances were the result of American economic conditions, especially its huge budget deficit. American goods were not competitive, at home or abroad. If the United States adopted policies to cure its internal deficits, the market would reflect such decisions, and American goods would be competitively priced—or so ran the theory (which several years later turned out to be wrong). Many other observers countered that the real problem was the unique character of Japan: a rigid, hierarchical, closed society, antagonistic to foreigners and foreign influence, while superficially accommodating. Japan was not susceptible to the laws of the market or economic forces. Americans, this view claimed, refused to recognize that Japan was different, and the various trade deals therefore were all destined to fail.

Antagonism was increasingly evident on both sides. "Japan-bashing" had become a Washington pastime, while Japan clawed back with occasional outbursts against the United States. *The Japan That Can Say No*, by Shintaro Ishihara, was a popular book in Japan. American handling of the Gulf War became a major irritant. The Japanese were shocked by the crisis. They were dependent on Middle East oil but were never really consulted by Washington. At the end of the war, however, the United States insisted that Japan pay its "share" of the costs, which in the end amounted to thirteen billion dollars. It was a humiliating demand. One Japanese observer compared Japan's position to that of an ATM machine that dispensed money on demand. In Tokyo the affair signified that Japan was clearly subordinate to American policy and politics, regardless of what was said by American officials. On the other hand, it was irritating to American officials that the Japanese seemed to take it from granted that the United States would look after Japan's global security interests.

President Bush's last visit to Japan had been particularly unfortunate. He had brought along the leading American automobile manufacturing executives, which the Japanese resented. He also became ill at a banquet—which quickly became a metaphor for troubled Japanese-American relations. Even the public mood was becoming more hostile; leading American commentators were highly critical of official policy, or the lack thereof.

As in many other aspects of its foreign policy, the Clinton administration's decision to adopt a tougher trade policy reflected what Washington believed was popular opinion. A more considered analysis would have revealed two important new factors. First was the weakness of the Japanese economy. The boom of the 1980s, the so-called "bubble economy," finally burst in 1992. Stock prices disastrously plummeted, as did real estate prices. As this became evident, there was no little gloating in the United States. The Clinton administration's lack of Asian experience was responsible for its ignoring this critical change in Japan. For three years the administration's economic officials treated Japan as the behemoth of the 1980s.

A second important change was the political revolution under way inside Japan. For almost forty years Japan had been governed and dominated by the Liberal Democratic Party (LDP), which was neither liberal nor democratic. It was a conservative oligarchy, if an effective one: it had restored Japan after the physical and psychological devastation of World War II. Gradually it had been infected by corruption and scandal and then by significant disaffection; new factions were formed by former LDP officials. The LDP had struggled to maintain its grip on power by shuffling premiers and leaders, but it was seriously weakened. Thus, the American stereotype of an alliance between the conservative political power structure and its economic counterpart was already obsolete by the time Clinton came into office.

Neither of these two important trends seemed to play any role in the early policy formulation of the Clinton administration. One of its first acts was to announce that it would insist on a new round of trade negotiations with Japan, which would be a test of the administration's new harder policy to open Japanese markets. The American side also proposed agreement on numerical indicators; that is, that American imports should constitute a fixed percentage of Japanese imports, or a percentage of the overall Japanese economy. As usual the Japanese agreed to the talks, but they resisted the administration's new criteria for measuring success. The Japanese had been through this before with Reagan and had conceded on certain sectors of trade, but without any blanket agreement.

The idea of holding new "Framework" talks was launched by President Clinton and Prime Minister Kiichi Miyazawa when the annual G-7 meeting was held in Tokyo in July. It seemed in the summer of 1993 that the administration was off to a reasonably good start. The Tokyo summit was Clinton's first important foreign outing; he was obviously on display. The

American press was upbeat in its predictions of Clinton's ability to deal with the issues: "He possesses an almost tactile awareness of the big cutting-edge economic issues and their impact on the politics and psychology of a nation," wrote Jim Hoagland in the *Washington Post*.

Before leaving for Tokyo, Clinton told reporters that he was not trying to take a "sledgehammer" to Japan. He also singled out Japan as the one member of the G-7 that might become a "natural partner" of the United States.[7] At the start of his visit Clinton said that the two sides ought to go beyond "finger-pointing." He ate a meal of sushi with the Japanese prime minister at the Okura Hotel and attended other scheduled events, such as a baseball game in downtown Tokyo. He gave a major speech at Waseda University in which he talked frankly about friction over trade. What the United States wanted, he said, was not managed trade or so-called trade by the numbers, but "better results from better rules of trade."[8]

At the end of the visit the two sides published an agreement in which the United States retreated from its insistence on numerical targets while Japan agreed to reduce or eliminate barriers to increased imports. The agreement did state that the two sides would agree on "objective criteria" to measure the opening of Japanese markets. This, of course, was a time bomb. The American side meant specific, measurable numbers, but the Japanese thought the issue had been finessed.[9] In any case, the United States claimed a victory. Warren Christopher said that while he wanted to avoid "bugling," Clinton had arrived on the world scene with a great deal of éclat. Rather condescendingly, Clinton commented that he had found more "energy and zip" than he had expected.[10]

Within days of the Tokyo summit, however, the LDP suffered a major defeat in the elections, and the Miyazawa government had to resign. It was replaced by a new coalition of parties, led by a former LDP leader, Morihiro Hosokawa. His government reaffirmed the commitment to the Framework talks, pledging to "redouble" Japanese efforts (the talks had not even begun). But his attention was compelled to the consequences of the growing recession and the bursting of the bubble economy.

Hosokawa was struggling to put together an internal incentive package, including tax cuts, to restart the Japanese economy. Nevertheless, he was subject to growing pressure from the Americans to buy more American automobiles. There was an obvious conflict between his domestic concerns and American insistence on opening up Japanese markets. Hosokawa was the kind of reform-minded leader that Washington had wanted; nevertheless, Clinton decided on a showdown when he met Hosokawa the week of February 11, 1994. After an hour of fruitless talk, Clinton and Hosokawa announced that they had not agreed. It was unprecedented! Both had agreed not to paper over their differences—"a welcome sign of candor," Warren Christopher lamely explained.[11]

There was nevertheless a sense of shock. For the first time a Japanese leader had, in fact, said "no." The Clinton administration began talking of retaliatory measures. Confronted by ominous predictions of a trade war, the Japanese agreed to resume the talks, and there was some progress. The stubborn automotive issues could not be resolved, and Kantor vowed to keep up the pressure. Again there was talk of sanctions.

The prospect of another showdown finally compelled the Department of State to intervene (albeit clandestinely). In May 1994 an internal "letter" from Assistant Secretary Winston Lord to Warren Christopher was leaked to the press. In this document, Lord noted several indicators of a downward drift in Asian relations. He deplored the state of American policy: a confrontation with China over MFN, a confrontation with Japan over trade, and a confrontation with North Korea over its nuclear weapons program. The confluence of these diverse situations was fostering a sense of "malaise." Americans actions, whether threatened or actually taken, were giving ammunition to those who saw American policy as an "international nanny, if not bully." Lord charged that the administration was too preoccupied with the near term at the expense of a longer-term strategy. Lord's critique also attacked economic officials in the administration who wanted to employ punitive measures without regard to overall regional policy. Finally, Lord argued for toning down the rhetoric and weighing more carefully the cost and benefits of unilateral action. All of this was spelled out in news stories, though the actual document was not released.[12]

This was a powerful indictment, especially since Lord was no Clinton amateur but an official with valid credentials stretching back to the Kissinger era. Outsiders joined in. One Asian specialist concluded that the administration had shown "little evidence that they understand the dynamics of Asia or have devised a comprehensive long term strategy for the region." Much of the blame, it was argued, rested on Clinton's uninterest and his unwillingness to spend political capital on Asian issues.

The net result, at least on the surface, was the adoption of a "new" Asian policy, loosely called "engagement." The administration announced that it would no longer pursue an all-or-nothing approach; trade talks with Japan, then in recess, were resumed. One reason may have been the growing crisis over North Korea's nuclear weapons program. Clinton had inherited intelligence estimates that the North Koreans were indeed embarked on a program to develop nuclear weapons. After the shock of discovering how far Iraq had progressed in its primitive programs, such intelligence had to be taken seriously. Moreover, as the Clinton administration took office, Pyongyang announced that it would withdraw from the Non-Proliferation Treaty (NPT). This meant it would not be subject to inspections. The prospect of the dangerously erratic regime of Kim Il-sung possessing these deadly weapons was a major threat to the United States and to both South Korea and Japan as well. Obviously, if the United States was forced into a confrontation—or even a war—with North Korea it would need unstinting Japanese support. This made the tactic of bullying Japan on trade even more short-sighted.

At first the Clinton administration did little to deal with the Korean problem, partly because key officials in the Pentagon were skeptical of the evidence. Some outside analysts, who knew even less, assured the public that there was no real threat and no need to panic. This view was echoed in both South Korea and Japan, where neither the governments nor public opinion wanted to face the ominous consequences. Gradually, however, a confrontation developed, as the North Koreans grew intransigent. By the spring of 1994 there was a growing chorus of demands inside the United States for military action against the North Korean nuclear facilities. At this point Jimmy Carter went to see Kim Il-sung and made a deal by which North Korea would not proceed with its weapons program, and in return the United States would negotiate and even supply peaceful nuclear reactors to the North. There was a palpable sense of relief, but there were also serious questions about the bargain, which was later translated into a formal agreement.

It might have been thought that this sobering passage would have ended the bickering over trade with Japan, which had by now helped to bring down the reform government of Hosokawa in April 1994. In its place, for the first time came a socialist-led government. Given the long and bitter opposition of the socialists to the United States, this was another setback for the brash tactics of Mickey Kantor.

Predictably, another confrontation developed over opening the Japanese market for American autos and automotive parts. Kantor was quoted as saying that the administration was going to open Japanese markets "one way or the other." It was a high-stakes game. The prevailing opinion was that Clinton seemed to have the upper hand. His threat to target Japanese luxury cars for higher duties was a shrewd maneuver, since it would scarcely affect middle-class American buyers. The American economy was in a strong recovery, while the Japanese were still in trouble. To be sure, there were voices of dissent raised against these hard-line tactics. Some Clinton officials warned against spillover from trade to security issues. The new ambassador to Japan, Walter Mondale, also joined in warning against using the American military presence as a bargaining chip in the trade negotiations.

Perhaps these admonitions had an effect. At the last minute (July 1) before the imposition of the new American tariffs, a deal was made between Kantor and the Japanese trade chief, Ryutaro Hashimoto. At first this new bargain was hailed as an American victory—to the amusement of Japanese commentators, because on closer examination the deal did not look so good. The Japanese government had guaranteed nothing. *Newsweek* commented, "Clinton talked tough on trade. But when the car talks came to a head, Washington blinked." Much of the credit in Japan for outfoxing the Americans was given to Hashimoto, who thereby improved his chances of becoming prime minister (as he did in January 1996, resigning after election defeats in July 1998).

Relations in the fall of 1995 were still troubled. At the last minute President Clinton canceled a trip to Japan, where he was to participate in an APEC summit. Allegedly the cancellation was necessary because of his involvement with the budget battles in Washington. His foreign policy advisors had told him that his attendance in Japan was critical, but others had urged him not to go abroad at a time when the American government was shut down by the lack of a federal budget and federal workers were laid off. Insult was added to injury when Warren Christopher cut short his participation at the Osaka summit to go to Dayton, Ohio, to oversee the negotiations on Bosnia. Observers were quick to point out that such behavior would have been unthinkable had the meeting been a NATO summit in Europe. Supposedly, Clinton's cancellation proved how little attention the United States gave to Asia. This was an ironic turn, because the opposite case had been made in Europe the year before, that the United States was turning to the Pacific.

Nevertheless, as the American economy boomed and the Japanese economy weakened, the Clinton administration retreated from its confrontational trade policy. The shift to a more conciliatory line may well have reflected the growing antagonism between the United States and China as well as between the United States and Russia. Clinton's eventual visit to Japan in April 1996 coincided with Jiang Zemin's trip to Moscow. During Clinton's stay in Japan trade was scarcely mentioned, except when Clinton visited a Chrysler dealership and poked around under the hood of one of the cars in the showroom. An important new declaration of principles emphasized the enduring security partnership as the "cornerstone" of U.S.-Japan relations; this was the basis for a series of cooperative defense agreements negotiated later.[13] The shift in emphasis back to security issues on Clinton's part was widely welcomed. Thus, in his Japanese policy the president came full circle, much as he had done in his China policy. After three years the administration had "finally got it right," wrote *Washington Post* columnist Charles Krauthammer.

Nevertheless, well-placed observers (former ambassador Michael Armacost) believed that elements of rivalry had become more visible and that the psychological underpinnings of the relationship "were shaky." The trade talks had been marked by "bitter recrimination, threats and counterthreats." Mutual dependence had been weakened. Armacost concluded that "few thoughtful Americans and Japanese could take the future of the bilateral relationship for granted."[14]

NOTES

1. News briefing by Winston Lord, "Vision for a New Pacific Community," Washington, D.C., August 31, 1993, in U.S. Department of State *Dispatch*, Vol. 4, No. 36, September 6, 1993.

2. Mickey Kantor, remarks to the Annual Meeting of the Trilateral Commission, Washington, D.C. 1993, pp. 9–12.

3. Mickey Kantor, testimony before the Senate Finance Committee, March 9, 1993, in *Dispatch*, Vol. 4, No. 11, March 15, 1993; David R. Sands, "Kantor's Only Trade Philosophy," *Washington Times*, May 6, 1993.

4. Dan Goodgame, "Trading Punches," *Time*, June 21, 1993.

5. Jeffrey E. Garten, *The Big Ten* (New York: HarperCollins, 1997), p. 141.

6. Kantor, *Dispatch*, March 15, 1993.

7. Hobart Rowen, "Tokyo Summit Presents Clinton an Opportunity," *Washington Post*, July 4, 1993.

8. President Clinton, remarks at Waseda University, in *Washington Post*, July 8, 1993.

9. Andrew Pollack, "U.S. Appears to Retreat from Setting Targets to Increase Japan's Imports," *New York Times*, July 11, 1993.

10. R. W. Apple Jr., "A Clinton Debut: Fancy Footwork and a Bow," *New York Times*, July 11, 1993.

11. Address to the Japan Association of Corporate Executives, Tokyo, March 11, 1994, in *Dispatch*, Vol. 5, No. 11.

12. Daniel Williams and Clay Chandler, "U.S. Aide Sees Relations with Asia in Peril," *Washington Post*, May 5, 1994.

13. Kevin Sullivan, "Feeling Good and the Trade Talks Are Easy," *Washington Post*, April 19, 1996.

14. Michael H. Armacost, *Friends or Rivals* (New York: Columbia University Press, 1996), pp. 195, 227.

10

Watershed

The first great turning point for the Clinton administration was not a foreign success or a foreign crisis but a domestic defeat. In the congressional elections of November 1994 the Democrats were repudiated by the electorate to the point that control of both houses of Congress passed to the Republicans for the first time since 1952. Most of the blame landed squarely on the White House. It was a vote of no confidence in Bill Clinton and especially his "liberal" advisors. Clinton himself acknowledged that it was a "national sea change." In a parliamentary system, he would have been forced to resign immediately.

Early in 1994, barely a year after he had taken office, a journalist had warned that unless Clinton became a foreign policy president he would jeopardize his chances for reelection. The president had rejected such advice. Even if he had been so inclined, after the disaster of the midterm elections of November 1994 much of the power in Washington passed to Congress and its new Republican majority. For two years the president was engaged in almost daily battles with them.

At first his tactic was to fight back, which meant stalemate, or as Washington preferred to call it, gridlock. This shifted some of the public frustration back onto Congress, but the Clinton presidency was widely regarded as wounded, perhaps mortally so. What he needed was a strategy, and he found it with the return of his old political comrade, Dick Morris. Clinton lowered his own sights and began to adopt Republican programs and even some of his opponents' rhetoric.

Foreign policy had played no special role in Clinton's defeat. Indeed, just before the elections foreign policy seemed one of his stronger points. The successful landing of American troops in Haiti, for example, had given the president a "bump" in the polls, so that he stood about even between approval and disapproval. White House officials went so far as to say that the president's activities as a foreign policy leader were more likely to benefit his party in the November elections than campaigning across the country would. Before the midterm elections, a *Time* magazine interviewer began by saying to the president, "You've had a string of successes overseas lately." Clinton himself said that his foreign policy had become a more disciplined, tightly focused process than it had been the previous year. He explained that he was spending fifteen to twenty minutes more each day on foreign policy, which made an "amazing" difference. It was later reported that in late 1993 Clinton's advisors—Christopher and Lake—had joined in a memorandum urging him to give more attention to foreign policy. He had written on the memorandum that he agreed to spend more time, but he had added—"if possible."

Nevertheless, the Clinton administration was never free for long from attacks on its foreign policy. At first, critics conceded the administration's good intentions. Even the debacles in Somalia and Haiti were ascribed to noble ideas gone bad. Some of the administration's most persistent critics, however, feared that good intentions were no longer good enough: a three-year interval of extraordinary international calm had ended with the "thunderclap" of the Russian elections of December 1994 and the threat of a new cold war.[1]

The administration saw it differently. Anthony Lake, in a candid admission that the administration's first year in office had been an "extraordinarily difficult" period, attributed the problems to a failure to explain persuasively the administration's reasons and goals as well as to a lack of timely information from all sources.[2] For example, in Somalia the White House had been misinformed about the situation in Mogadishu and had not pressed for a political compromise. All the turmoil abroad had invited Congress to encroach on the president's authority, and this reaction in turn had persuaded some foreign leaders that the United States was in retreat. Not surprisingly, Lake concluded that the White House saw no need to change any of its procedures; no shakeup in Clinton's foreign policy team was anticipated (Les Aspin was shoved out of the Pentagon two months later).

After the midterm election, the criticism not only resumed but was much sharper edged. The London *Economist*, while noting Clinton's successes before the elections, wrote in January 1995 that he had been blown off course:

> Clintonian diplomacy is back to its old, unhappy state—a weak team, a distracted president, an unsettled world—with extra buffeting from the newly empowered Republicans. . . . America's response to a messy world comes at the moment from an enfeebled administration that has never been terribly coherent on foreign policy and from the equally incoherent Republicans who now control congress.[3]

The article was entitled "Calling Dr. Kissinger." It was an apt point, for Kissinger as well as a number of others were increasingly critical of Clinton's foreign policy—and not because he had been distracted, as Clinton's own diagnoses suggested. His critics were bothered more by substance than by how little time he had invested. According to Kissinger, Clinton had failed to articulate an operational theory of foreign policy for the post–Cold War period and to relate individual events and crises to such a theory. One reason for this failure, Kissinger wrote, was that the Clinton team was led by officials whose convictions had been formed in opposition to the Cold War consensus. Their views, rooted in the 1960s, were badly out of date; thus, their distrust of the use of American power inhibited a realistic response to the new challenges. Moreover, their views were so "opaque and academic" that operational policies could not be devised from them; one of their principal policies, "enlargement" of democracies, could not be given any realistic content. The Clinton administration's tendency toward abstraction was compounded by an extraordinary obsession with public relations, Kissinger argued. Finally, Haiti and Bosnia illustrated the gap between the administration's convictions and its willingness to run risks, according to the former secretary of state.[4]

Kissinger was not alone in his critique. The former *New York Times* columnist Leslie Gelb, normally inclined to be sympathetic to Democrats, wrote that Bosnia exemplified Clinton's foreign policy woes: "No ethical ballast, no strategic center, no convictions, no steadiness and a tendency to blame others."[5]

Another usually sympathetic critic was E. J. Dionne, a columnist for the *Washington Post*. He noted that Bush had to bear some blame for the legacy he had left, but that nevertheless Clinton's foreign policy was rated a failure, not only by political opponents and specialists but by the American people. The reason was that many of his strongest statements on policy in the 1992 campaign did not square with what he was actually willing to do in office.[6] The editors of the prestigious quarterly *Foreign Policy* placed themselves in the critical column in their Spring 1995 issue: "It is the firm belief of the editors that the United States has yet to develop a foreign policy relevant to this post–Cold War world."[7] Finally, Professor Michael Mandelbaum, who had known the president since Clinton's Oxford days, summed up the administration's failures in an article significantly entitled "Foreign Policy as Social Work." Mandelbaum wrote that the "seminal events" of Clinton's foreign policy were "three failed military interventions," which had set the tone of the foreign policy agenda.[8]

At the end of his first year, Clinton had scored better than 50 percent approval in polls on his handling of foreign policy. By mid-1994 the number had fallen to 39 percent, and by September to 34 percent. Another poll showed that 58 percent were "uneasy" over Clinton's ability to deal with a difficult international situation. Similar polls, however, found little public support for giving high priority to foreign policy. The most important foreign issue, the surveys suggested, was stopping the illegal flow of drugs into the United States.[9]

A devastating summing-up of Clinton's failings was provided by James Schlesinger, secretary of defense under Gerald Ford and secretary of energy under Jimmy Carter:

> Our policies have been changeable rather than consistent. Our commitments do not appear to be reliable. Our policies appear excessively driven by domestic constituencies. The result is that the call for American leadership is diminishing in strength. Increasingly, American leadership appears to be a problem rather than a solution.[10]

Clinton, of course, had his defenders. Too often, however, his administration's spokesmen resorted to the simplistic argument that the alternative to Clinton was rampant isolationism. Even though most opinion polls refuted the myth of a prevalent isolationism, Clinton's close friend and political advisor Dick Morris warned him that 40 percent of the public was isolationist. A cogent defense came from a surprising source, Owen Harries, the editor of the conservative *National Interest*, who wrote for the *New Republic*:

> How bad, really, is Clinton's foreign policy? Is it bad enough to carry the weight of responsibility for the deteriorating state of the world that is thrust upon it? I think not. In fact, I believe that it deserves a kind of Wagner's music defense: it is not anything like as bad as it sounds when virtually all its critics chant in unison: "Somalia-Bosnia-Haiti-China-Korea [and now] Cuba" which is just about all

that many of them have been doing. Clinton's foreign policy is not an unmitigated disaster. It is not even a mitigated disaster. It is merely quite bad in certain ways that have limited consequences.[11]

If, on the one side, such critics as Kissinger, Brzezinski, and Jeane Kirkpatrick wanted a return to some version of realpolitik, the pressures on Clinton on the other side were illustrated during the visit of the South African hero Nelson Mandela. Addressing the United States Congress in October 1994, Mandela said:

> If the world is one stage and the actions of all its inhabitants part of the same drama, does it not follow then that each of us as nations, including yourselves, should begin to define the national interest to include the genuine happiness of others, however distant in time and space their domicile might be?[12]

When he took office, President Clinton might well have easily adopted Mandela's humanitarian prescriptions, but after more than two years of buffeting he was ready to soften if not drop his Wilsonian idealism. Pragmatism was becoming "more visible than Wilsonianism."[13] He could not completely abandon liberal internationalism, for it was ingrained in his character, but to a significant degree he moved to his right, in both domestic and foreign policies. In part he was forced to do so by the Republican majority in Congress, led by Georgia congressman Newt Gingrich. The new Republicans were determined to enforce their own agenda and ride roughshod over the White House if necessary. Bipartisanship, always something of a Washington myth, was clearly a thing of the past for the time being.

Clinton had to confront some harsh facts. With an election for the presidency pending, he could no longer expect automatic support on key foreign policy issues. The majority leader in the Senate, Robert Dole, had helped Clinton on several issues; now he was getting ready to run for the Republican nomination for president. Moreover, the Republicans in the new House of Representatives had their own blueprint, called the "Contract with America." It was devoted mainly to domestic policy; it had little to say about foreign policy but it did have a section on national security. It called for increased defense spending, was sharply critical of subordinating American troops to UN command, and strongly advocated a new version of the Strategic Defense Initiative (SDI), Reagan's "Star Wars." It specifically called for admitting new members to NATO by January 1999.

Clinton eventually worked out an effective response to the Republican challenge, mainly by preempting certain key issues. A target for expanding

NATO, for example, was set for April 1999, the fiftieth anniversary of NA-TO's founding. While not prohibiting American forces from serving under a UN commander, in Bosnia they were specifically placed under a NATO command (not surprisingly, the commanding officer turned out to be an American general). Clinton balked at one issue, as he had since the 1992 campaign; he would not fund Star Wars, preferring development of a shorter-range antimissile system to protect American troops in the field. When SDI funding was pressed to an early vote in February 1995, to everyone's surprise the Republican majority lost; several key members had defected, including the chairman of the Budget Committee, Congressman John Kasich.

There was little doubt that the administration was dispirited. There was speculation about replacing Warren Christopher, who in fact offered to resign. In a conversation with Dick Morris, Clinton suggested Senator Sam Nunn as a possible secretary of state, but instead he sounded out Colin Powell for the job. Powell turned him down, and Christopher remained—not exactly a vote of confidence. Much of the early enthusiasm for an internationalist foreign policy began to wane. In particular, the UN seemed less the focal point for a new world order and more an obstacle to American policy. Boutros Boutros-Ghali, the Secretary-General, had alienated key Clinton administration officials, who quietly began to work against his reappointment. Little was heard now of the infamous doctrine of "assertive multilateralism." Instead, the administration discovered the virtue of acting alone, at least on some issues.

Nevertheless, Clinton's policies were in trouble. NAFTA was turning sour because of the massive Mexican financial bailout. The Middle East peace negotiations had suffered a severe setback with the assassination of Yitzhak Rabin. Yeltsin was on the warpath over NATO expansion. The Chinese were increasingly suspicious of a new American policy of containment. The Japanese were digging in against further trade concessions. By the spring of 1995, foreign policy was dragging down an administration already in trouble, confronting both a hostile Congress and a disenchanted electorate. Clinton was needled by Dick Morris about being too young to run foreign policy: Christopher and Lake, he asserted, had established a "regency" over foreign policy until the president "came of age." Clinton responded bitterly: he told Morris that he never got policy options from the National Security Council, and he invited Morris to become involved behind the scenes. Morris concluded that the NSC staff did not understand that even foreign policy needed public support, which meant politics. This earned him an "evil rodent" look from Lake.[14]

A turning point came over the summer of 1995. Clinton had more or less accepted the Republican scheme for balancing the budget by the year 2002 but had protested that he would not abandon his social programs. He thus inaugurated a long negotiation, in which his Republican opponents became bogged down in infantile debates over how to measure the balance of a budget. In the end the Republicans insisted on shutting down the government rather than compromising; this proved a calamitous mistake, and Clinton reaped the benefit. Eighteen months after his failure in the midterm elections, his own reelection prospects had improved dramatically, and pundits were beginning to speculate that the Democrats might regain control of Congress.

This recovery was helped, ironically, by a major achievement in foreign policy—the Dayton peace agreements on Bosnia. The semi-official explanation was that Clinton had finally broken out of his self-imposed straitjacket over Bosnia. In 1994 he had admitted that he had been surprised at the resistance to his first plan in May 1993 to lift the arms embargo and launch air strikes; he had not understood how reluctant the British and French would be. At one point, he said, Prime Minister John Major told him that he doubted that his government could survive if he had supported Clinton's plan in 1993: no government would risk falling to satisfy pressure from the United States, Clinton said. Perhaps Clinton was right that he could not have forced his plan down the throats of reluctant allies. But over the next eighteen months he was subjected to constant second-guessing, as the war continued.

Matters finally came to a head in the summer of 1995. Frustrated and exasperated by a policy that "wasn't working," Clinton ordered his staff to find a way out of the Bosnian impasse. Dick Morris reinforced the message, telling the White House staff that if Bosnia was not settled it would threaten the 1996 campaign. Nevertheless, it would not be so easy. A political success in Bosnia would probably mean an American commitment of troops—a risky option for a president facing reelection. On the other hand, if successful in ending the fighting, Clinton would go into the election campaign with a major foreign policy gain, a prospect that few would have predicted at the beginning of 1995. Clinton gambled, and it paid off. He launched a new, and ultimately successful, initiative to settle the war in Bosnia. Clinton had at last found a role he found congenial—"Peacemaker in Chief."[15]

NOTES

1. Charles Krauthammer, "Good Intentions Gone Bad," *Washington Post*, December 24, 1993.

2. Adam Nagourney, "Key Aide Acknowledges Blunders in Foreign Policy," *USA Today*, October 21, 1993.

3. "Calling Dr. Kissinger," *Economist*, January 14, 1995.

4. Henry Kissinger, "At Sea in a New World," *Newsweek*, June 6, 1994.

5. Leslie H. Gelb, "Can Clinton Deal with the World?" *Washington Post*, March 6, 1994.

6. E. J. Dionne Jr., "Clinton's Promise Problem," *Washington Post*, May 3, 1994.

7. "Editor's Note," *Foreign Policy*, Spring 1995.

8. Michael Mandelbaum, "Foreign Policy as Social Work," *Foreign Affairs*, January/February 1996.

9. John E. Riley, "The Public Mood at Mid-Decade," *Foreign Policy*, Spring 1995.

10. James R. Schlesinger, "The Second Paul Nitze Award: A Lecture," *Center for Naval Analyses Occasional Paper*, May 1995, p. 13.

11. Owen Harries, "My So-Called Foreign Policy," *The New Republic*, October 10, 1994; Stephen Rosenfeld, "Clinton's Foreign Policy: Better Than It Looks," *Washington Post*, August 12, 1994.

12. Nelson Mandela, "The Oneness of the Human Race," *Washington Post*, October 7, 1994.

13. Stanley Hoffmann, "The Crisis of Liberal Internationalism," *Foreign Policy*, Spring 1995.

14. Dick Morris, *Behind the Oval Office* (New York: Random House, 1997), pp. 244–265.

15. R. W. Apple Jr., "Clinton's Peace Strategy," *New York Times*, December 2, 1995.

11

Endgame

The 1996 presidential campaign became a minor political legend. The successful candidate of four years earlier, overwhelmingly repudiated in the midterm elections of 1994, underwent a Svengalilike change. A new Bill Clinton emerged, a man who had moved so far toward the center that he was becoming a "neo-Republican." The front cover of *Newsweek* featured a large photo of the president with the caption, "The Makeover."

It was generally agreed that his comeback was a combination of luck and shrewd advice from Dick Morris, plus Clinton's own uncanny ability to calculate the political currents. The public and politicians liked a winner, and Clinton seemed to be more and more a winner, whether in Bosnia or in the legislative battles with the Republicans. Clinton had never been much of a contrarian, but now he had become a consensualist, much more attuned to what the country wanted. The high point of this transformation was the signing of the welfare reform bill, legislation that many of his supporters thought he should have vetoed. His decision to sign it prompted some bitter rebukes from the Democratic left.[1] But it seemed to help him with the general public, adding to his strong position as the Democratic Convention began in Chicago the last week in August 1996.

Clinton seemed to have more confidence in foreign policy as he became comfortable as a "deal-maker and statesman." A *New York Times* public opinion poll of July 1996 showed that 50 percent of those asked approved the president's handling of foreign policy.[2] In his address to the Democratic Convention (August 29, 1996) he said he recognized that foreign policy was not a matter of great interest in the debates in the "barber shops and the cafes of America, on the plant floors and at the bowling alleys," but that America could make the "difference between life and death"; he continued to list foreign policy among his successes.[3] His first campaign pamphlet in 1992, *Putting People First*, had concentrated on criticizing Bush's foreign policy. His new brochure for 1996, *Between Hope and History*, asserted a string of successes in saving America from the dire fate of isolationism. (The first booklet had been attributed to Clinton and Gore, the next was supposedly written by Clinton himself.)

Some Republican gurus believed that Clinton's foreign policy record was vulnerable and that the Republicans ought to build a major campaign around foreign affairs. Given the drumfire of criticism of Clinton's foreign policy, this approach had some merit. What the pundits offered, however, was warmed-over Reaganisms, a so-called conservative internationalism that advocated such bromides as "standing by our ideals" or "expressing confidence in American power."[4] While shrewdly evoking the spirit of Reagan, in practice these platitudes seemed not much different from the new Clinton. In fact, the Republicans were divided, and Senator Dole was buffeted by clashing prescriptions. (Many conservatives were writing off Dole as early as April.) The activists wanted a form of "benevolent interventionism," while the more moderate wing wanted a "selective pragmatism." Dole tried to bridge the gap between "drastic neo-isolationists and hyperactive global crusaders." A practical man, oriented toward results rather than theory or ideology, Dole finally chose to downgrade foreign affairs and concentrate his campaign on Clinton's character, or lack thereof.[5]

To be sure, there were disagreements between Clinton and the mainstream Republicans, but there were also areas of agreement on some key issues—more agreement than in 1992, when Clinton had been reticent. By 1996 both the Republicans and Democrats agreed that NATO ought to expand and take in the countries of Eastern Europe (at least Poland, Hungary, and the Czech Republic). The real difference was over how quickly to move: the Republicans wanted to move immediately, whereas Clinton preferred to proceed more slowly. Both agreed that Yeltsin and Russian reforms had to be supported, but the Republicans were more skeptical of Yeltsin's commitment to genuine democracy and to a moderate foreign policy. Both agreed that the China trade issue (MFN) should be separated from questions of human rights; Dole's help had been critical to Clinton on this issue. They agreed on the pursuit of free trade, but the Republicans would emphasize "fair" as well as free; Dole had supported NAFTA but in the campaign he retreated slightly on future trade agreements. They both supported Israel and agreed that Saddam Hussein had to be contained, if not removed.

There was not much daylight between the Republicans and Democrats, especially between Robert Dole and Bill Clinton.

Dole's most frequent charges against Clinton were that he had squandered the foreign policy legacy he had inherited, had failed to give the country a clear direction, and had made "inconsistency, confusion, and indecision" the characteristic features of his diplomacy.[6] The Republican campaign drew support from academic sources. A prestigious group of scholars and former diplomats (largely Republicans) issued in summer 1996 under the auspices of the Kennedy School of Government at Harvard a report that stated, "We have seen five years of ad hoc fits and starts. If it continues this drift will threaten our values, our fortunes and indeed our lives. The defining feature of American engagement in the world in the years since the Cold War has been confusion."[7]

Thomas L. Friedman, a respected columnist for the *New York Times*, pointed out that Clinton had been "so lucky" the past four years because he had the help of a number of major international figures, such as Helmut Kohl, who were not likely to be around for another four years. He made the additional point that Bob Dole had been helpful as majority leader, and that a reelected Clinton might miss him most of all.[8]

The Clinton camp, of course, saw things its own way. Indeed, it was confident enough of its position that some observers speculated the administration's foreign policy would simply coast until November. Memories of the first setbacks and defeats were banished. Responding to new complaints over the timid and minimal political role of American peacekeeping troops in Bosnia, Anthony Lake said that Clinton had avoided a Vietnamlike quagmire in Bosnia, that Clinton's limited use of force in Bosnia also proved that selective but substantial use of force was sometimes more appropriate than "massive use." This was a slam at the Bush-Powell doctrine of Desert Storm. The implication was obvious: if Bosnia worked, it would be a repudiation of Bush and a vindication of Clinton. Lake also said that any new peacekeeping operations involving American troops had to be "tightly tailored mission [with] sharp withdrawal deadlines the norm." This was an interesting claim in light of the speculation that after the elections the duration of the Bosnian mission might be extended beyond Lake's "sharp withdrawal deadline."

Dole tried to sharpen his attacks on Clinton. He questioned how the country could have turned foreign policy over to Clinton, a "would-be statesmen, still suffering from a post-Vietnam syndrome."[9] Dole said that in Bosnia the administration had wasted two years before adopting Dole's position (that is, lift and strike) and had permitted the Iranians to gain a "foothold" in Europe. As for Russia, Dole supported Yeltsin but ridiculed the U.S. administration for harboring romantic illusions and giving a "green light to the most dangerous tendencies in the New Russia." Dole also attacked Clinton for his "vacillating and incompetent" Asian policy, especially toward China. After "considerable confusion and embarrassment," Dole claimed, Clinton had come around to the view that punishing China by withdrawing MFN would not help human rights in China. (This happened also to be Dole's position.)

Nevertheless, it was difficult for Dole to concentrate on foreign policy issues. One news account, for example, was headlined, "Dole Attacks Clinton Asia Policy Although He Supports Part of It." Another news story reporting his foreign policy attacks on Clinton in June noted that "his [Dole's] differences with the President on foreign policy were more in tone than substance." "Bob Dole is finding it hard to pick a foreign policy fight with President Clinton," editorialized the *New York Times* on July 7. According to the editorial, Dole had more in common with Clinton than his campaign wanted to admit. It was becoming difficult for Dole to distinguish himself from an incumbent president who had moved to capture the center of American politics. Similar points were made by other observers more sympathetic to Dole.

The secondary role of foreign policy in the Republican campaign was confirmed at the party's convention in August. It was addressed by two veterans, Jeane Kirkpatrick and James Baker. Their speeches were given minimal attention, since they were not scheduled in television prime time. On August 14, Baker described "four years of drift, not direction. Four years of rhetoric, not resolve. Four years of flip-flops and photo-ops passing as foreign policy." While Baker's speech was largely ignored, one by Colin Powell was given major attention. He paid little attention to foreign policy, however, saying only that he had become a Republican because a Republican president would bring "greater conviction and coherence to our foreign policy."[10] In his acceptance speech at the convention Dole addressed foreign policy only in passing.

There was, however, one major security issue raised by Dole, and seconded by Kirkpatrick at the convention: the building of an antimissile defense system (SDI) to protect the United States from missile attacks by "maverick" states. At the convention Dole said that on his first day in office he would put the country on a course that would end American vulnerability to a missile attack. This was the old Reagan "Star Wars" reborn in a more modest garb and addressed to a threat from pariah nations, such as Iran, Libya, or North Korea. A new SDI had been a feature of the "Contract with America," and it had been proposed as a specific addition to the defense budget by Dole. The Republican Party's national platform advocated a missile-defense system by the year 2003. But some Republicans were wary of the high cost and the debatable effectiveness of SDI; consquently the issue was never put to a clear legislative test.

In wrangling with Congress Clinton had opposed the program as premature, arguing that any such threat was more than a decade away. Clinton also emphasized the prohibitive cost—sixty billion dollars over seven years. Democrats pointed out that the huge cost of such a system hardly squared with Dole's proposal for a 15 percent tax cut. At the Democratic Convention Clinton shifted slightly saying he favored a "sensible" program of antimissile development but would not "squander" sixty billion dollars on an "unproved, ineffective" program that could be "obsolete tomorrow." It was the one issue on which differences were starkly drawn, but Dole never pressed it; a large, expensive defensive system was obviously not going to be a vote-getter.

Another disputed issue was the United Nations. The Republicans insisted that no American troops serve under a UN command, and even went so far as to claim that American soldiers could not be ordered to wear a UN uniform (that is, blue berets). Having decided to force the UN Secretary-General, Boutros Boutros-Ghali, out of office, the Clinton administration was in a weak position to defend the authority of the organization. It took refuge in stressing UN reform. Indeed, Clinton never even mentioned the UN in his acceptance speech to the Democratic Convention.

In any case, foreign policy played no special role as the two parties headed into the more formal phase of the election after Labor Day. This confirmed what had been suggested in 1992: that the end of the Cold War had led to a shift in opinion from foreign to domestic concerns and that this shift was indeed a genuine one, not a reflection of tactics or campaign styles.

From the Willkie-Roosevelt campaign of 1940 through the 1992 campaign, foreign policy had played some role, occasionally a major one. It had surely helped elect Eisenhower after he promised to go to Korea in 1952; it had helped him again in 1956, when Europe and the Middle East were caught in crises over Hungary and Suez. In 1960 Nixon and Kennedy had debated the menace of Chinese attacks against the offshore islands. They had also tangled over how to deal with the new dictator in Cuba, Fidel Castro. Johnson's campaign advertising had virtually destroyed Goldwater with a television clip showing a little girl plucking petals from a flower and counting down until she disappeared in an atomic mushroom cloud. Vietnam had wrecked Hubert Humphrey's campaign in 1968, just as a different side of the same issue had crippled McGovern's call for America to "come home." Jimmy Carter probably never had a chance after the hostages were seized at the American Embassy in Iran and his rescue mission failed. On the other hand, the amazing victory of the Gulf War had not saved George Bush, proving the old adage that a good foreign policy is of no value, but a bad one can be trouble.

In 1996, as the post–Labor Day campaign opened, Clinton could take comfort that he would not be saddled with a "bad" foreign policy. Rather surprisingly one poll indicated that if Americans were forced to go to war again with Iraq, 52 percent would rather be led by Clinton, while only 36 percent favored Dole's leadership. The mini-crisis with Iraq, however, demonstrated that foreign policy was playing a "meager" role.[11] Clinton's editorial endorsement by the New York Times (October 27) stressed that he was regarded internationally as a "leader with a sophisticated grasp of a superpower's obligations to help the world manage its conflict and economic contests." Pundits of various political persuasions, however, deplored his lack of interest in foreign affairs, and some warned that this attitude would be regretted when the inevitable crises blew up in a second Clinton term. Nevertheless, public interest in foreign affairs did not catch on. At one point in the second presidential debate, Jim Lehrer, a respected TV anchor, acting as the moderator, had to plead with the audience to ask a foreign policy question.

This low level of interest probably helped the president. There was considerable turmoil abroad during the 1996 presidential contest—the Taiwan Straits confrontation with China, the gradual disintegration of the Middle East peace process, new tensions with Iraq (again), and the Russian elections—any of these could have affected the vote. Candidate Clinton, however, headed into the final weeks of the campaign almost beyond criticism for his foreign policies. Opinion polls also showed a high level of confidence in his presidency at the outset of his new term, and his poll ratings on foreign affairs were relatively good. Indeed, postelection polls showed that the public's confidence in his handling of foreign affairs now registered 54 percent compared to his low point of 37 percent only two years earlier.[12] The pundits were already predicting that the second term would be more about foreign policy—"It's the world, stupid!" editorialized the Financial Times of London. An editorial judgement of the Washington Post (January 19, 1997) offered a caveat: "In his first term President Clinton was slow to find his foreign policy way, and in Bosnia, Haiti and Somalia a price was paid, though in the first two places he recouped. His team was not always sure handed."

Almost immediately after the election Clinton began to change his foreign policy and national security team. Warren Christopher resigned within days, ostensibly so that his successor could be in place as soon as possible. William Perry followed soon thereafter. Christopher was replaced by Ambassador Madeleine Albright, who became the first woman to hold the position of secretary of state. Perry was succeeded by retiring Republican senator, William Cohen. Clinton replaced Anthony Lake at the White House with Lake's deputy, Sandy Berger, Lake was nominated to become director of the CIA; he withdrew after a bitter wrangle with the Senate Intelligence Committee and was replaced by George Tenant, acting director since the departure of John Deutsch, who was now passed over entirely.

It was a highly political team—much more than that of the first term. Clinton's choices were interpreted to mean that the president was looking not so much for innovation in policy as a steadier implementation and for more support both from the public and from Congress.[13] Whereas members of the original team had been distinguished by their prior service, their replacements owed their appointments to Clinton's favor. Commentators and critics were favorably impressed by the new group, especially by Albright.[14] She was adept at public relations and articulate, expounding her views in engaging sound bites. She was criticized by Owen Harries, however, for having shown too much zeal in her previous post at the UN, for having a "passion" for an activism "unattached to or controlled by an overarching strategy." According to Gary Wills, she seemed to "yearn back toward cold-war certitudes and swagger."[15] Some critics wondered to what degree this new team could count on Clinton's support if they encountered heavy weather.

With the election safely behind him, Clinton proceeded to reinvent the history of his foreign policy. He said that he had originally entered office with three objectives: (1) to finish the business of the Cold War (Russia, China, North Korea, and Europe); (2) to deal with new threats, ethnic hatreds, and other internal bloodbaths (the Middle East, Bosnia, Northern Ireland, and Haiti); and (3) to build a new "structure" of opportunity through trade, investment, and commerce (NAFTA, GATT, and APEC). Nowhere in the speeches, proclamations, or directives of the first three years, however, could such a clear structure of policy be found. In those years the objectives had been quite different: upgrading the UN, practicing assertive multilateralism, and pursuing the enlargement of democracy.

As was to be expected, his outgoing team was expansive in its praise. Secretary Christopher claimed that the administration had built "an enduring basis for our engagement in a more secure and prosperous world."[16] Secretary Perry was more sober in his parting remarks, warning against further cuts in defense spending lest the United States find itself unable to carry out its avowed strategy of fighting two regional wars. Moreover, he said, further cuts would mean that United States would have to "scale back our aspirations and our rhetoric to accommodate that."[17] Commentators echoed Perry's admonitions.

Clinton's four years was summarized by the *New York Times* as an "odd journey" from idealism to pragmatism—a journey from a chaotic beginning through some extraordinary lows, finally arriving at a position more reminiscent of his Republican predecessor than of the last Democratic president. This judgment seemed to be borne out by Clinton's second inaugural address: he sounded more like Bush than the Clinton of four years earlier. While he was wise enough not to adopt Bush's much-maligned codeword of "prudence," Clinton's new pragmatism was evident throughout his speeches and interviews around the time of his second inaugural.

In his first State of the Union address (February 4, 1997) after his reelection Clinton said that the "enemy of our time is inaction." After his inauguration he went further: "The decisions we make in the next few months will set America's course in the world for the next fifty years."[18] He supported this expansive hyperbole with rather modest goals: the ratification of the Chemical Weapons Convention (which was achieved) and expanded authority to seek trade agreements (which was defeated)—issues scarcely likely to dominate the next fifty years.

NOTES

1. Mary McGrory, "A Man You Can't Count On," *Washington Post*, August 25, 1996.

2. Steven Erlanger and David E. Sanger, "On Global Stage, Clinton's Pragmatic Turn," *New York Times*, July 29, 1996.

3. Text of Clinton's address in *Washington Post*, August 30, 1996.

4. Editorial, "It's Foreign Policy, Stupid," *Weekly Standard*, March 18, 1996.

5. Owen Harries, "Bob Dole's Calculated Pragmatism," *New York Times Magazine*, September 22, 1996; Jim Hoagland, "Campaign Expediency—Or the National Interest?" *Washington Post*, September 26, 1996.

6. Katharine Q. Seelye, "Dole Attacks Clinton," *New York Times*, May 10, 1996.

7. "America's National Interests," *The Commission on America's National Interests*, July 1996, sponsored by the John F. Kennedy School of Government, Harvard University, the Nixon Center for Peace and Freedom, and the RAND Corporation.

8. Thomas L. Friedman, "Help Wanted: Bulldozers," *New York Times*, October 23, 1996.

9. Robert Dole, speech to the World Affairs Council of Philadelphia, in *New York Times*, June 26, 1996; also the related news story by Adam Nagourney, "Dole Portrays Clinton as 'Misguided,' " *New York Times*, June 26, 1996.

10. Excerpts from convention speeches printed in *New York Times*, August 14 and 15, 1996.

11. R. W. Apple Jr., "Voters Pay a Price for a Campaign of Domestic Issues," *New York Times*, September 24, 1996.

12. An ABC–*Washington Post* poll summarized by Richard Morin, *Washington Post*, January 19, 1997.

13. Editorial, "The New National Security Team," *Washington Post*, December 6, 1996.

14. "Bright Light," *Newsweek*, February 10, 1997; David Broder, "Albright's Difference," *Washington Post*, February 23, 1997.

15. Owen Harries, "Madeleine Albright's 'Munich Mindset,' " *New York Times*, December 19, 1996; Gary Wills, "The Clinton Principle," *New York Times Magazine*, January 16, 1997.

16. Warren Christopher, "Investing in American Leadership," address at the John F. Kennedy School of Government, Harvard University, Cambridge, Mass., January 15, 1997.

17. Bradley Graham, "Perry Resists Cuts," *Washington Post*, January 16, 1997.

18. James Bennet, "Clinton Urges an Expanded U.S. Role," *New York Times*, April 12, 1997.

12

Oslo and Beyond

The formal 1996 election campaign in the United States had barely begun when two crises in the Middle East erupted—again. The first was another confrontation with Iraq. The second was a new clash between Israel and the Palestinians. Each was serious enough to threaten the president's prospects in his campaign for reelection. The Clinton administration's handling of these two crises illustrated its strengths and weaknesses. In the confrontation with Saddam Hussein, the administration acted quickly and advertised the outcome as a victory; but it was in fact a failure, as would become clear later in the second term. American intervention in a growing standoff between Israel and Palestine was also only partly successful. During the second term it too would turn out to be an illusion.

Throughout the Cold War the United States had had to wrestle with the conflict between Israel and the Arabs. The nature of the problem that confronted Clinton in 1993, however, was significantly different. For the first time, the prospects for a peaceful settlement seemed promising. The Clinton administration's involvement with the Middle East peace process began with a genuinely dramatic and historic moment on the afternoon of September 13, 1993. Hollywood could not have staged it better.

The scene was the South Lawn of the White House, sun drenched, of course. In the background was the Oval Office and the Rose Garden. Stretched along a small raised platform was a heavy table adorned with weighty, leather-bound documents. Behind the table, standing center stage, was President Clinton. On his right was the prime minister of Israel, Yitzhak Rabin; on Clinton's left was Yasir Arafat, the longtime leader of the

PLO, decked out in his olive-drab dress uniform but without his pistol. As if on signal, Clinton stepped slightly forward, softly nudging Arafat while putting a gentle hand on Rabin's back. Arafat extended his hand. Resigned to his fate, Rabin reluctantly extended his hand, while Clinton spread his arms as if to embrace both of them. This historic handshake between life-long enemies symbolized the bargain they had struck. Minutes before signing the documents, awkwardly entitled "Declaration of Principles on Interim Self-Government Arrangements," Rabin had summed up the moment: "Enough. Enough blood and tears."

The formal documents, usually called the Oslo Accords, were the culmination of a process that had begun during the Yom Kippur War of 1973. It was after that conflict that the first American-sponsored political breakthrough had occurred, as a result of the diplomacy of Henry Kissinger. In 1973, Kissinger had seized the moment after the Egyptian-Israeli cease-fire which he had arranged with the Soviet leader Leonid Brezhnev in Moscow. That cease-fire had led eventually to the first Arab-Israeli disengagement agreement along the Suez canal territory (the Kilometer 101 Agreement, as it was called).

Thereafter the United States had assumed the role of honest broker in urging, cajoling, pushing, pulling, and even threatening in an effort to keep the peace process alive. It was always called a "process," in recognition that peace would not be achieved in one grand bargain but would be evolutionary. Of course, the United States was never truly an honest broker, in the sense of being uncommitted or evenhanded: Washington tilted toward Israel, sometimes only slightly, sometime outrageously. But only the United States had the power and influence to act as an intermediary. During the Cold War, the other superpower, the Soviet Union, had had no credibility in Israel and had been regarded with suspicion even in the Arab world.

America's role was central to the Arab-Israeli peace process. President Carter had achieved a breakthrough in the Camp David agreement in 1979, which solidified peace between Israel and Egypt. The successful formula was land for peace—Israel would withdraw from certain areas in return for guarantees of peace with its respective neighbors. Under Reagan, little progress was made, but the end of the Cold War and the outcome of the Gulf War changed everything. The Arabs, especially the radicals, lost their great-power protector in Moscow. Gorbachev did not disavow Russia's historic interest in the Middle East, but he subordinated it to his relations with Washington. As a consequence, when Iraq attacked Kuwait in 1990, Moscow aligned itself with Bush, going so far as to authorize the use of force against its onetime client, Saddam Hussein. The United States intervened and defeated a major Arab power, proving to both Israel and the

Arabs that it could and would fight in the Middle East. The decisive defeat of Iraq was the first strategic turning point since the Yom Kippur War.

Bush and Baker appreciated the opportunity. The Soviet Union had virtually bowed out of the area. The PLO and Jordan, to their everlasting chagrin (and regret), had initially supported Iraq, and they were now eager for a chance to recover from this blunder. It all added up to a chance for another American-led breakthrough in the Arab-Israeli peace process. The Palestinians had shored up their claim to an independent state when George Shultz opened a direct dialogue with the PLO for the first time. James Baker took this a step further in the wake of the defeat of Iraq in Desert Storm: he promoted an international conference in Madrid, which seated a Palestinian delegation; Israel attended under pressure from Washington. Madrid represented another step toward the recognition of the PLO, even though the Palestinian delegation was composed only of inhabitants of Palestine, not the leaders of the PLO. It led to the creation of several working groups to negotiate specific issues, such as water rights, that would be involved in the transfer of territory from Israeli occupation to Palestinian self-rule.

Thus, the Clinton administration inherited a more promising position than had any of its predecessors. The Clinton administration also inherited a relatively new government in Israel. The Labor Party, led by Yitzhak Rabin, had won an unexpected victory in the elections of June 1992. The Labor coalition cabinet included Shimon Peres as foreign minister. Rabin was regarded as the more conservative hawk, while Peres had the image of a more liberal dove. Both were committed to the concept of land for peace. Peres and Rabin were not impressed by the slow, desultory meetings that followed the Madrid conference.

The future of the area was not being decided in Geneva, or for that matter in Lebanon, London, or Washington. The real action was in the incongruous setting of Oslo, Norway. Two professors from Israel had made contact with representatives of the PLO. They had begun meeting them to discuss a declaration of principles that might be adopted by the two sides. The talks made progress and were eventually taken seriously by the Labor government and the PLO. By August a text was worked out that was virtually agreed to by both Arafat and Peres. Rabin was still suspicious and reluctant but went along with the effort. Peres, using the subterfuge of an official visit to Norway, attended the final secret signing in Oslo, after which it was announced to the world. It was this agreement that was restaged for the ceremonies at the White House in Washington.[1]

The United States played no role in this historic breakthrough. State Department representatives had been informed by the Norwegians early in

the Oslo meetings, but they had airily dismissed them as of no consequence. Periodically the State Department, including Warren Christopher, was briefed and brought up to date, but it chose to ignore the Norway
channel—much as Rabin and Peres did. There is no indication that President Clinton knew anything at all. Thus, the breakthrough in Oslo had
come as a surprise, a pleasant but also embarrassing one. When Christopher and his aide Dennis Ross perused the final document they were impressed; they arranged the Washington ceremonies, especially urging
Rabin to attend.[2]

The Declaration of Principles on Interim Self-Government Arrangements was a complex, carefully worded document, spelling out an agreed
framework for an "interim period" not exceeding five years. Its essence was
that Israel would withdraw from Gaza and Jericho, transferring its authority to a Civil Administration of Palestinians. Whenever peace was characterized in such documents there was always attached to it the adjective
"comprehensive." This reflected the belief that peace could not endure if it
did not eventually include all of Israel's neighbors. This meant subsequent
agreements with Jordan, Lebanon, and Syria. An agreement with Jordan
followed reasonably soon; preliminary agreements were signed in July at
the White House.

The toughest nut to crack was Syria. The United States assumed that it
had to be the catalyst for an Israeli agreement with Syria. There was a touch
of arrogance in America's near-obsession with Syria, as if Israel could not
achieve an agreement with the wily Assad. Every recent administration
had tried to rope in Assad and had failed. Syria was an extremely elusive,
difficult, and tiresome burden. Even Israeli officials were dismayed by
Washington's insistence on taking up the mediation with Syria; they
thought the United States was a trifle naive.[3] The territory involved, the
Golan Heights, was critical, however. Though a narrow strip of land, it was
high ground that overlooked all of northern Israel. From it Syria had
launched a devastating attack in 1973. Israel required stringent security
guarantees if it were to yield this territory back to Syria. For its part, Syria
wanted all of the Golan Heights returned, as a matter of honor and prestige.

Over the next three years Warren Christopher trudged back and forth
between Washington and Damascus. If he made any progress it was so min-
uscule that only experts could detect it. Clinton also met with Assad twice.
They were weird encounters: Syria was still on the list of terrorist nations
published annually by the Department of State, and it was well known that
Syria was the sponsor of the terrorist attacks coming out of southern Lebanon. Nonetheless, in late October 1994 when he visited the Middle East,
Clinton traveled to Damascus. Assad was his usual prickly self, refusing to

make any statement condemning terrorism as Clinton had hoped. Assad later even denied that terrorism had been discussed. This was a disappointing outcome. In both of Clinton's meetings Assad simply repeated his position that the establishment of "normal relations" with Israel would be linked to the "full withdrawal" from the Golan, back to the line of June 4, 1967, plus a withdrawal from the south of Lebanon. [4] Observers were dubious that Syria could be coaxed into an agreement. For Syria, as one commentator wrote, peace was still a "spectator sport."[5]

The Syrian dimension became largely academic, as the peace between the PLO and Israel unraveled under the attacks of the extremist grpi[Hamas, which Arafat seemed unable to control, and others from Lebanon by the Hizbollah, which Syria might be able, but was not disposed, to control. The Labor government in Israel was also under attack from opposition parties in the Likud coalition. Nevertheless, in September Israel and the PLO reached a new agreement, dubbed Oslo II, concerning further withdrawals from the town of Hebron in particular. Arafat had also agreed (again) that the PLO would repudiate its charter provisions that called for the destruction of Israel.

Inside Israel criticism of the Oslo concept grew more vehement. The leader of the opposition, Benjamin Netanyahu, said that the Rabin's government had crossed every "red line" it had set for itself and had been blackmailed into a hurried, timid, and irresponsible negotiation. The mood inside Israel was turning ugly. Everything was tragically changed on November 4, 1995, when Yitzhak Rabin was assassinated, not by an Arab terrorist but by a crazed twenty-five-year-old Israeli fanatic. Netanyahu was blamed for creating the atmosphere that had spawned the crime.

Rabin was succeeded by Shimon Peres, who was committed to the Oslo formula he had helped to negotiate. The internal security situation was deteriorating badly; terrorism was spreading, including rocket attacks from the Hizbollah forces in southern Lebanon. Clinton responded with a weak, theatrical gesture. He convened a summit meeting on terrorism, attended by the Middle East leaders, minus Syria, and by the Europeans and Boris Yeltsin. Held in Sharm el-Sheik, it issued the usual declarations. There was a particularly vicious series of rocket attacks from southern Lebanon, followed by a major Israeli retaliation. The return fire struck a UN refugee camp in southern Lebanon. Israel insisted that the rocket attacks on Israel had been launched from this very site (which was later confirmed). The resulting publicity, however, was quite bad for Israel.

Christopher was galvanized into action to bring about a cease-fire. A strangely limited cease-fire was arranged in which the sides agreed not to attack civilian targets, apparently leaving them free to attack "military" ones. The incidents and firefights declined, but the practical result was to weaken still further Peres's position. In the Israeli May elections, Peres received close to an outright American endorsement. For Clinton it probably looked like a safe gamble. Peres's opponent, Benjamin "Bibi" Netanyahu, seemed to have only an outside chance, especially since his campaign was become increasingly harsh and vitriolic.

The outcome was extremely close: Netanyahu was elected by a margin of about thirty thousand votes, less than 1 percent of the total. Peres's defeat was widely regarded as a defeat for Clinton, who was "shaken" by the results. Critics attributed Peres's loss to his reliance on reciprocity from Arafat. Peres promised peace at the end of a long process, but Netanyahu insisted on peace "now" and vowed to take action against Palestinian violations.

Netanyahu had to prove that he could produce results with a new, tougher approach. In his first meeting with Clinton (July 8), nothing concrete emerged. All the old issues were reopened, however. Netanyahu was backing away step by step from Israeli commitments in the Oslo agreements. It was not a blatant and outright challenge but a series of maneuvers. Netanyahu, for instance, was reluctant to evacuate the town of Hebron, as agreed by Rabin and Peres. Arafat finally reacted by staging a demonstration, which turned violent and bloody. It was followed by a series of violent incidents.

Clinton decided to intervene. He invited Arafat and Netanyahu to Washington to meet face to face; he also invited President Mubarak, who refused to attend. The subsequent summit achieved very little, despite face-to-face meetings (October 1–2). The *Washington Post* in an editorial (October 3, 1996) characterized the summit talks in Washington as a "disaster." The peace process, the editorial concluded, was "floating into a perilous realm of stagnation and uncertainty." Arafat gained almost nothing, and Netanyahu reinforced American doubts about his hard-line policies, partly because prior to the talks various pundits had defined success as Israeli concessions. Netanyahu's strategy was to stall and play for time, resisting withdrawal from Hebron and dragging out the negotiations. Inevitably this tactic led to new pressure from Washington, in what was becoming a disturbing pattern.[6] Prior to the American elections there was no progress in the talks, but there is no doubt that Clinton's intervention had helped his own reelection. He had seemed to American voters a concerned president in action for peace.[7]

Under new prodding from Washington, as well as new and strong assurances of American support for Israel, the Hebron withdrawal agreement was finally signed by Israel and the Palestinians shortly before Clinton's second inaugural. The deal was clinched by a crucial letter from Christopher assuring Israel that America's commitment to Israel's security was not only "ironclad" but the fundamental cornerstone of American policy; the United States was, he added, committed "cooperatively to seek to meet the security needs that Israel identifies." This went beyond any prior American commitment, particularly in that Washington had conceded to Israel alone the determination of its "security needs."[8] Christopher's letter helped Netanyahu win a grudging cabinet agreement on the Hebron withdrawals; nevertheless, he paid a high political price within his own party.

With each step the dilemma produced by the Oslo Accords deepened: how to proceed became ever more complex and risky. For over a decade the Arab-Israeli peace process had been based on the concept of building trust and creating commitments piece by piece. This had been the original idea behind Kissinger's diplomacy that began after the Yom Kippur War with Israel's withdrawal from the Sinai. The Oslo agreement was the logical endgame of this gradual approach. It turned out to be too little and too late. It rested on the skill and determination of Rabin, and it assumed that Arafat would cooperate in seeing the process through to the end, even though the end was never really defined.

As progress had faltered, the old concept was challenged. Ironically, the challenge was first issued by Henry Kissinger. In the fall of 1996 he wrote an article asserting that gradualism had run its course. He argued that the time had come to address the "unmentionables": statehood for the Palestinians; the definition of Israel's final frontiers; and the status of Jerusalem.

> The United States must shift the discussion from procedures to goals. Israel must face the implications of its own policies, and the Palestinians, perhaps intoxicated by the heady wine of global solicitude, must be reminded that they have no military prospects and that their people require not just coexistence but Israeli cooperation in day-to-day living.[9]

Kissinger's appeal was a watershed, even though the initial reactions were negative. Gradually if gingerly, each party would move in this new direction.

At first the idea of a final settlement was brushed aside by the Clinton administration. Christopher was still in office and totally caught up in the Oslo process. He and his aide Dennis Ross refused to contemplate a leap toward a final round; not only were they dubious of success but they recognized that it would be tantamount to an admission that their previous efforts had failed. Moreover, the Hebron agreement seemed to vindicate their faith in the piecemeal process.

For his part, Netanyahu saw a Palestinian state as a mortal threat. Once inside their own internationally recognized boundaries, the Palestinians could resume terrorism as they chose, but Israel could not retaliate without committing "aggression." Netanyahu opted instead for "self-rule" without true sovereignty.

After the Hebron agreements Netanyahu began to modify his position. He resurrected an old idea—creating the necessary "depth" of security for the defense of Israel, which implied something other than a return to the old 1967 boundaries. His ideas came to be called "Allon-plus," so named for the former Israeli deputy prime minister Yigal Allon, who had put forward a plan for defining a Palestinian entity in the 1970s. It essence was the establishment of two belts of land separating Israel and the Palestinians (thus security in depth): one belt in the east along the Jordan river, and another in the west. It had never been treated very seriously, mainly because there seemed no chance of Arab acceptance.

The seeds sown by Kissinger and others were beginning to bear fruit. Leapfrogging the intermediate stages and moving on to negotiations for a final settlement was virtually adopted by Netanyahu. He tacitly accepted a Palestinian entity bounded by the two security zones of the Allon plan. This shift got almost no attention in the United States; Washington chose to ignore it because it did not fit its preconceived view of the centrality of the incremental Oslo process. The PLO, however, recognized that Netanyahu's plan would be disastrous and immediately rejected it. By going into a final settlement the PLO would not only lose the advantage of periodic American intervention but would also have to specify its own final goals—which probably would split the PLO.[10]

American opinion was beginning to sour as well. For example, one *Washington Post* editor confused cause and effect: "Palestinian terrorism is in some measure a response to Israeli policy and will diminish as Israeli policy moderates."[11] Ever sensitive to shifts in public opinion, and frustrated by what one official called clearing away the underbrush to get at the underbrush, the Clinton administration in June began a "basic rethinking" of its position, including a reexamination of the idea of tackling the most nettlesome issues in a final negotiation. By early August, the administration adopted a compromise: first to support Netanyahu's proposal to move into negotiations for a final settlement, but second, to continue the interim process of withdrawals as anticipated by the Oslo agreements.[12]

The public unveiling of the new plan came in a speech on August 6 by Secretary Albright shortly before her first visit to the area. Much of it was boilerplate, but in one passage she came close to adopting the Netanyahu-Kissinger approach: "If the parties have a clear, mutual, and favorable sense of the ultimate direction of negotiation, it will be easier for them to over-come setbacks and avoid distractions along the way. This will require accel-erating permanent status negotiations."[13]

It was soon apparent, however, that the administration was having sec-ond thoughts. On the flight over to the Middle East, Secretary Albright briefed reporters and specifically rejected the notion that the Oslo process had failed and should be scrapped in favor of permanent-status negotia-tions.[14] In her major address in Israel, she barely mentioned accelerating the permanent-status negotiations; she called for both sides to refrain from "unilateral acts." Her call for a "time out" was rejected by Netanyahu, ac-cording to press reports of their meetings. At a joint news conference be-tween Albright and Netanyahu their "wide differences" were laid bare.[15]

Gradually, a contrast emerged between Christopher's patient persis-tence and Albright's emotionalism. After visiting the West Bank town of Ramallah and taking an unproductive side trip to Syria, she told reporters that the situation was even worse than she thought—"It's fairly tattered." She peevishly complained that she could not be occupied with the Middle East full time; if the parties decided to get serious she would return, other-wise she would spend her time on more important issues. Rarely had a sec-retary of state spoken so harshly.[16]

Clinton also was "increasingly frustrated and impatient."[17] He refused to meet Netanyahu on an occasion when the latter was unofficially in Wash-ington. The White House weakly denied that this was an intentional snub; Netanyahu, however, characterized it as an "insult." Washington's irrita-tion was aggravated by its poor showing in the Iraqi crisis; the United States had been isolated in the UN Security Council, and American offi-cials were eager to blame Israel. They claimed that Netanyahu's hard line had alienated the moderate Arabs, who had accordingly deserted the United States in the confrontation with Iraq.

What followed was a bewildering series of proposals and counterpropos-als that only the experts could follow. Netanyahu shifted slightly.[18] It was time to start "swimming," Albright said after meeting with Netanyahu in Paris (December 5). Arafat, however, turned down Netanyahu's revised formula, and a senior Palestinian official confused matters by calling for a full withdrawal from the West Bank. Netanyahu countered by saying that the West Bank was part of Israel "proper." This is not "an alien land," he said, "this is the land of our forefathers."[19]

To break yet another impending stalemate, Secretary Albright an-nounced that Clinton would receive both Arafat and Netanyahu in Wash-ington in mid-January 1998. The impression was growing that the Clinton administration had indeed shifted from its pro-Israeli posture to a more neutral stance. A *New York Times* editorial noted this change and called on Israel to offer new withdrawals that would give the Palestinians 40 to 50 percent of the West Bank; this would "reassure Palestinians."[20] It was this kind of pressure for piecemeal concessions that Netanyahu had hoped to avoid by moving toward the final status. Once again, however, Israel found itself confronted by the same combination of international pressure—from the United States, from the Arabs, and from world opinion.

The Clinton administration was relying on an old diplomatic two-step. First Netanyahu and Arafat would visit Washington, and then Secretary Albright would follow up. There was, however, an important difference: for the first time Washington sketched the outline of a plan of its own. In his January 19 meeting with Netanyahu the president laid out a detailed plan for a phased withdrawal from the West Bank linked to the beginning of final-status talks. The plan included timetables, percentages of territorial withdrawals, reciprocal actions to be taken by the Palestinians, and a specific date for beginning the final talks. The United States had once again switched its position: it had returned to a plan of small steps, albeit phased and linked, abandoning apparently the idea of grand move to the final talks but—oddly enough—firmly insisting on a date for these final talks.

This was a clever but convoluted gambit. Despite some serious reservations expressed by Netanyahu, the Clinton plan was presented to Arafat (January 22, 1998). Arafat was shrewd enough not to turn down all of Clinton's plan; his spokesman suggested some different formulas for the degree of Israeli withdrawal. He agreed to phased withdrawals and a link to the final talks. American officials again said that there had been some progress, but the gap was still wide. As he left Washington on January 23, Arafat rejected Netanyahu's offer, dismissing it as "peanuts."

Subsequently, Secretary Albright, who was touring the Middle East to shore up the American position on Iraq, met with both Arafat and Netanyahu. After her meetings Albright vented her frustration, once again rebuking both sides: "We have been stalled at this point in the peace process, negotiating the same issues for a long time—frankly far too long. There is far too much at stake for this to go on."[21] Clinton and Netanyahu continued to exchange letters and telephone calls; Netanyahu offered a withdrawal of 9 percent, plus some other concessions, but the American initiative of the previous summer was virtually dead. There had been no breakthrough on any significant item on the agenda; there was nowhere to go. The peace process, an Israeli journalist wrote, was on "artificial respiration."[22] A former Clinton administration official who had been responsible for the Middle East as assistant secretary in the State Department, Robert Pelletreau, called it a time of "pessimism and uncertainty" in the Middle

East; negotiations were at an impasse, mistrust was rampant, and peace-makers were spending all of their energy "bailing just to keep the boat afloat."[23]

Clinton officials began to sound more and more apocalyptic. Assistant Secretary of State (and former ambassador to Israel), Martin Indyk testified before Congress that the "strategic window for peacemaking was closing."[24] Secretary Albright wanted to crack down hard on Israel, but President Clinton intervened against her, it was reported. Soon, however, the United States resumed its pressure on Netanyahu. The American "plan" was widely leaked, although the Israeli government had asked it to be kept private. Washington was insisting that Israel give up 13.1 percent of the West Bank, which would bring the total concession by Israel to about 40 percent of the disputed territory. Though dubious at first, when it became clear that Netanyahu was against the American plan Arafat decided to endorse it, thereby making him Secretary Albright's ally in the bargaining still to come.

Amid great ballyhoo, the British prime minister, Tony Blair, acting at Clinton's behest, arranged a crucial meeting in London of Netanyahu, Arafat, and Albright. The three never actually met, however. This time Albright was clearly aligned with Arafat against Netanyahu, a tragic and historic reversal of America's role. In effect, she repudiated Secretary Christopher's letter promising that Israel would decide its security requirements alone, without American dictation. The meetings ended with an American ultimatum: a proposed summit meeting three days hence (May 11) in Washington was conditioned on Netanyahu's acceptance of the American plan.

Albright's ultimatum and threat of an agonizing reappraisal backfired. Netanyahu dug in, refusing to accept American conditions or to attend the projected summit. His resistance may well have been strengthened by the publication of informal remarks by Hillary Clinton, that she believed it would "be in the longer term interests of the Middle East for Palestine to be a state." White House spokesmen tried to soften her remarks and distance the president, but there was a widespread view that she had weighed her words carefully and reflected the president's private views.[25] The confrontation with Netanyahu was quickly described as a test of wills. Despite some conciliatory remarks by Clinton, who insisted the United States would not impose an agreement, administration officials insisted that they would not back down and in fact vowed to turn up the heat if their overtures were rebuffed.

Quite predictably, there was a domestic backlash in the United States. A *Washington Post* editorial (May 12, 1998) noted that the United States was no longer a "facilitator" but a full participant, drafting compromises. Netanyahu garnered support from Republicans, and several commentators complained about Clinton's repudiation of Warren Christopher's commitment to Israel at the time of the Hebron agreements. Faced with congressional and other political attacks, however, Clinton characteristically retreated from his ultimatum. Albright was "ordered" to patch up differences with Netanyahu, which she more or less did. The stalemate resumed, interrupted by occasional hand-wringing that time was running out, by leaks of new American plans, and by half-hearted predictions of another breakthrough.[26] The stalemate was not broken until October 1998; in a meeting with Clinton in Washington, Arafat and Netanyahu agreed to a compromise version of the American plan for further Israeli withdrawals. Clinton then visited Gaza, thereby virtually recognizing an independent Palestinian state. Political pressures, however, shattered Netanyahu's coalition and forced new Israeli elections. Thus, the entire effort pressed by Clinton throughout 1998 was in jeopardy. But it may well have been too late to turn back. Indeed, during Clinton's term of office, there were major changes, including a subtle but significant transformation of American post–Cold War policy.

In the Cold War the primary interest of the United States had been to exclude or reduce Soviet influence in the area and to support and protect Israel. Promoting peace between Israel and its Arab neighbors served both major American interests. Diplomacy had focused on the Arab states, Egypt, Jordan, Syria, and Lebanon, but not the PLO. Israel understood the strategy; both the Labor party and the Likud sympathized with it and cooperated within certain limits.

Once the Cold War ended, however, American interests began to change. The fear that an Arab-Israeli war would escalate into a Soviet-American confrontation, as had happened in 1973, receded. It was inevitable that the Arab-Israeli conflict would assume less urgency and less significance. The Oslo agreements shifted the focus from Arab states, where the United States still had some leverage, to the Palestinians. The new focus engaged indigenous interests and elements that were less susceptible to American influence. As the sides came closer to the core issues, it was inevitable that the Oslo process would slow down. Frustration in Washington came to center more on Israel than on the Palestinians. This change in attitude finally broke into the open under Madeleine Albright, who made it clear she blamed both sides for their recalcitrance. What had begun as a subtle shift under Reagan and Bush turned into a scarcely concealed American-Israeli rupture under Clinton. To be sure Clinton was regarded as a friend of the nation of Israel, but he was openly hostile to its government under Netanyahu.

Tensions between Israel and the United States also reflected American frustration over the erosion of American power after the Gulf War. In the wrangling over Iraq the United States found itself isolated. The Russians reasserted their claim to a role in the area as a counterweight to American power, and they earned some sympathy from the French. Far more important was the rise of Arab nationalism and Islamic fundamentalism. Friendly Arab states found it politically more difficult to support Washington against Saddam Hussein as Israeli-Palestinian tensions revived. They justified their refusal by claiming that the United States was pursuing a double standard: sanctions against Iraq but appeasement of Israel. It was an unfair comparison but an insidious linkage. It was also indicative of latent fears in the Middle East that America would not stay the course after punishing Saddam.

The Middle East itself was changing. It was no longer the relatively self-contained area bounded by the Arab-Israeli dispute. The area was coming to resemble the nineteenth-century arena defined by the imperial powers. The liberation of the Caucasus and Central Asia from Soviet dominance opened a new dimension. American policy—and Russian and European policy for that matter—could not be confined to the Arab-Israeli front or even the Gulf. The Caspian Sea and Central Asia were the setting for a new and complex strategic competition, not in the confrontational sense of the Cold War but more like the "Great Game" of the nineteenth century. The new game was made all the more important by the existence of huge oil reserves. Thus, America's expanding interests reduced American concern for Israel. Washington still had a moral obligation to remain involved in the peace process, but wider interests began to drive policy.

Finally, a new international dimension transcended geography—the proliferation of weapons of mass destruction. It was feared that Iran and Iraq would both become nuclear powers; Israel already had such a capability. India revived its nuclear program, and Pakistan soon followed. It was the frightening new prospect of a multinuclear world as much as the older Arab-Israeli confrontation that propelled American policy in the Middle East.

Nevertheless, all of this was overshadowed by a more fundamental and more positive change: all of the parties were beginning to look beyond the next minor, tactical steps. For the first time since the founding of Israel, the outline of a final settlement with its Arab neighbors, as well as the Palestinians, was beginning to take shape. It too was one of the major consequences of the end of the Cold War.

NOTES

1. Yigal Carmon, "The Story behind the Handshake," *Commentary*, March 1994; Shimon Peres, *Battling for Peace: A Memoir* (New York: Random House, 1995), pp. 281–306.

2. "Risking Peace," *Time*, September 13, 1993; Peres, *Battling for Peace*, pp. 305–306.

3. Uri Savir, *The Process* (New York: Random House, 1998), pp. 279–280.

4. U.S. Department of State *Dispatch, Supplement*, November 1994.

5. Peter W. Rodman, "Waiting for Assad," *The New Republic*, August 8, 1994.

6. Connie Bruck, "The Wounds of Peace," *New Yorker*, October 14, 1996; Norman Podhoretz, "The Tragic Predicament of Benjamin Netanyahu," *Commentary*, December 1996.

7. Jim Hoagland, "Damaging What He Would Protect," and Stephen S. Rosenfeld, "Hardening Against Peace," *Washington Post*, October 4, 1996; Charles Krauthammer, "Arafat's War Card," *Washington Post*, October 3, 1996.

8. Thomas Lippmann, "Accord Assures," *Washington Post*, January 16, 1997. The text of Christopher's letter is in "Looking Ahead: Two U.S. Documents," *New York Times*, January 17, 1997.

9. Henry Kissinger, "The Mideast Deal," *Washington Post*, November 7, 1996; Charles Krauthammer, "The Road from Hebron," *The Weekly Standard*, February 3, 1997; Henry A. Kissinger, "The Oslo Piecemeal Process," *Washington Post*, August 24, 1997.

10. Charles Krauthammer, "Netanyahu's Map," *Washington Post*, June 13, 1997; Douglas Feith, "A Strategy for Israel," *Commentary*, September 1997.

11. Stephen Rosenfeld, "Mideast: Before Things Get Worse," *Washington Post*, June 13, 1997.

12. Steven Erlanger and Alison Mitchell, "A Meeting That Transformed," *New York Times*, August 9, 1997.

13. Madeleine Albright, "Finding the Path to Peace in the Middle East," *Dispatch*, August/September 1997.

14. Thomas W. Lippman, "Albright Takes Balanced Approach," *Washington Post*, September 10, 1997.

15. The texts of Secretary Albright's remarks in the Middle East were published in *Dispatch*, August/September 1997.

16. Peter W. Rodman, "The Mideast Impasse," *Washington Post*, September 15, 1997; Charles Krauthammer, "Oslo Endgame," *Washington Post*, September 19, 1997.

17. Steven Erlanger, "U.S. Pushes Israel," *New York Times*, November 24, 1997.

18. Serge Schmemann, "Israel Suggests New Pullback," *New York Times*, November 26, 1997.

19. Joel Greenberg, "Netanyahu Reasserts Israeli Claims to West Bank," *New York Times*, December 22, 1997.

20. Editorial, "Glimmerings in the Middle East," *New York Times*, December 22, 1997.

21. Stephen Rosenfeld, "The Fatal Flaw in Netanyahu's Policy," *Washington Post*, February 6, 1998.

22. Serge Schmemann, "Israelis Worry," *New York Times*, February 3, 1998.

23. Robert Pelletreau, "European-American Cooperation in the Middle East," in *Advancing Common Purposes in the Broad Middle East: A Report to the Trilateral Commission: 52* (New York: The Trilateral Commission, April 1998).

24. Barton Gellman, "Turning Point with Israel," *Washington Post*, May 10, 1998.

25. James Bennet, "Aides Disavow Mrs. Clinton," *New York Times*, May 8, 1998; William Safire, "Hillary's Palestine," *New York Times*, May 11, 1998.

26. Serge Schmemann, "Reports of U.S. Plans," *New York Times*, June 5, 1998.

13

Iraq

Just as the Bush administration had been defined by its confrontation with Saddam Hussein, so too was the Clinton administration. For Bush the Gulf War had been a triumph, marred only by the survival of Saddam Hussein. For Clinton Saddam's survival would become a nightmare he could not exorcise. Six months after taking office, Clinton too confronted Saddam's reckless and aggressive behavior and ordered a small, punitive air strike. Three years later, as Clinton's campaign for reelection began, another crisis with Iraq erupted, and then another, and another.

Time and time again Iraq compelled Clinton to face the most agonizing question of the post–Cold War era—how the United States would employ its overwhelming military advantages. There were two obvious areas for the use of force—Bosnia and Iraq. In Bosnia, American military power was a last resort, to be employed when all other alternatives had been exhausted by the Europeans. In Iraq, the situation was different: the United States was the only power that could contain Saddam Hussein. In Bosnia, once American forces became committed Washington insisted on using the NATO umbrella, thereby casting aside several years of UN efforts. In Iraq, however, the crisis was centered on the United Nations rather than NATO.

In both cases, Clinton was reluctant to use, if not opposed to using, American military action. His ambivalence guaranteed that the crises in both Bosnia and Iraq would drag on. Clinton's obvious wariness gave Saddam a freedom to choose when and how he would challenge the UN and United States. Moreover, the so-called "Clinton doctrine" held that any use of force should be limited in time and scope and would be relatively safe, with cruise missiles the weapon of choice. This approach also encouraged Iraq to believe that it could run significant risks.

In Bosnia, the United States shared a common interest with its allies and Russia in ending the war; in Iraq, the common interest was increasingly difficult to define after the Gulf War. In Bosnia, America's allies wanted it to intervene, while in Iraq there was growing resistance to American threats of force. Containing Saddam began to wear thin.

In neither Bosnia nor Iraq could the United States act unilaterally when it finally chose to act. Dealing with Iraq was also complicated by two other factors: the effect of American actions on the Arab-Israeli conflict, and the other regional power, Iran. Clinton adopted a rather prudent and effective collective strategy toward Iran and Iraq. Rather than leaning toward one or the other, the Clinton administration announced a policy of dual containment, opposing both Iraq and Iran. On the whole, dual containment seemed to work.

Clinton first struck out at Iraq, after an incident during former President Bush's tour of Kuwait in April 1993. There was evidence that Iraqi intelligence had planned to assassinate the former president. When this was determined to be the case, Clinton ordered an air strike against Iraq: on June 26, over twenty cruise missiles were fired against intelligence headquarters in Baghdad. It was later reported that after ordering the strike the new president was "tense and wobbly" and kept asking his aides whether they were *sure* it was the right thing to do.[1]

It was a minor show of force, yet a reminder that the United States was still the arbiter of events in the Middle East. Washington had not sought UN approval for its retaliatory strike. These small demonstrations evidently did not impress Iraq. Saddam continued to evade effective inspections of his weapons programs and to make threatening gestures toward Kuwait. His most serious series of challenges, however, began in the summer of 1996 in northern Iraq.

It was a strange area. Though still a part of Iraq, Saddam's influence and presence had virtually disappeared. It was under a "no-fly" zone, declared as such by the United States in 1991 after Iraqi forces had crushed a Kurdish uprising in the wake of the Gulf War. The area was overwhelmingly Kurdish, but the Kurds were divided into warring factions. The Kurdish Democratic Party (KDP), led by Massoud Barzani, was favored by the United States and bitterly opposed by Saddam. The second large faction, the Patriotic Union of Kurdistan (PUK), headed by Salal Talabani, was thought to be supported by neighboring Iran. A third faction, the Kurdistan worker's party (PKK), inhabited areas that extended well into Turkey.

The United States had shied away from advocating Kurdish independence, partly because of violent Turkish opposition. Washington, however, sponsored an umbrella Kurdish political organization operating out of London. Using Kurdish territory as a sanctuary, the United States was trying to create an anti-Saddam organization of Iraqi dissidents (the Iraqi National Congress). The CIA also gave support to another group, the Iraqi National Accord. There was a growing American civilian and military presence, including intelligence agencies, in northern Iraq. It was later reported that the CIA had spent 120 million dollars in abortive efforts to overthrow Saddam.

Fighting among the Kurds began in mid-August 1996, when Barzani's forces attacked the city of Irbil, then held by the Talabani faction. To everyone's surprise Barzani was supported by Saddam Hussein. Baghdad moved to the area a large number of troops, which participated in the fight for Irbil. At first it appeared to outsiders that this was an Iraq invasion of Kurdistan. It was Saddam's engagement in the crisis, rather than the Kurdish fighting, that prompted a major American reaction—warnings to Baghdad to withdraw its forces were quickly followed by two cruise missile strikes against Iraq, launched from aircraft carriers and B-52 bombers. In addition, the Clinton administration announced the expansion of the no-fly zone in *southern* Iraq—not the north.

It was a bizarre affair. The Barzani faction, supposedly pro-American, admitted that its leader had invited the support of Iraqi forces. Barzani justified his actions by insisting that the pro-Iranian faction had first begun a military offensive; this offensive was later verified, and it probably included assistance to Talabani from Iran. The facts were established too late to have any effect on the crisis. Barzani subsequently claimed that his alliance with Saddam was only a temporary tactic. The United States found itself opposing Saddam, but thereby also opposing Barzani and, in effect, supporting the pro-Iranian faction of Talabani.

Before the crisis American policy had assumed northern Iraq was virtually immune from Iraqi interference. The no-fly zone in the north excluded Iraqi aircraft but did not explicitly exclude Iraq ground troops. The American response to the new crisis muddied the waters. Washington treated the Iraqi troop movements toward Irbil as "aggression"; it justified its punitive strikes on that claim, even though the Kurdish region was within the sovereign territory of Iraq and the local leader Barzani (an American client) had invited the Iraqis to intervene.

Rather than striking at the offending Iraqi forces in the Kurdish area, the United States inexplicably attacked targets in southern Iraq. The rationale was that the terrain in the north was too rugged for precise attacks, and that the targets in the south had been selected to avoid interfering in the Kurdish internal fighting. The American aim was not to reverse the military situation in Kurdistan but to undermine and intimidate Saddam Hussein.

Clinton's critics insisted that Saddam had acted because he thought that Clinton was weak. Senator Dole, in an offhand comment, said the situation betrayed Clinton's weak leadership. Dole, however, softened his criticism by pledging his support for U.S. naval and air forces that were already in action. The Senate, voting ninety-six to one, endorsed Clinton's military response.

There can be no doubt that the administration was determined to impress not only the Iraqi leader but the voters in the presidential campaign. Clinton's advisors admitted the domestic political aspect: by ordering military action they hoped to gain a "bump" in the opinion polls.[2] Many analysts concluded that Saddam was indeed probing U.S. resolve and testing Clinton, while trying to recover his own authority in an area threatened by the expanding influence of Iran and growing American political infrastructure. American reaction, however, was too slow to prevent bloody purges of Saddam's opponents. Iraqi intelligence killed a large number of pro-Talabani forces after the capture of Irbil and other smaller towns. The Americans stationed in the area had to flee. The infrastructure that had been created for the Iraqi opposition to Saddam was thoroughly demolished, and the Kurdish coalition was split. After doing considerable political damage to Saddam's opposition, Iraqi military forces pulled back.

Observers friendly to Clinton thought his performance was to his credit, because he had used force in a measured and limited manner. The New York Times, which would endorse Clinton for reelection, editorialized (September 4, 1996) that he had "handled the quicksilver of Saddam Hussein with the right mix of America power and restraint." Dole attacked Clinton for "timidity," but the issue never rose to the level of a major campaign debate. Opinion polls gave strong support to Clinton's handling of the crisis. On balance, therefore, it was probably a net gain for the president in his reelection campaign.

Over the longer term, however, the crisis may even have helped Saddam: the coalition put together by George Bush in the Gulf War was falling apart. Jordan, France, Turkey, and Russia were cool to American policy in the Kurdish affair. Jordan refused the use of air bases for attacks against Iraq. The French criticized Clinton's resort to military means. The Turks refused to let American aircraft use their bases inside Turkey, but they then took advantage of the crisis to pound the Kurdish faction that opposed Ankara. Russia threatened to veto a British UN resolution condemning Saddam, and the resolution had to be withdrawn. Subsequently, the UN adopted a partial lifting of sanctions against Saddam, permitting him to begin selling oil for food.

The Kurdish crisis was over quickly, and it centered around an area too distant to cause much alarm in the United States. The administration's questionable performance, however, was a portent of trouble to come. The "Clinton doctrine" of the limited use of force raised some disturbing questions. Clinton rationalized the cruise missile attacks as not a punitive measure but a means of "educating" his adversary. (Critics charged that this meant there was no clear red line between diplomacy and force.) The administration's military riposte therefore had "the feel of an abstract staff study on air strategy." Others attacked the administration's "moral and intellectual lameness" in responding to unexpected events in Iraq. The net result, some critics concluded, was to undermine the idea of a strategy in which the threat of force created leverage.[3]

In the fall of 1996, after Iraqi forces retreated from Kurdish areas, the Clinton administration had crowed about its success. Washington insisted that Saddam was locked in a strategic "stranglehold"; Clinton said that Saddam had been put back in his "box." He was now deterred from moving against Kuwait, and his overall position had been weakened. Unfortunately, the hapless new director of the CIA, John Deutsch, dissented: he testified that Saddam had emerged stronger than ever. (Deutsch was not reappointed for the second term.)

Not surprisingly, in light of Deutsch's assessment, Iraq turned out to be the first serious test of Clinton's new national security team in the second term. The indefatigable Saddam Hussein once again challenged the UN, even more directly confronting the United States by refusing to admit American members of the UN Special Commission (UNSCOM) to inspect his suspicious weapons facilities. With that rather simple assertion of defiance, another crisis errupted in the fall of 1997. Saddam's motives often seemed baffling; observers, in despair, wrote him off as a madman. But his maneuvering was shrewd and effective in breaking up the coalition, led by the United States, arrayed against him.

After President Clinton's reelection, the administration had continued to assert that its position vis-à-vis Iraq was a strong one, that the international coalition was working and was agreed on "principles," even if not marching in lockstep. True, some states in the region had chosen not to speak out publicly while supporting the United States privately, but that was "immaterial," according to the State Department's briefing officer. The message was clear: Saddam had to live up to his international obligations;

the United States would be watching and would act to make sure that a price would be paid by Saddam Hussein for misbehavior.

The new secretary of state, Madeleine Albright, took a tough line in the spring of 1997. In a major speech (March 26, 1997) at her former teaching home, Georgetown University, she said,

> While Iraq's lawless policies are failing, our policies of law and firmness are working. As long as the apparatus of sanctions, enforcement, inspections and monitoring is in place, Iraq will remain trapped within a strategic box, unable to successfully threaten its neighbors and unable to realize the grandiose ambitions of its ignoble leader.[4]

The American position boiled down to a simple proposition: as long as Saddam was in power there could be no end to the confrontation. Saddam's intentions would "never be peaceful," but a change in the Iraq government could lead to a change in U.S. policy. President Clinton enunciated this same position. The implication was that Washington was committed to a perpetual state of belligerency with Saddam Hussein. Some observers went so far as to claim that this tough line in itself provoked Saddam, because he saw no way out of his dilemma.[5]

In fact, the political position of the United States had eroded. The first sign of trouble for American policy had emerged in the UN Security Council. When the Clinton administration proposed new sanctions to punish Iraq for its recalcitrant resistance to UN inspection of its chemical and biological weapons production, there was opposition from both France and Russia. A resolution was voted in April, but its implementation was delayed. When it was raised again in October, the United States found that it had even less support. France and Russia were joined by Egypt, which had one of the rotating seats on the Security Council. The proposed sanction itself was pathetic—a restriction on the travel of specific officials blocking new inspections. Nevertheless, the United States retreated, thus exposing its own weakness but avoiding an open split in the coalition. Under pressure from its allies, Washington had grudgingly agreed that Iraq could sell limited amounts of oil to earn hard currency for the purchase of food and medical supplies.

In the summer of 1997, the CIA had produced its estimate of Saddam's strengths and vulnerabilities. Overall, the CIA concluded, Saddam was vulnerable and that his regime was faced with the "constant possibility of a sudden and violent change." Nevertheless, Saddam, relying on his pervasive security services, remained entrenched. Any successor regime, the CIA speculated, might move to conciliate international opinion but would probably insist on a strong military establishment. The army's potential, however, had declined "marginally" over the past four years of sanctions.[6]

Saddam, however, decided once again to gamble, taking risks to test the international coalition. During September 1997 Iraqi officials put several sites off limits to UN inspectors. A few days later, Saddam announced that no Americans would be allowed in the inspection team and a few days later ordered all American inspectors stationed in Iraq to leave forthwith. The Iraqis claimed that all they wanted was "balance" in the inspecting teams. Baghdad also warned against any U-2 surveillance flights. Saddam's timing was "brilliant," some Arab commentators wrote, because the poor state of Israeli-Palestinian negotiations made it hard for Arabs to oppose Saddam.

Washington took these moves as a direct challenge. Various military preparations were announced, including ordering a second aircraft carrier from the eastern Mediterranean to the Gulf. Public opinion seemed supportive of military action, if necessary. Critics, however, warned Clinton against another series of "pin-pricks." From the right, Clinton was advised by former Republican officials to strike hard—"put a lid on Saddam."[7] Others, however, doubted that air power alone could bring down Saddam's regime, and such an attempt in any case would have to be a prolonged and costly effort.

The UN Security Council flinched; it agreed only to warn Iraq of "serious consequences." Moreover, America's allies saw the crisis as an opening for negotiation. Instead of taking a tougher line, the Security Council dispatched three mediators to Baghdad for discussions. Clinton argued that the United States needed no further approval from the Security Council for the use of force, but the Russian representative disagreed. The Chinese representative to the UN offered the Delphic comment that three feet of ice could not be created in one day of cold, meaning—apparently—that the confrontation had deep roots and would take time to thaw. Clinton acquiesced in the dispatch of the UN mediation mission rather than force a confrontation in the Security Council. The UN mediating team achieved nothing, but the Security Council, led by France and Russia, continued to back down. On November 12 it voted for the sanctions limiting the travels of Iraqi officials, as the United States had first proposed seven months earlier. The Council warned of "further measures," but despite a major diplomatic blitz by Albright and Berger, the United States failed to get a stronger statement.

President Clinton clearly wanted to avoid a military campaign. It was reported that he was on the telephone to both the French and Russian leaders urging them to find some diplomatic way out. These countries, in turn, took the position that Iraq had to be offered an eventual solution that would end all sanctions—light at the end of the tunnel, as Jacques Chirac of France put it to Clinton. At one point Clinton vowed that sanctions would be in place until the "end of time," but he immediately backed down, telling French and Russian leaders that the United States did not want sanctions to last forever.[8]

Clinton was once again buffeted by his advisors. Albright and Berger argued that the aim of American policy should be to get rid of Saddam Hussein. His new secretary of defense, William Cohen, supported by the new Chairman of the Joint Chiefs, General Henry H. Shelton, argued that not backed by ground forces, an air campaign would not bring down Saddam. Any air campaign would have to involve "many more than dozens" of sorties. This analysis virtually ruled out military measures. Saudi Arabia hinted that it would not allow American planes to fly from land bases in that country. Jordan argued against any military solution.[9]

The Clinton administration was nearly isolated. If the United States was to attack, it would probably have to do so unilaterally, without international support except for the British. Clinton decided to retreat even further. With the agreement of the British, the administration announced (November 17) that it was willing to consider additional Iraqi sales of oil for food. Privately, the administration argued that this humanitarian gesture would strengthen its position should military action become necessary. It was just a "little carrot," a source in the secretary of state's traveling party said.

The effect was to encourage the Russians to intervene, which eventually led to a deal: Saddam would permit inspections, and Russia would work to lift all sanctions. The inspections team did in fact return to Iraq on November 21. The Security Council met the same day to hear Russia's pleas for a speedy end to all sanctions, but that view was rejected by the United States. On December 4, however, the Security Council once again voted unanimously to extend Iraqi oil for food sales for six months.

Realizing that he could not claim another victory, the president said that he would "wait and see." Clinton's supporters nevertheless insisted that his handling of the crisis had been admirable—Saddam had had to reverse himself in the face of American firmness. In contrast to the style of Clinton's first term, in this crisis the administration had avoided freewheeling and inconclusive meetings. Administration officials emphasized that this time the president knew his own mind and used the meetings to gather information. This time his team had displayed more "poise."[10]

Critics, however, focused on the longer-term political damage inflicted by Clinton. First, he had let the Russians back into Gulf diplomacy, thus abandoning more than two decades of American policy. It was pointed out that even Warren Christopher had firmly refused Russian help in the Middle East. Clinton's reversal was characterized as typical of his disregard of balance-of-power diplomacy. That, his advisors countered, was "Old Think"; the administration had acquiesced in a Russian political intervention in order to show that it had gone the last mile if, subsequently, it had to resort to military actions.[11]

The Arab leaders were relieved not to have to choose sides. Their conclusion was that the United States would once again only "wound" Saddam, and leave him in power to plot his revenge. Clinton administration officials, however, shifted the blame to Israel: the degeneration of the Arab-Israeli peace process was having a centrifugal effect.[12] The administration's hints that the real problem was Netanyahu's alienation of moderate Arabs, who in turn refused to support Clinton, drew heavy fire. Blaming Israel was a feeble excuse for "inept and weak diplomacy"; the real problem, observers concluded, was that Clinton had backed down. His team had managed the crisis as if it had been in a "fog."[13]

The Clinton administration insisted that the crisis was not over. It would wait to test the new arrangements. Having taken the measure of the Clinton administration, Saddam decided that he could resume his pressure against inspections. First, he denied entry to a specific inspection team that was led by an American, but he shrewdly permitted other teams to continue operating. He was adamant, however, that his so-called "presidential palaces" were still off limits. A familiar pattern then repeated itself. The head of the UN inspection teams, Richard Butler, traveled to Baghdad to negotiate but got nowhere. He reported back to the Security Council, which passed the usual anodyne resolutions of condemnation.

The Clinton administration was reaping the unfortunate harvest of years of indecision and weakness in dealing with Iraq.[14] Faced with a credibility gap, the administration apparently decided to play this round strictly by the book, as an exercise in brinkmanship. First, it sharpened its warnings. Administration officials said that the United States was ready to act alone; the president ordered a buildup of military and naval forces. In his State of the Union address, Clinton said that the "world" would not stand for Saddam's defiance: "You cannot defy the will of the world." He gained broad Republican support for strong measures, including an invasion if necessary.[15] Then the administration began to weaken its case. It admitted that even a "sustained" bombing campaign would not eliminate all weapons sites or remove Saddam; it disavowed, however, any plan for a ground invasion. Finally, the president and others kept repeating their desire for a diplomatic solution.

Secretaries Albright and Cohen embarked on missions to Europe and the Middle East to "explain" the military option. In the Senate a Tonkin Gulf–style resolution was introduced (but not immediately voted). Republicans issued tough statements advocating an invasion, but they also raised questions about the administration's lack of a clear statement of objectives. The rationale for air strikes seemed less and less convincing: the most that could be expected was to destroy "some" of Saddam's military facilities and "put his regime under heavy political stresses."[16] The dilemma was obvious: if air strikes would not be fully effective, the administration could either compromise or launch a ground invasion, which had been virtually ruled out. Finally, unnamed White House officials said that removing Saddam from power was a goal that went much further than the Clinton administration was willing to commit to.

The administration stuck to its traditional tactics: turning the military screws, increasing the rhetoric, but keeping the diplomatic door open. Every few days some new military deployment was announced, and every few days the timetable for action was extended. The president was almost pleading for a "genuine" diplomatic solution. He protested (February 5) that military action was not inevitable. While Secretary Cohen warned against any "unrealistic expectations" of the results of a bombing campaign, Republicans leaders (Newt Gingrich) were warning against "incremental timidity." The French, Turks, Russians, and members of the Arab league all sent diplomats to Baghdad; compromises plans were eventually forthcoming, but they were turned down by Washington.

Under pressure from congressional Republicans for a clearer statement of objectives, the administration struggled to find a convincing formula that justified military action even if such action would not lead to the resumption of inspections or remove Saddam Hussein. Had he acted quickly and early in the confrontation, President Clinton probably could have carried public opinion and even garnered international support. His commitment to psychological warfare and brinkmanship, however, meant that he had to build public support to demonstrate he was not bluffing. The Republicans were wary; a supportive congressional resolution was put on hold, because many preferred a different route: they wanted to recognize a government in exile and establish an insurgency rather that inaugurate a bombing campaign.

The administration finally offered a formula to the effect that the air strikes would "substantially reduce or delay" Iraq's stockpiles of chemical and biological weapons; moreover, if they were rebuilt, the United States reserved the "right" to strike again. This weak statement of objectives was a substantial retreat, which led some observers to predict Clinton would back down. The White House, however, continued to announce new troop deployments and more naval forces—the "most telegraphed punch" in history, one observer commented. It was leaked that the president had decided on a four-day, around-the-clock bombing campaign, a decision made as early as January 24.[17]

The president launched a public-relations campaign to gain support, beginning with a speech at the Pentagon in which he sought to explain the high stakes if Saddam obtained biological or chemical weapons. But he confused matters by announcing that the aim of his policy was to "seriously reduce" Saddam's ability to threaten his neighbors. Stung by criticism that its goals were confusing, the administration escalated its public-relations campaign to sell its policies.[18] Clinton's first-line national security team—Albright, Cohen, and Berger—was dispatched to Ohio State University in Columbus to participate in a televised town meeting. They got a rough reception from the audience. Suddenly it seemed that the administration was losing the public, even though the polls suggested otherwise.

Perhaps because of this adverse incident in Ohio as well as indications of lack of international support, the United States reluctantly agreed to a mission by the new UN Secretary-General, Kofi Annan, to visit Baghdad. The administration had been divided over a such mission: Albright and Berger favored it, Cohen was skeptical, and Ambassador Richardson had been opposed. American officials had blocked such a mission earlier, fearing Annan would negotiate a deal (he had said publicly that there was no need to humiliate Saddam). Faced with the likelihood that Annan would go to Baghdad despite American opposition, Clinton was won over to a new peace mission, but insisted on a written set of instructions. Annan could not negotiate, and his bottom line had to be a demand for unconditional resumption of inspections. The Security Council, however, failed to agree on any written instructions, and settled for "agreed advice."[19]

While his mission was treated in the media as a cliffhanger, in fact Secretary Albright had met secretly with Annan on Sunday, February 15, to draft his precise mandate, including the terms of a compromise settlement—"red lines," as they were called. While Annan was in Baghdad, the White House and State Department leaked details that they had reason to assume would be in the agreement.[20] Once Annan announced his agreement with Saddam (February 22), there was a sigh of relief, disguised by stern statements that the agreement would have to be tested in practice.[21] It seemed that Saddam had blinked: inspections would be resumed without restrictions, but at the same time a new administrative regime was created to supervise the inspections.

At first the Annan agreement met sharp criticism in the United States. Clinton officials insisted that the policy of containing Saddam remained unaffected. But the protestations were wearing thin; the UN Security Council refused American demands for automatic sanctions if Saddam reneged. It was increasingly apparent that the administration had no strategy for dealing with Saddam; it was rebounding from crisis to crisis, settling for one compromise after another.

American policy began to change. There was no dramatic announcement, but the signs accumulated that the old strategy of containment and confrontation was being abandoned. There was, for example, a new tilt toward Iran; the shift was justified on the grounds that while it was unlikely the United States could get rid of Saddam in any near term, courting Teheran would supposedly increase pressures on him.[22] Containment of Saddam was itself giving way to the pursuit of a semi-covert program to overthrow him. By September, Saddam broke off contact with UN inspectors. Clinton ordered retaliatory air attacks but at the very last minute, after Saddam agreed to new inspections, he called them off. His invasion soon resumed and in mid-December Clinton ordered air and missile attacks that lasted for four days. The timing of his decision to invade was criticized as an effort to engineer a crisis to save his presidency, as the attacks coincided with the House of Representatives debate on his impeachment.

The Iraq crises brought to an end the post–Cold War era. The Bush-Gorbachev coalition of 1991 had finally expired. In the UN, the lineup was the Anglo-Americans versus Russia, France, and China. So, too, had the idea of collective security finally collapsed. At the same time, the Clinton administration had to act alone. On August 21 Clinton ordered American forces to launch a cruise missile attack against a terrorist camp in Afghanistan in retaliation for the bombing of American embassies in Kenya and Tanzania; the attack proved that America could use its power, even during the president's domestic crisis. But on the whole the usefulness of American military power was limited in trying to impose the nation's will. It could not bring down Saddam; it could not dictate peace to the PLO and Israel; it could not isolate Iran. Middle East policy was an obvious candidate for an agonizing reappraisal.

NOTES

1. Evan Thomas et al., eds., *Back from the Dead* (New York: Atlantic Monthly Press, 1997), p. 1.

2. John F. Harris and Bradley Graham, "After Quick Response to Iraq," *Washington Post*, September 8, 1996; R. W. Apple Jr., "How to Slap Iraq," *New York Times*, September 2, 1996; Neil Macfarquhar, "To Baghdad, Kurd Raid Was Sure-Fire Gamble," *New York Times*, September 6, 1996.

3. Henry Kissinger, "No Objective, No Will," *Washington Post*, October 6, 1996; Jim Hoagland, "Saddam Prevailed," *Washington Post*, September 29, 1996.

4. Madeleine K. Albright, "Preserving Principle and Safeguarding Stability: United States Policy Toward Iraq," in U.S. Department of State *Dispatch*, March/April 1997.

5. Phebe Marr, "Why Saddam Hussein Craves a Crisis," *Washington Post*, November 23, 1997.

6. Walter Pincus, "Iraqi Leader Vulnerable," *Washington Post*, December 5, 1997.

7. Robert Zoellick, "Strike Hard," *Washington Post*, November 18, 1997; Zalmay Khalilzad and Paul Wolfowitz, "We Must Lead the Way in Deposing Saddam," *Washington Post*, November 9, 1997.

8. Elaine Sciolino, "Tough Questions and Shrewd Mediating," *New York Times*, November 23, 1997.

9. Ibid.

10. Barton Gellman, "New Frame of Reference for U.S." *Washington Post*, November 23, 1997.

11. Charles Krauthammer, "Munich on the Tigris," *Washington Post*, November 19, 1997, and "Deflecting the Blame," *Washington Post*, November 28, 1997; Stephen S. Rosenfeld, "Attentive to the Human Factor," *Washington Post*, November 21, 1997.

12. Douglas Jehl, "Arab Capitals Relieved," *New York Times*, November 21, 1997.

13. Jim Hoagland, "Crisis-Managing in a Fog," *Washington Post*, November 26, 1997; A. M. Rosenthal, "Time for Repairs," *New York Times*, November 25, 1997.

14. Jim Hoagland, "Serious about Saddam," *Washington Post*, January 28, 1998.

15. William Kristol and Robert Kagan, "Bombing Iraq Isn't Enough," *New York Times*, January 30, 1998.

16. Editorial, "Our Allies," *Washington Post*, February 1, 1998.

17. Eric Schmitt, "White House Using Candor," *New York Times*, February 14, 1998; Michael R. Gordon and Eric Schmitt, "U.S. Plan for Iraq Envisions 4 Days of 24-Hour Bombing," *New York Times*, February 21, 1998.

18. Elaine Sciolino, "U.S. Builds Its Case on Shifting Assertions," *New York Times*, February 15, 1998; Peter W. Rodman, "Show Business," *National Review*, March 9, 1998.

19. James Traub, "Kofi Annan's Next Test," *New York Times Magazine*, March 29, 1998.

20. Michael R. Gordon and Elaine Sciolino, "Fingerprints on Iraqi Accord Belong to Albright," *New York Times*, February 25, 1998.

21. Editorial, "Iraq: Future Policy," *The Nation*, March 16, 1998.

22. Thomas Friedman, "Let's Play," *New York Times*, June 9, 1998.

14

Crisis Management

Every administration has had its share of crises. How well the president and his colleagues handle a crisis is often a measure of the entire presidency. The Cuban missile crisis is the obvious example, but there are crises that have been spread over a number of years. Vietnam is the obvious example of that test. In retrospect, an administration is judged not only by its conduct but by its responsibility for provoking crises: whether it could have acted differently and averted a crisis or changed its outcome.

The two crises in Asia during Clinton's second term fell into a mixed category: perhaps both challenges might have been avoided, and certainly both could have been handled much better. Both challenged the stability of Asia, which was the watchword of the Clinton administration. From the first months, the Clinton administration argued that American engagement would contribute to Asian stability and that if the entire region remained stable, prosperity would grow, American businesses would flourish, and democracy would progress, perhaps even in China.

ASIAN FINANCES

By the autumn of 1997, such optimistic evaluations seemed pathetically naive. Asia was overwhelmed by a severe financial and economic crisis. The "Asian tigers" were sick. Japan's economy was staggering. The "Asian way" and "Asian values," which had been tirelessly cited to American statesmen for most of the 1990s, seemed almost burlesques of reality.

The financial crisis should have been foreseen and could have been mitigated, if not avoided altogether. The Mexican bailout two years earlier should have been a warning; indeed, the chairman of the Federal Reserve, Alan Greenspan, had described the Mexican crisis as only the first "casualty" of the new international financial system. On the other hand, Secretary Rubin had reassured Congress that restoring confidence in Mexico would "head off the spread of financial distress around the world" (January 25, 1995). He was quite wrong, of course. IMF officials later admitted that for over a year they had been concerned about the economic situation in Thailand, but in November 1996 the IMF reports were praising South Korea's "enviable fiscal record."[1] American bankers, with the advantage of hindsight, claimed that they had been concerned since the spring of 1997. After the crisis broke Greenspan said that the potential risks should have been "spotted earlier and addressed."[2]

The promise of an American bailout, should trouble occur, encouraged investors and bankers to run irresponsible risks. The leaders of the world's major economies, meeting as the G-7, agreed in June 1995 that a new plan was needed to deal with future crises. Of course, as with many of the G-7's pronouncements, nothing special was done.

The Asian crisis demonstrated the failure of the Clinton administration's and the G-7's post-Mexican bailout policies. Under prodding by the United States, the international community had informally agreed to three prescriptions: that all countries should share more data about their financial situations; that the central banks should be prepared to act more quickly in making emergency funds available; and finally, that the IMF should take the lead, with national governments backing the IMF. The preference for an IMF leading role was consistent with President Clinton's warning that the United States could not act as the lender of first resort. It also reflected the political judgment that Congress would resist any future financial bailouts.

These prescriptions proved unreliable. Far from sharing data, banks in Thailand concealed their deteriorating position for months if not years. Most observers accordingly remained enthusiastic about Asia as an investment opportunity right up to the crisis.[3] Even Robert Rubin, the father of the idea of sharing more information, admitted that the post-Mexico "rules" of disclosure had failed.

The crisis broke in Thailand and then spread to Malaysia, the Philippines, Indonesia, Korea, and—ultimately—to Japan. At first the experts brushed aside the Thai crisis as a run on shaky banks. Many economists believed that the Thai economy was badly in need of reform, and they argued against propping up a faulty system. This was the prevailing sentiment in

Washington, where little attention was paid to Thailand.[4] American experts insisted what was happening was a short-term run on local banks rather than a long-term crisis of regional growth.[5] Washington's position was in part disingenuous. American officials—especially Rubin and Greenspan—wanted to force reforms in Asia and pressed the IMF to set stringent terms for loans to Thailand.

The Clinton administration seemed catatonic, insisting that everything would turn out all right. The United States did not begin to stir even after the contagion reached Indonesia. At that point Washington agreed to a three-billion-dollar commitment, but it was a political token. The IMF insisted on a series of stringent reforms; after some resistance President Suharto had to agree, under strong pressure from the United States. The IMF subsequently acknowledged in a "confidential" report that its rescue strategy had backfired, causing a bank panic that actually inflamed the crisis.[6] After the initial Indonesian bailout, the head of the World Bank, James Wolfensohn, announced that the "worst was over." Early in the crisis, President Clinton had even described it as a "few glitches in the road."[7]

It was already very late in the game when the crisis spread to Korea, the world's eleventh-largest economy. Any bailout for Korea therefore would be massive. The depth and speed of the Korean collapse surprised and shocked the Clinton administration, the IMF, and the international markets. Nevertheless Rubin, supported by Greenspan, stuck to his hard line against bailing out weak institutions. In a speech on December 2, Greenspan argued that it was high time to stop protecting banks in developing countries from the forces of the market.

The situation was too critical for such academic theorizing. Korea was only days away from a complete collapse and repudiation of debts, which of course would have included debts owed large American banks. Even Rubin could not maintain the aloofness he had affected during the IMF intervention in Thailand and Indonesia. To improve the IMF's offer to Korea, Rubin announced that the United States would put up funds, but still only as a "second line of defense." He assured his audiences that the American funds would not be used, that not even the whole IMF package would be needed. The outcome was a fifty-six-billion-dollar rescue. In February, the number-two official at the IMF, Stanley Fischer, a former MIT professor, said that there could be a few more hiccups, but that the "worst was over." He could not have been more mistaken.

Rubin insisted that the Korean-IMF agreement was a strong one, supported by the "second line of defense" of other countries; in fact, both the first and second lines of defense had already crumbled. The crisis escalated, and at this point secretaries Albright and Cohen finally bestirred themselves and tried to convince Rubin to do something. Private U.S. banks also began to put pressure on the Clinton administration and to discuss their own bailout plans. The major American banks affected by the crisis were J. P. Morgan, Chase Manhattan, and Citicorp. As later studies would demonstrate, the banks themselves had panicked, trying to cut their losses and thereby contributing to the crisis.[8] Their involvement was a critical turning point, because bringing in the private banks allowed the administration to claim that some of the burden was being borne by the "rich" bankers whose loans the IMF and Treasury were trying to save.

Nevertheless, the crisis continued. At long last, Rubin decided to act. He met with Alan Greenspan on December 18; they finally decided that Washington had to become a front-line player and give up its pretense of remaining in the second line. Rubin proposed accelerated U.S. loans, on the condition that the private banks would negotiate a restructuring of their own loans to Korea. Clinton approved the package, and the announcement was made by Rubin on December 24. The Clinton administration had executed a complete about-face.

There were heavy casualties from this crisis. Suharto had second thoughts about the stringent IMF terms and was toying with setting up a currency board to lock in exchange rates; in private telephone calls on February 13, Clinton and the IMF chief Michel Camdessus threatened to halt aid if he proceeded with his currency board. Suharto was obviously paying a price for being a military dictator, compared to the soft treatment of Korea, where former dissident Kim Dae Jung had been elected president. Secretary Albright called for political reforms in Indonesia, on the grounds that economic stability would not be restored without political stability. Clinton's comments bordered on outright silliness as advice for a leader besieged by violent demonstrations: Clinton suggested Suharto "open a dialogue with all elements of the society." The London *Economist* in an editorial urged the withdrawal of the IMF package—"no matter what"—if Suharto did not bend to the IMF's demands.[9] Washington would not go quite that far, but an American official hinted that IMF assistance would be withheld. The left wing in Congress joined in the attack. Senator Paul Wellstone said that American "silence" was a betrayal: "We have to be on the side of the students." Senator John F. Kerry (D-Massachusetts) said the message should be simple and direct: "President Suharto has got to go."[10] The *Washington Post* editorialized (May 20) that "Mr. Suharto has run out his string and should be replaced promptly by the popular choice." (How such a "popular choice" would be selected was never explained.) Suharto resigned on May 24, 1998. The World Bank then promptly agreed to a rescheduling of Indonesian debts. The Clinton administration now completely reversed its position of only a few days earlier. Having undermined Suharto and in effect encouraged the political upheaval, it now took the position that the most important step in economic recovery would be political "stability."

The international financial system itself, especially the IMF, was also a casualty. Rubin was criticized not for his disastrous hesitation early in the crisis but for trying to save private American investors. He claimed that he would not spend a "nickel" to help investors, but he did acknowledge that it was virtually impossible to save Korea from default without saving those who had invested there. Helping investors and creditors was therefore a "byproduct," he said. Clinton also lamely admitted that he hated to see the bankers "get their money back, plus a profit," but failing to subsidize the Asians would have led to a worse crisis.[11] Not surprisingly, the bailouts came under attack in Congress. Influential congressmen and senators complained that the Clinton administration seemed bent on reimbursing Wall Street's losses at the taxpayers' expense.

In this hostile atmosphere the administration proposed to increase the overall funding for the IMF by eighteen billion dollars; it ran into a buzz saw of opposition. It did not help that new crises were forecast. The president of the World Bank predicted that in "five or seven years" there would be another crisis that "we don't anticipate." Alan Greenspan went further, suggesting that the virulent episodes in Mexico and Asia might be a defining characteristic of the "new high-tech international financial system." In other words, the system "may fail" and future crises were inevitable.[12] Such prominent observers as George Shultz claimed that the promise of massive intervention by the IMF had spurred a global meltdown: the IMF was "ineffective, unnecessary and obsolete," Shultz and coauthors William Simon and Walter Wriston argued.[13] Shultz testified to Congress that the world's financial system would work better without the IMF. Politicians Steve Forbes and Jack Kemp were also highly critical of the IMF's conduct. Reagan's chief economic advisor, Martin Feldstein, attacked the IMF for trying to impose on recipients fundamental changes in economic policy not necessary to deal with the immediate crisis.[14] A *Wall Street Journal* editorial (May 7, 1998) agreed that Rubin had failed to make his case for the IMF.

The third casualty was Japan. It was faced with a banking crisis of the sort that the United States had endured with the collapse of its savings and loan industry. Japan would have to bail out its banking system and use public monies to do so; the estimated cost was staggering, about three hundred billion dollars. At the same time, Japan faced an even more basic crisis, as the economic stagnation of 1992 lengthened into a major recession that would require a major stimulus to reverse. By the late spring of 1998 Japan had officially slipped into recession, the first in twenty-three years. The yen fell to record lows, 44 percent against the dollar compared to early 1995. Once again Rubin's bizarre behavior seemed to provoke a crisis. In comments to Congress on June 11 he implied that the United States would not intervene to support the yen; the currency markets virtually collapsed. On June 17 he completely reversed himself: the United States was forced to buy yen on the open market for the first time in more than six years. Clinton announced that this action was the result of a telephone conversation with Prime Minister Hashimoto and was conditioned on Japanese "reforms." There was considerable speculation that Rubin had deliberately driven down the yen, to increase pressure on Tokyo to agree to American-proposed reforms.[15]

The hectoring of Japan seemed particularly hypocritical to certain seasoned American observers. Lawrence B. Lindsey, who had served on the Federal Reserve Board, wrote that at the very time the United States was bragging about ending its own deficit, it was urging Japan to increase its deficit spending: "The administration's lectures on how the Japanese should behave in their fiscal affairs contrasts markedly with the same administrations' rhetoric and behavior in its own fiscal conduct."[16]

American officials, having bungled the Asian crisis, were not reluctant to press Japan with constant advice, which of course was resented in Tokyo. Washington bragged that President Clinton had taken Hashimoto to the "woodshed" in insisting that he restart the Japanese economy. In April Washington revealed a "blunt" private letter from Clinton to Hashimoto. The chances that Japan would open its markets as American officials kept insisting was obviously and increasingly remote. Six years of pressure from Washington had made little impact on the American trade balance, which became worse as the impact of the financial crisis was felt. The Deputy Secretary of the Treasury, Lawrence Summers, openly derided the Japanese administration for engaging in "virtual policy." Japanese officials, who had been reacting to American pressure, now grew increasingly offended and began to speak out. The Clinton administration finally admitted that its "jawboning" had exhausted its influence in Tokyo.[17] The conventional wisdom was that the government of Hashimoto would hold off decisive action until after the elections of July 12, which the LDP was expected to win easily. In fact, it suffered a humiliating defeat. Hashimoto immediately resigned and was eventually replaced by his foreign minister, Keizo Obuchi. It was a defeat for Clinton as well. American harassment and badgering of Japan had not produced a plan for economic revival but had contributed to the political turmoil. Japanese officials insisted that the United States, in its obsession with economics, had failed to appreciate the nuances and complexities of changing politics in Japan. Obuchi, for example, pointed out to American reporters that the United States had pulled out of the Great Depression in the 1930s by increasing defense spending; he insisted he would not consider such an option and pledged to take whatever measures necessary but short of a "wartime economy." His allusion to defense spending was obviously a riposte to American complaints that Japan was not doing enough to stimulate its economy. Now Clinton faced both an economic and political crisis.

Thus, the foundations of American policy for Asia and for the international economy were badly damaged. Clinton administration officials badly mismanaged the rolling crisis. They were slow and late in recognizing its seriousness. How they could have missed the accumulated warning signs is simply inexplicable. Once it saw them, the administration was hesitant and indecisive in responding. Its remedies were weak and inadequate. The net result was that far greater funds were required than if the government had undertaken preventive action earlier.

The Clinton administration abdicated its responsibilities, allowing fundamental political decisions to be made by international banking bureaucrats. Asians were dismayed by Washington's passivity until so late in the Korean emergency. There were suspicions that the United States welcomed the crisis, as a way to wring out weak banks and institutions. There was a palpable rise in anti-American sentiment. To some in Asia it seemed obvious that America was imposing austerity measures to protect its own investors and to enable American banks and firms to buy failing Asian firms at rock-bottom prices.

The financial crisis threatened the very stability that American policy makers had sought. Allowing the Asian crises to slide was extremely shortsighted. Thailand had been one of America's few allies in the Vietnam War; Suharto had stabilized a volatile and radicalized Indonesia; and South Korea was, after all, one of the few countries that might embroil the United States in a shooting war. Neglect of the political aspects was a major failure of secretaries Cohen and Albright.

It would be months, if not years, before the final verdict was in. The direct price for the bailout was at least a hundred billion dollars and climbing. The geopolitical price was likely to be much higher. The Pacific Century was over.

INDIA

If the financial crisis caught Washington largely unawares, so too did the next crisis. The second Asian crisis—the explosion of nuclear weapons by India—was as serious as the financial crisis, if not more so. India's actions answered one overriding post–Cold War question: had the nuclear age ended with the Cold War? India provided the stunning answer on May 11, 1998, when it exploded three nuclear "devices" underground at a test site near the village of Khetlai, in the Thar desert of northwestern India: a fission explosion, a low-yield device, and one thermonuclear test (about forty-three kilotons, considered relatively "small"). One Indian spokesman, an aide to the new prime minister Atal Bihari Vajpayee, said that India had a "proven capability for a weaponized nuclear program." Vajpayee put it better in an interview: "We have the capacity for a big bomb now." Although Vajpayee had campaigned as a Hindu nationalist, vowing to test atomic weapons, the actual test came as a shock to the international community, except for Pakistan, which had warned the United States and expressed its dismay at the naivete of the Western world. The Pakistani warning had reportedly been brushed off as a case of "jitters."

The United States found itself in a bind. Two years earlier it had headed off a similar test, and a Hindu nationalist government had fallen before its plan could be carried out. This time there was adequate intelligence, but the analytical system collapsed; the White House was taken by surprise. Clinton was indignant, because he believed that he had been lied to by Indian officials, who had assured American representatives that no tests were planned. Clinton had no choice but to invoke economic sanction against India, as mandated by law.

On the whole, American reaction was negative. Senator Jesse Helms even went so far as to say that India's action "clearly constitutes an emerging nuclear threat to the territory of the United States." On the other hand, Newt Gingrich pointed to the contrast between Clinton's outrage against India, a democracy, and his complacency toward the Chinese dictatorship. A *New York Times* editorial (May 13, 1998) was almost hysterical: "For a paltry and short-lived domestic gain, India now faces a ruinous cutoff in foreign aid, a self-defeating arms race with Pakistan and isolation even from its friends."

Clinton was also criticized for not having anticipated the tests and having trusted too much in Indian reassurances. He was also attacked for fueling the India-Pakistan arms race by courting China and pursuing a soft response to repeated violations of the nonproliferation regime by Russia and China.[18] The *Times* of India editorialized that by the time the United States woke up to what it called the Pakistan–North Korean–Chinese axis it would have been too late for India.[19] One Indian spokesman attacked the United States for sitting on a mountain of nuclear weapons and "pontificating" to India and the world. There was even some sympathy for India's security dilemma, confronted as it was by one nuclear power, China, and another potential power in Pakistan. Secretary Albright's proclamation of a new Chinese-American strategic "partnership" no doubt encouraged the Indians to proceed with their tests. But the Indian motive also reflected a growing trend of nationalism. While President Clinton complained that it was unnecessary for India to test to manifest their national greatness, Indians claimed that in fact the test gave India *shakti*, a Hindu term meaning power and respect. There were two more tests on May 13.

Clinton was disturbed and deeply disappointed by the Indians, but attention quickly shifted to Pakistan. Would Pakistan follow suit, especially after the second set of Indian tests? The Clinton administration made a major effort to head off a Pakistani test; a special team led by Deputy Secretary of State Strobe Talbott was dispatched to Pakistan. Clinton called the Pakistani prime minister three times. The G-8 meetings in England appealed for restraint, but because of Russian (a new member added to the G-7) and French dissent no strong condemnation was forthcoming despite vigorous lobbying by Clinton. "Frankly," Yeltsin said in Moscow on May 13, "India is a very good friend of ours." In any case, Clinton's efforts were futile gestures: what Pakistan wanted was an ironclad security guarantee from a nuclear power. Clinton would not and could not give such a guarantee. Pakistan turned to China with the same objective. There was speculation that China might sponsor a multilateral guarantee that nuclear powers would not attack nonnuclear powers. But after several days of talks, China too declined to make a commitment.[20]

So on May 28 Pakistan exploded several atomic devices (five tests were announced in Islamabad, but American experts were skeptical of that total number, because one test may have been a failure). A single additional test was conducted on May 30. Pakistan's rationale was like India's highly nationalistic, but it was shrewdly couched in strategic terminology designed to appeal to the West: its tests had restored the "strategic balance" and were intended to "deter aggression, be it nuclear or conventional." Pakistani officials credited Clinton with having made the right arguments but complained that the international community had been "filing its fingernails" after the Indian tests. Pakistan announced on June 11 a moratorium on further testing.

Nevertheless, the outcome was a humiliation for Clinton. He could not muster an international coalition, and his unilateral efforts had been in vain. Indeed, his statements showed naivete. He claimed that India was repeating the "worst mistake" of the twentieth century—an odd remark for a nuclear power that had deterred war for over fifty years. He also claimed that the world was moving away from nuclear weapons—which was scarcely the case in Iraq, North Korea, Libya, India, and Pakistan. Observers countered that proliferation was a reality, to be regulated and moderated by political means, including an attempt to resolve the old Indo-Pakistani dispute over Kashmir. But this ignored China: it was China that India designated its number-one potential enemy. The Clinton administration's response, beyond mandatory sanctions, was to insist on U.S. Senate ratification of the Comprehensive Test Ban Treaty (CTBT). The failure of the Senate to ratify that treaty was embarrassing, but ratification was scarcely likely to deal with the fundamental problems of geopolitics and nationalism, the moving forces behind proliferation.

The tests by India and Pakistan unleashed a torrent of warnings and worry throughout the world. Initially at least there was the widespread conclusion that the world had become more dangerous, that the "prospect of nuclear war was once again real."[21] The UN Security Council demanded an end to any further testing, a demand that India dismissed as "grotesque" coming from five nuclear powers. There was widespread fallout for American policy. The probability that China had helped Pakistan over the years was cited in renewed attacks on Clinton's China policy. In the one other location where there was a palpable nuclear danger, Korea, the reaction was baffling. The new South Korean president, Kim Dae Jung, called on Washington to relax sanctions against North Korea and adopt a policy of "reciprocity" in order to move toward reconciliation. But North Korea, true to its reputation, brazenly announced that it had sold missile components to other countries and intended to keep doing so.

Asia was clearly entering a new era of increased turmoil. Nationalism was emerging as the major threat to American interests. America's commitment to stability as the precondition for prosperity and democracy was a wreck, as was the policy of giving priority to commercial and economic interests.[22] Indeed, it was difficult to imagine a worse combination than massive economic recession and nuclear proliferation—two threats that might have been averted by skillful and prescient diplomacy.

NOTES

1. Paul Blustein, "At the IMF, a Struggle Shrouded in Secrecy," *Washington Post*, March 30, 1998.

2. Richard Stevenson, "Greenspan Urges More Attention," *New York Times*, December 3, 1997.

3. Brett D. Fromson, "The Lionized Tigers," *Washington Post*, January 11, 1998.

4. Clay Chandler, "Critics Challenge IMF," *Washington Post*, November 29, 1997.

5. Steven Radelet and Jeffery Sachs, "Asia's Bright Future," *Foreign Affairs*, November/December 1997.

6. David E. Sanger, "I.M.F. Now Admits Tactics in Indonesia Deepened the Crisis," *New York Times*, January 14, 1998.

7. Paul Blustein, "President Upbeat About Asian Economic Woes," *Washington Post*, November 24, 1997.

8. Edmund Andrews, "Study Shows How World Banks Panicked," *New York Times*, January 30, 1998.

9. "Asia's Coming Explosions," *Economist*, February 21, 1998.

10. David E. Sanger, "Halting Loans Isn't Enough," *New York Times*, May 19, 1998.

11. Steven Pearlstein, "Administration Urges New Bailout," *Washington Post*, January 22, 1998, and "On the Table," *Washington Post*, January 30, 1998.

12. Alan Greenspan, Testimony before the House Committee on Banking and Financial Services, January 30, 1998, in *Federal Reserve Bulletin*, March 1998; Jeff Gerth and Richard Stevenson, "Poor Oversight," *New York Times*, December 22, 1997; Paul Blustein, "IMF Seeks to Be More," *Washington Post*, April 18, 1998.

13. George P. Shultz, William E. Simon, and Walter B. Wriston, "Who Needs the IMF?" *Wall Street Journal*, February 3, 1998.

14. Martin Feldstein, "Refocusing the IMF," *Foreign Affairs*, March/April 1998.

15. Jonathan Fuerbringer, "Deliberately Or Not, Rubin Set Up a Fall," *New York Times*, June 18, 1998.

16. Lawrence B. Lindsey, "Clinton to Japan: Do As I Say," *Wall Street Journal*, May 6, 1998.

17. Stephanie Strom, "Ruffled, Japan Advises U.S.: Mind Your Own Business," *New York Times*, April 9, 1998; David E. Sanger, "Adrift in Japan's Sea of Unknown Intentions," *New York Times*, June 16, 1998.

18. Charles Krauthammer, "Clinton's China Grovel," *Washington Post*, June 5, 1998; Michael Kelley, "To Be Ignored," *Washington Post*, May 13, 1998.

19. Henry Sokolski, "A Blast of Reality," *New York Times*, May 13, 1998.

20. John Pomfret, "Pakistani-Chinese Talks," *Washington Post*, May 20, 1998.

21. R. W. Apple Jr., "Wake-Up Call: Truisms of U.S. Policy Totter," *New York Times*, May 30, 1998.

22. Ibid.

15

Between Hope
and History

William Jefferson Clinton enjoyed a unique opportunity. When he was inaugurated on January 20, 1993, he became the first post–Cold War president. Unlike his predecessors, he faced no serious foreign threats; he was relatively free to reconstruct America's role in the world. Unfortunately, he demonstrated little interest in foreign affairs, leaving too much of it to his subordinates. They in turn hijacked his foreign policy in the name of a neo-Wilsonian internationalism, and for more than two years they engineered a series of failures and disasters. To both foreign and domestic audiences his performance seemed erratic and raised doubts about his credibility, doubts that complicated relations with his allies and adversaries. Shifting with the winds of popular opinion, he executed a remarkable public reversal, saying in effect that it was time to drop the "abstractions and dogma" and pursue a policy based on "trial and error." This conversion from idealism to trial and error became the story of his foreign policy.

During his tenure the post–Cold War transition ended. In that transition Clinton had to confront the basic questions that would define the next historical period: (1) How would the United States relate to a world that was increasingly complex and complicated, but far less threatening? (2) How would the United States relate to an international economic structure that, though built largely by the United States after World War II, was now increasingly global and perhaps more threatening? (3) How would the United States relate to a world of nuclear weapons that seemed likely to spread, despite the end of the Cold War, and might once again become a threat to American security?

These were fundamental questions, but the answers were never really in doubt. The United States would remain globally involved, as the dominant political, economic, and military power. For a time, however, it seemed that the new administration would reorient the geostrategic focus of American policy. In both Europe and Asia there were apprehensions over American intentions. To Asians, Clinton seemed preoccupied with NATO and Russia; to Europeans, however, Clinton seemed obsessed with correcting trade imbalances and opening Asian markets. Clinton's willingness to fight for NAFTA supported a notion that the treaty might well be the first move toward a new architecture of American policy. Finally, to both Europeans and Asians, Clinton seemed to elevate internationalism over America's regional commitments; his policy of assertive multilateralism in the United Nations contributed to the idea that the focus of American policy was changing.[1]

In the end, American policy was not reoriented. By the end of Clinton's first term, many of the uncertainties had been dispelled. America would remain first and foremost a European power, and there was a contingent of American combat troops in the Balkans to prove it. In Asia, however, there was no NATO to anchor American security policy. Relations with both Japan and China inevitably deteriorated, in part because there was no longer a strategic context for these links, and in part because policy was increasingly affected by domestic American politics. Year after year American trade imbalances grew, and year after year the Clinton administration attacked the culprits—mainly Japan, and to a lesser extent China. The administration's obsession with commercial interests and with its own popularity made it virtually impossible to conduct a policy based on geopolitics. Ironically, it would be the quest for commercial advantage in the China market that undermined Clinton's policy of "engagement."

The Clinton achievement most likely to define his legacy was the expansion of NATO to include three new Eastern members. This brought the old Atlantic alliance to an end and opened a new chapter in the historic saga of European security. It signified that the United States would remain committed to Europe beyond the Cold War. It was the creation of NATO that had marked the definitive end to American isolationism in 1948–1949, and it was the expansion of NATO that marked the end of any temptation toward a new disengagement from Europe.

But still unanswered was yet another major historical question, perhaps equally important—would Russia be drawn into the new European system or once again remain outside of it, as a potential predator? Relations with Russia deteriorated after an initial high point in 1993–1994. The Clinton administration gambled that it could reconcile Russia to the expansion of a military alliance directed against it, and that it could do so without jeopardizing the prospects for Russian democracy. However, Clinton's projected "strategic partnership" with Boris Yeltsin gradually disintegrated, partly because of the conflict over NATO and European security, partly because of the revival of Russian nationalism, and partly over the absence of timely and effective Western economic assistance. On balance, the future of Russia was never up to Clinton, but America had a great deal of influence and leverage. His Russian experts recognized the limits and opportunities, but they played their strong hand erratically.

The post–Cold War period ended more or less where it had begun—in Iraq. Saddam Hussein posed a prolonged test of Clinton's national security policy. The periodic crises over Iraq undermined and finally ended the hopes for an international security system based on a new United Nations. Saddam's repeated challenges gradually split the Gulf War coalition. It was not so much a question of Saddam's craftiness as a matter of growing resistance to American dominance. Two critical allies, France and Russia, moved into virtual opposition to American hegemony. So too some of the Arab states that had been favorable to the United States edged toward neutrality. Too often Clinton found himself isolated. Thus, the policy pursued since the Gulf War had run its course, and so too had the post–Cold War period.

More serious perhaps than the tactical maneuvering, was Clinton's strategic failure to persuade his friends and allies that the issue with Saddam—the proliferation of sophisticated weapons—was not merely a regional quarrel but a fundamentally serious international challenge. The Indian and Pakistani nuclear tests finally provided an international wake-up call, but they came very late in the game. Key international players, Russia and China, had flirted for years with proliferation. There was also another aspect to these tests that the United States had been slow to recognize: it was not until after his reelection that Clinton acknowledged that the real threat to international stability was not neo-isolationism but a virulent nationalism in a world of proliferating nuclear weapons. It was disconcerting that at century's end the most likely nuclear war was one not between the two nuclear giants that had adopted some rules of engagement, but between two poor, backward countries with no strategic experience. The era that had begun in Hiroshima would not end with the Cold War.

Even if the world had been a far more placid place, the Asian financial crisis would have ended the post–Cold War transition. The conventional wisdom had been that after the Cold War the balance of power would be replaced by the balance of accounts. For several years these predictions turned out to be misleading. Japan and Germany gradually dwindled into second-rate powers, barely able to cope with their own economic problems, let alone play a major international role. Then, Asia was engulfed by a huge financial crisis. In effect, the crisis confirmed America's dominance of the international economy. As the Asian crisis developed into a global crisis, it also signaled the beginning of the end of the international economic order created by the United States at the end of World War II, one based on the IMF and other international structures. Clearly, those institutions would have to be either drastically reformed or abandoned. Even free trade seemed a relic of forlorn hopes. The Asian financial crisis therefore became a huge black cloud: it threatened Russia and Latin America and pointed up the increasing vulnerability of the American economy. Thus, foreign affairs, which Clinton had initially disdained, were becoming a serious threat to his legacy of a long run of domestic prosperity.

Another international pillar of the Clinton presidency was the enlargement of democracy. This policy too produced no significant breakthroughs. Reeling from the disaster in Somalia, the administration virtually ignored a horrible bloodbath in Rwanda; supported in Zaire the rebellion of Laurence Kabila, a man whose record of atrocities rivaled that of Pol Pot; and tolerated military dictatorships elsewhere in Africa. In Russia, antidemocratic extremists on the right and left were in the majority, and in Ukraine the communists scored impressive electoral victories. Throughout the Middle East the United States tolerated and befriended antidemocratic regimes. Finally, of course, the administration paid only lip service to the advance of democracy in China. To be sure, the the broad trend toward democracy is stronger near the end of Clinton's tenure, but only in one country had the United States effected change—Haiti.

Of course, Clinton had not been elected to be the world's policeman, as he kept reminding the American public. It was probably just as well, because from the outset Clinton was a prisoner of his own instinctive aversion to the use of military force; the administration invariably preferred various forms of economic or political sanctions. But behind the scenes, American officials, including Clinton, treated sanctions as window dressing or evaded their imposition, even in cases mandated by law. Clinton privately explained that he needed a certain flexibility in deciding how and when to impose sanctions. This, of course, was what all of his predecessors had claimed, but they had done so in the name of realpolitik, not ideology. Averse to the use of force and reluctant to enforce harsh sanctions, Clinton found time and again that he had little leverage.

As his second term unfolded, Clinton seemed mesmerized by his place in history. He cited both Thomas Jefferson and Theodore Roosevelt as his models, while noting that they had had conflicting philosophies. Clinton had shown a particular affinity for Jefferson; he had visited Monticello just before his own inauguration in 1993 and had ostentatiously retraced Jefferson's route from Monticello to Washington for his inauguration in 1801. Jefferson's concept of an empire of liberty found an echo in Clinton's enlargement of democracies.

Clinton explained that his newfound admiration for Theodore Roosevelt was because the times were most like the turn of the last century, and Roosevelt had shaped an era of dramatic change without the catalyst of a war. The first Roosevelt had made a major change in the way people worked, lived, and related to each other and to the rest of the world: that is what Clinton hoped would be his own legacy.[2] Critics, however, doubted that Clinton had an agenda to match his Rooseveltian ambitions: what had characterized Theodore Roosevelt was his willingness to run large risks—almost the opposite of Clinton's style.[3]

Clinton's historical musings were an interesting manipulation of symbols. Traversing from the idealism of Jefferson and Wilson to the realism of Roosevelt, from a visionary to an activist, was quite a switch. During his first term, however, Clinton had damaged the idea of realistic foreign policy that Theodore Roosevelt had symbolized. Too often the first Clinton administration had glorified internationalism and mulilateralism, the UN and collective security, and the necessity of achieving a moral consensus while scoffing at such crude concepts as the balance of power. Too often had Clinton tailored his foreign policy to popular opinion, which he mistakenly believed was the foundation of a legitimate foreign policy.

It is not easy to strike a balance sheet of Clinton's foreign policy. Too many large question marks hover over his major achievements and his presidency. Understandably, however, uncertainty is the hallmark of transitional periods. Moreover, as for most presidents, it might be years before a clean verdict can be rendered. One observer has compared Clinton to Harry Truman and Warren Harding.[4] Truman left office under a barrage of criticism, but decades later he ranked among the truly great leaders; Harding died a popular president, but his legacy was scandal, isolationism, and ultimately a worldwide depression.

The influence of the United States declined under Clinton, but it was bound to decline from the high point of 1989–1991 and the end of communism in Europe. The decline was neither precipitous nor fatal; for the foreseeable future America will remain the only superpower. More serious than the loss of influence was the erosion of the president's moral authority, a decline that undermined American leadership in foreign affairs. Fortunately, international politics was no longer the infamous zero-sum game of the Cold War, in which any and every American loss was an automatic gain for its adversaries and enemies.

President Clinton is a transitional figure wedged between the end of the Cold War and the beginning of a new century. The historian Alan Brinkley noted that the president who actually presided over the turn of the last century was William McKinley, not Roosevelt. Unless Clinton could find a way to challenge the "dreary ethos" of his own era, Brinkley concluded, Clinton would be likely to close the century in the same undistiguished way as McKinley.[5]

After the elections of 1996, an interesting poll was taken of a group of American historians, who were asked to rate all the presidents (Lincoln, Washington, and FDR were rated at the very top).[6] Arthur Schlesinger, who had supervised the poll, took stock of Clinton: "a rare combination of talents and infirmities." On the one hand, he was man of "penetrating intelligence," who could master complicated issues, and a skilled and resilient political leader with a genuine intellectual curiosity. On the other hand, Schlesinger wrote, he lacked self-discipline, his judgment of people was "erratic," and his resilience struck many observers as "flagrant opportunism." (These observations came well before the House of Representatives voted on impeachment in December 1998.)

In that 1996 poll, Clinton was lodged in a category of "average (low)," along with Reagan, Bush, Ford, and Carter. Other polls of historians ranked him lower, though mainly because of personal scandals, not his foreign policy. He was judged to be essentially a status-quo president, riding a strong economy and a bull market in stocks, putting off tough issues for his successors. In the Schlesinger poll, Norman Graebner, a diplomatic historian at the University of Virginia, found Clinton flawed but possessed of some "good qualities of leadership." Another diplomatic historian, Walter MacDougal, brushed Clinton aside as a complete failure, for making a "hash" of his policies toward Asia and Europe and destroying the morale and preparedness of the armed forces.[7] A harsh judgment was also rendered by the distinguished professor of American history Forrest McDonald. He conceded that with end of the Cold War America no longer needed the kind of leadership that had been necessary during the preceding five decades, but he concluded nevertheless that Clinton's presidency was "more corrupt" than those of Grant and Harding combined. Clinton himself, he argued, was "more deceitful than any of his predecessors." The significance of Clinton's "chronic mendacity," according to McDonald, was that it would be difficult for Americans to trust their presidents for a long time to come.[8]

Despite such indictments of his administration, Clinton remained popular. After a shaky start in his first two years, Clinton absorbed much of George Bush's prudence and Robert Dole's savvy. His ratings in popular opinion polls remained strong; the approval rating of his conduct of foreign policy was about 60 percent well into 1998. This was not surprising, because what distinguished Clinton was his near-obsession with doing the popular thing. The public wanted American leadership, and Clinton gave it to them—but too sporadically and often too hesitantly.

In the end, Clinton adopted foreign policies that could be grouped under the rubric of selective engagement, again not unlike Bush or Dole. Selectivity, however, required criteria for defining the national interest. This was Clinton's weak point. He was not temperamentally or intellectually geared to such a complex task. In the absence of an overall perspective, most issues were bound to degenerate into tactical manipulations, some successful some not. Clinton stumbled from crisis to crisis, trying to figure out what was popular, what would be effective, and what choices would pose the lowest risk to his presidency, and, especially, to his reputation. After some years when he seemed to be "floundering, reacting rather than imposing American leadership on world events," there were reports that Clinton had become much more comfortable and confident in the handling of foreign and defense policies.[9] But he also faced the jinx of a second term. Rarely in American history has a president enjoyed a successful second term, at home or abroad. Bill Clinton was no exception.

No one could have foreseen just how severe that second term jinx would turn out to be. By the end of 1998, President Clinton was impeached by the House and faced a Senate trial. Whatever the outcome of the crisis, the institution of the presidency had already been badly damaged. If the Cold War created the imperial presidency, the post–Cold War period resulted in new limits on the office, caused by Clinton's impeachment and a series of confrontations that led to court decisions significantly weakening the president's powers and prerogatives (e.g., the president could be sued while still in office; the claim of executive privilege was diluted).[10]

At first the weakening of the presidency applied more to domestic powers than to the conduct of foreign affairs. When Clinton ordered a retaliatory air strike against a terrorist base in Afghanistan, and then against Iraq, even though his own political crisis was intensifying, he received strong political support from the public and both political parties. Moreover, his international popularity remained strong as evidenced in the standing ovation he was accorded at the United Nations when he addressed the General Assembly on September 21, 1998. There was, nevertheless, a growing apprehension abroad that Washington's political quarrels would impair America's ability to provide international leadership—especially on such matters as the burgeoning global economic crisis.[11] Fears of an international political vacuum led some foreign critics to call for the president's resignation. ("Just go" was the headline of the *Economist's* editorial and front cover of September 19, 1998.) Some observers also noted that Secretary Albright's authority had suffered, partly because her style was wearing thin and was less effective, and partly because she lacked the support of the president on such issues as the conflict with Iraq and the Middle East negotiations.[12] All of this added to the difficulty of arriving at an objective evaluation of Clinton's foreign policies.

Even before the impeachment crisis, the second term had seemed more and more like an eerie rerun of the first.

It was George Shultz, Ronald Reagan's secretary of state, who said that the conduct of foreign policy was not one thing after another but the same thing over and over. Clinton's second term had indeed included most of the issues of the first term; Bosnia, China, Yeltsin, NATO, Middle East peace, debates on trade, and clashes with Saddam were still on the active agenda. The two chief differences were the international context and Clinton's political weaknesses. In 1993, Clinton was the leader of an unrivaled superpower; six years later he was a badly crippled lame duck, and the opportunity to mold a new international order had closed. The post–Cold War period was over. The new global order that was emerging was in many ways antagonistic to American interests and designs. A magnificent historical opportunity to shape the international system had been missed.

NOTES

1. Jim Hoagland, "Scorecard for '97," *Washington Post*, December 29, 1997.

2. "An Interview with the President," *Washington Post*, January 19, 1997.

3. Alan Brinkley, "Why Clinton Is No TR," *Newsweek*, January 27, 1997; Richard Norton Smith, "Please Stop Thinking about Tomorrow," *New York Times*, January 19, 1997.

4. Paul Wolfowitz, "Clinton's First Year," *Foreign Affairs*, January/February 1994.

5. Alan Brinkley, *Newsweek*, January 27, 1997.

6. Arthur M. Schlesinger, "The Ultimate Approval Rating," *New York Times Magazine*, December 16, 1996.

7. James Piereson, "Historians and the Reagan Legacy," *The Weekly Standard*, September 29, 1997; Walter A. MacDougal, "Rating the Presidents," *National Review*, October 27, 1997.

8. Forrest McDonald, "Unmaking the Presidency," *National Review*, March 23, 1998.

9. Steven Erlanger and David E. Sanger, "On Global Stage, Clinton's Pragmatic Turn," *New York Times*, July 29, 1996; Richard L. Berke and John M. Broder, "A Mellow Clinton at Ease," *New York Times*, December 7, 1997.

10. Arthur Schlesinger Jr., "So Much for the Imperial Presidency," *New York Times*, August 3, 1998.

11. William Greider, "Breakdown of Free Market Orthodoxy, *Washington Post*, October 7, 1998; Thomas Friedman, "Forgive and Forget," *New York Times*, August 11, 1998; Fred Hiatt, "A Nation in Retreat," and Jim Hoagland, ". . . And Counting on 'Soft power,' " *Washington Post*, August 16, 1998; Jim Hoagland, "America Undermined," *Washington Post*, August 20, 1998; George Will, "Contagious Clintonitis," *Newsweek*, August 31, 1998. See also evaluations by several commentators in *The Nation*, September 7/14, 1998, pp. 13–17.

12. Thomas W. Lippman, "Albright Loses Luster," *Washington Post*, August 30, 1998; Steven Erlanger, "Albright, a Bold Voice Abroad, Finds Her Role Limited at Home," *New York Times*, September 1, 1998; John H. Miller, "Half Bright," *National Review*, October 12, 1998.

Selected Bibliography

Armacost, Michael H. *Friends or Rivals.* New York: Columbia University Press, 1996.

Beckner, Steven K. *Back from the Brink: The Greenspan Years.* New York: John Wiley, 1996.

Brzezinski, Zbigniew. *The Grand Chessboard.* New York: HarperCollins, 1997.

Callahan, David. *Between Two Worlds.* New York: HarperCollins, 1994.

Carpenter, Ted Galen, and Barbara Conry, eds. *NATO Enlargement.* Washington, D.C.: CATO Institute, 1998.

Clarke, Walter, and Jeffrey Herbst, eds. *Learning from Somalia.* Boulder, Colo.: Westview Press, 1997.

Clemens, Clay. *NATO and the Quest for Post–Cold War Security.* New York: St. Martin's Press, 1997.

Clinton, Bill. *Between Hope and History.* New York: Random House, 1996.

Crowley, Monica. *Nixon Off the Record.* New York: Random House, 1996.

Delong, Kent, and Steven Tuckey. *Modgadishu!* Westport, Conn.: Praeger, 1994.

Dionne, E. J. *They Only Look Dead.* New York: Simon and Schuster, Touchstone edition, 1996.

Drew, Elizabeth. *On the Edge.* New York: Simon and Schuster, Touchstone edition, 1995.

———. *Showdown.* New York: Simon and Schuster, Touchstone edition, 1996.

Foreign Affairs Agenda: The New Shape of World Politics. New York: Foreign Affairs, distributed by W. W. Norton, 1997.

Garten, Jeffrey E. *The Big Ten.* New York: HarperCollins, Basic Books, 1997.

Holbrooke, Richard. *To End a War.* New York: Random House, 1998.

Huntington, Samuel P. *The Clash of Civilizations and the Remaking of World Order.* New York: Simon and Schuster, 1996.

Ishihara, Shintaro. *The Japan That Can Say No*. New York: Simon and Schuster, 1989.

Kurtz, Howard. *Spin Cycle*. New York: Free Press, 1998.

Kurzman, Dan. *Soldier of Peace: The Life of Yitzhak Rabin*. New York: HarperCollins, 1998.

Lieber, Robert J., ed. *Eagle Adrift*. New York: Longman, 1997.

Mandelbaum, Michael. *The Dawn of Peace in Europe*. New York: Twentieth Century Fund Press, 1996.

————, ed. *The New Russian Foreign Policy*. New York: Council on Foreign Relations, 1998.

Morris, Dick. *Behind the Oval Office*. New York: Random House, 1997.

Newhouse, John. *Europe Adrift*. New York: Pantheon Books, 1997.

Owen, David. *Balkan Odyssey*. New York: Harcourt Brace, 1995.

Parmet, Herbert. *George Bush*. New York: Scribner, 1998.

Reshon, Stanley A. *High Hopes*. New York: New York University Press, 1996.

Rodman, Peter W. *More Precious than Peace*. New York: Scribner's, 1994.

————. *America Adrift*. Washington, D.C.: Nixon Center for Peace and Freedom, 1996.

Savir, Uri. *The Process*. New York: Random House, 1998.

Schaller, Michael. *Altered States*. New York: Oxford University Press, 1997.

Simon, Roger. *Show Time*. New York: Random House, Times Books, 1998.

Thomas, Evan, Karen Breslau, Debra Rosenberg, Leslie Kaufman, and Andrew Muir, eds. *Back from the Dead*. New York: Atlantic Monthly Press, 1997.

Ullman, Richard H., ed. *The World and Yugoslavia's Wars*. New York: Council on Foreign Relations, 1996.

Vogel, Ezra, ed. *Living with China*. New York: W. W. Norton, 1997.

Walker, Martin. *The President We Deserve*. New York: Crown Publishers, 1996.

Woodward, Bob. *The Agenda*. New York: Simon and Schuster, 1994.

————. *The Choice*. New York: Simon and Schuster, 1996.

Zimmermann, Warren. *Origins of a Catastrophe*. New York: Random House, Times Books, 1996.

Index

About the Author

WILLIAM G. HYLAND was editor of *Foreign Affairs* from 1984 through 1992, and subsequently, was a research professor of international relations at Georgetown University's School of Foreign service. He pursued a long career in government, with the CIA, the National Security Council Staff, and as Assistant Secretary of State for Intelligence. He is the co-author of *The Fall of Khrushchev* (1968) and the author of *Mortal Rivals* (1987) and *The Cold War Is Over* (1989).